Myron Taylor

Myron Taylor

The Man Nobody Knew

C. Evan Stewart

TWELVE
TABLES
PRESS

To

W. David Curtis Jr.
Legendary law professor and the
original biographer of Myron C. Taylor

and

Walter F. LaFeber & Joel H. Silbey
Legendary scholars who inspired my
love of history

Contents

Preface

This biography of Myron C. Taylor has taken three decades. It was begun in the 1990s by my Cornell law professor, W. David Curtis Jr., after he went emeritus. Unfortunately, Dave became extremely ill and almost died. By 2002 he had substantially recovered, but he recognized that he could never finish what he had started.

On one of my many trips to Cornell in 2002, Dave asked me to stop by his law school office to chat. He did not flag in advance the reason for his request. And I did not need one, because David was the kindest and sweetest professor I had had at the Cornell Law School (two adjectives that usually do not go in the same sentence with an Ivy League law professor).

As was his custom, Dave got straight to the point. He explained the Taylor project and, given his health, that he could not bring it to fruition. Would I be interested in signing on to complete the biography of arguably Cornell's greatest philanthropist, the nation's greatest industrial leader of the first half of the twentieth century, and (in "retirement") a diplomat at the heart of some of the most important geopolitical issues of the World War II era? And not to worry, Dave assured me, the research was all done, all I would have to do is write it up.

Because of my high regard for my esteemed professor, I said "yes" without fully realizing what I was getting into. Unfortunately, Dave's representation about the research being fully done was not quite right. As an initial matter, Dave believed that all of Taylor's papers were stored at Cornell; but Taylor's papers are also housed at the Franklin D. Roosevelt Library in Hyde Park, New York, the

Myron Taylor portrait, painted by Frank O. Salisbury

Library of Congress (Washington, D.C.), the Annex to the Library of Congress (College Park, Maryland), and the Harry S. Truman Library (Independence, Missouri). In addition, the Oral History Project at Columbia University had also yet to be mined.

One benefit of the time it took me to go through all of the archives (including the Taylor Papers at Cornell) has been the enormous amount of relevant archival material and important scholarly work that has been released and published since 2002 (including works published in 2022). These materials have richly filled out the story of Taylor's life and works; put another way, a Taylor biography published in 2002 would have been woefully incomplete.

The absence of a Taylor biography to date (and why he is little remembered today) is in large part because of his intense personal distaste for publicity; indeed, for much of his business career, the national media called him "the man nobody knows." This lack of interest in self-promotion stemmed (I believe) from at least two sources: first, as the reader will see, Taylor was very much a nineteenth-century, Victorian gentleman; and second, Taylor was so successful in everything he had undertaken in his life, he felt no need to convince others of how great he in fact was.

Taylor's lack of a need for public ego-gratification would prove to be of immense importance in fulfilling his diplomatic work, initially for President Roosevelt and later for President Truman. Based on my research, there was only one other presidential advisor who shared Taylor's desire to do *only* what the president wanted. This is best illustrated by an incident in the Oval Office in January 1941, a meeting of FDR and his just vanquished Republican opponent, Wendell Willkie. President Roosevelt wanted Willkie's help in building public support for aiding Great Britain in its war with Germany. Willkie, however, first wanted to vent about FDR's closest political confidant, Harry Hopkins:

> "Why," asked Willkie, "do you keep Hopkins close to you? You must surely realize that people distrust him and resent his influence."

Roosevelt replied: "[S]omeday you may well be sitting here where I am now as president of the United States. And when you are, you'll be looking at that door over there and knowing that practically everyone who walks through it wants something out of you. You'll learn what a lonely job this is and discover the need for somebody like Harry Hopkins who asks for nothing except to serve you."[1]

Taylor was made of similar stuff, and (as the reader will see) Roosevelt knew that and thus trusted him with many tough tasks (as later did Truman). It is no surprise that Taylor and Hopkins formed a strong personal friendship while serving the president and the country.

By the time he was representing FDR as the president's "Ambassador Extraordinary and Plenipotentiary" to Pope Pius XII, Taylor was no longer "the man nobody knows"—he was, in fact, internationally famous and regularly received worldwide media coverage. But his approach to his task(s) remained the same. Ultimately, the pope would name Taylor a Knight of the Order of Pius IX, First Degree, in 1948, and President Truman awarded him the presidential Medal for Merit later that same year.

The process of writing Taylor's biography has not only given me a fascinating archival look into his brilliant, multi-faceted career, but it has also enriched my understanding of the political sagacity of Franklin Roosevelt. In addition, it has given me a far more nuanced understanding of Pope Pius XII's role vis-à-vis the Holocaust than was my prior (uneducated) understanding. With respect to this latter subject (as is true with many parts of the Taylor biography), the reader will need to consult some lengthy footnotes to get a complete picture of the historical record.

Note

1 R. Sherwood, *Roosevelt and Hopkins*, pp. 2-3 (Harper & Brothers 1948).

Myron Taylor

CHAPTER I

A Useful Life

On April 10, 1937, America's political elite gathered at the Statler Hilton Hotel ballroom in Washington, DC; remarks and skits roasting those elite would soon be performed by the Washington journalists who comprised the Gridiron Club. The star-studded guest list was headed by President Franklin D. Roosevelt and Chief Justice Charles Evans Hughes, and also included prominent members of both the Senate and House, cabinet officers, justices of the Supreme Court, chiefs of the armed forces, political leaders, and foreign dignitaries.

It was a tradition of the Gridiron Club to conclude its annual program with an off-the-record speech by the President of the United States, coming after remarks by a representative of the opposition party. On April 10, preceding FDR would be Myron Charles Taylor.

Who was Myron Taylor and why was he there? Taylor, who had once said that personal publicity should be limited to "a brief mention of birth, marriage and death,"[1] had never been elected to public office and was hardly the leader of the opposition party. He was, however, the Chairman and Chief Executive Officer of the United States Steel Corporation, one of the largest and most important commercial enterprises in the entire world. In short, Taylor was America's preeminent industrial leader. He was also the first person with such a professional background ever to be invited to speak at a Gridiron dinner.

Myron Taylor began his remarks that evening on a light note: "[I] hesitated a few days before deciding to put myself at the mercy of the press, but I concluded that I had tried nearly all the thrills in life and I would add one more great experience."[2] The principal insight Taylor wished to share with the Gridiron Club, however, was of a more serious nature, and he wasted little time in stating it:

> The weakest link in the chain of human events through the centuries has generally been the defects of human nature itself. The defects in human nature based on greed and anger and vanity have leveled to the very dust most of our great civilizations of the past. Through the years of my own experience, I have achieved the greatest results, small though they be, and have attained the greatest happiness, and great it has been, from considering the point of view of others and from fairly reconciling my own with theirs. Rarely have I found a man who had not some, and often many, good reasons for his own point of view, even though in the beginning to me it appeared wrong.
>
> For the permanent peaceful solution of all great problems, there must be a meeting of minds and an honest attempt to try to understand the objectives of the other side. Only by this frank method of approach can our problems be solved on a national scale, free of class distinction.[3]

Taylor's articulation (which did in fact guide his life) was well received that night. Jessie Jones, Chairman of the Reconstruction Finance Corporation, for example, called it "one of the most outstanding addresses he [had] ever heard." And Mark Sullivan, the noted columnist, was moved to write to Taylor because he was "so impressed with the spirit of it, its tolerance, and its emphasis upon understanding the points of view of the men or groups with whom a man finds himself in controversy."[4]

However appealing Taylor's remarks might have been to those in the audience, the more important question was how they were viewed by the man who followed Taylor to the podium. Franklin Delano Roosevelt left no doubt on that score:

> When I learned that my old friend Myron Taylor was to speak at the Gridiron dinner tonight, I realized, in the first place, that because he and I agree on so many factors and fundamentals in our Governmental, social and economic problems he had not been invited in the usual sense, that he was to speak for the opposition, and I for the Government. He was invited, I assumed, and since hearing him I know, to speak as a representative, successful, educated and thoughtful American. And I am grateful to him for his fine statement of American ideals.[5]

It was almost three years later, on December 22, 1939, when President Roosevelt underscored his confidence in Myron Taylor in more compelling and dramatic terms than those reflected at the Gridiron Club. The President made clear his conviction that his "old friend" was qualified not only to make a "fine statement of American ideals" but also to advance those ideals through one of the most controversial and important assignments in American diplomatic history. Taylor was asked to serve as the President's "Ambassador Extraordinary" to Pope Pius XII at the Vatican. In the words of one prominent FDR historian, "Taylor was one who really deserved [that] somewhat archaic title."[6]

During the dark and critical times just preceding America's entry into World War II, Roosevelt informed the Pope: "it would give me great satisfaction to send to you my personal representative in order that our parallel endeavors for peace and the alleviation of suffering may be assisted."[7] This proposal culminated in the Taylor Mission to the Vatican, which brought Myron Taylor again into the public limelight, but this time as diplomat rather than industrialist. And in his diplomatic role, Taylor grappled with some of the thorniest issues that arose over the course of World War II.

Taylor had long been one of FDR's confidants. One example of that role was demonstrated by the German submarine attack on an American destroyer, the USS *Greer*—an attack little remembered today, but one FDR manipulated to change American foreign policy: from relative adherence to the isolationist, Neutrality Act, to a confrontational stance with the Axis powers that brought the country to the edge of undeclared war.[8] The date was September 4, 1941, some three months before America's entry into World War II, when the *Greer* was en route to Iceland with a shipment of American mail. A German U-boat fired torpedoes at the ship without warning. The torpedoes missed their mark and the undamaged *Greer* counterattacked with depth charges.

The *Greer* incident was the subject of a major presidential radio address to the American people and indeed to the whole world on September 11, 1941.[9] President Roosevelt first recounted the facts surrounding the attack, noting that the *Greer's* "identity as an American ship was unmistakable" and that she was at the time "in waters which the Government of the United States had declared to be waters of self-defense, surrounding outposts of American protection." Without identifying by what authority he was claiming America's "defensive waters" to incorporate essentially the whole of the North Atlantic, FDR told the radio audience that the attack was part of a larger "Nazi design to abolish the freedom of the seas and to acquire absolute control and domination of these seas for themselves."

This brought the President to an announcement that made banner worldwide headlines the following day. FDR unilaterally proclaimed a preemptive doctrine (without seeking the formal advice or consent of Congress):

> Let us not say, "We will only defend ourselves if the torpedo succeeds in getting home, or if the crew and the passengers are drowned."

In the waters which we deem necessary for our defense of American naval vessels and American planes will no longer wait until Axis submarines lurking under the water, or Axis raiders on the surface of the sea, strike their deadly blow—first.

From now on, if German or Italian vessels of war enter the waters the protection of which is necessary for American defense they do so at their own peril.

In furtherance of this new "shoot-on-sight" policy, FDR used the unmistakable imagery of rattlesnakes to drive home his point to the listening radio audience: "When you see a rattlesnake poised to strike," he said, "you do not wait until he has struck before you crush him. These Nazi submarines and raiders are the rattlesnakes of the Atlantic."

Samuel I. Rosenman, one of FDR's main advisers and his principal speech writer, later identified Myron Taylor as the author of this rattlesnake simile.[10] Deducing that Taylor had discussed the *Greer* attack and the Nazi threat with the President during a weekend visit to Hyde Park, Rosenman uncovered a Taylor memorandum that had arrived at the White House shortly thereafter:

If I am armed and lawfully in a forest and suddenly along my path I hear the warning rattle of a rattlesnake, and though it has not otherwise disclosed itself, I would feel justified in discharging a shot into the apparent location of the snake. If I killed it, I would probably have saved my life, and no one would question my right to do so; no one would feel that I should wait until it had struck me, and bitten and perhaps killed me, before taking action.

One would consider this a parallel to the case of a vessel lawfully upon the high seas, which became aware of the underwater presence of any danger, be it submarine or other, and which used any instrument within its power to protect itself from attack.[11]

Taylor's contribution to the Roosevelt administration's pre-emptive "shoot-on-sight" policy was typically behind the scenes. Another example of Taylor's nonpublic, but historic, role took place at 10 Downing Street in London, the home of the Prime Minister of England. The date was October 5, 1942, and Winston Churchill then resided at that famous address.

The Prime Minister was hosting a small dinner party with a guest list limited to his wife, Clementine, their two daughters, Myron Taylor, and John G. Winant, the United States Ambassador to England. Taylor had come to London from his post at the Vatican because the President "had directed [him] to speak frankly to Mr. Churchill."[12] One of Taylor's goals was to persuade Churchill to spare Rome—and the Vatican—from British bombing, which could destroy the spiritual home of countless Catholics around the world.

Ambassador Winant later recalled the intensity of Taylor's plea. "No one who has seen Mr. Taylor," he wrote, "could ever doubt his tenacity of purpose. He has the kindly simplicity that comes of a Quaker ancestry.... What he said had great weight with Mr. Churchill...."[13]

Notwithstanding the force of Taylor's arguments, the prime minister could not see his way clear to accept them that night. To rule out Rome as a possible target for bombing might jeopardize the success of the Mediterranean campaign, give unacceptable aid and comfort to the enemy, and might not be well understood by Churchill's fellow residents of London, who themselves had been subjected to massive bombing by the Nazis.

As might be expected, however, the issue of sparing Rome from the destructive effects of bombing arose again and again in diplomatic exchanges by and among Taylor, Washington, London, and the Vatican. In the end, as Secretary of State Cordell Hull recorded in his memoirs, "the center of Rome was, in fact, not bombed, although Allied planes dropped bombs on the city's railroad yards.... The Allied advance on Rome was carried out so as to encircle the city and force the Germans to retire without contesting the capital street by street, which would have wrought great destruction. When the Allies reached Rome they found the city comparatively untouched...."[14]

Returning to Churchill and Taylor's attempt, albeit unsuccessful (at the time), to reach agreement on this subject at the prime minister's residence in the fall of 1942, and having listened to the Churchill–Taylor interchange, Ambassador Winant later remarked:

> It was the most civilized conversation I have ever listened to which involved both spiritual considerations and the use of the destructive tools of war. It was not a conflict between those two men. It had to do with man's continuing failure to establish peace and freedom through the power of love, and every time that breaks down the only answer must always be an agonizing compromise between the spiritual and the temporal. Similar conflicts arise and pass unnoticed in day-to-day life, but they are forever highlighted by the tragedies of war.[15]

These three vignettes—of the industrialist at the Gridiron Club, the contributor to Franklin D. Roosevelt's preemptive "shoot-on-sight" policy, and the diplomat at 10 Downing Street—provide only a teasing glimpse into Myron Taylor's fascinating life. Taylor's diplomatic contributions to America (and the world) were many and significant, as he was thrust into numerous critical geopolitical matters, including efforts to keep Italy, Spain, and Portugal from entering World War II (as Axis members); helping to secure Lend-Lease aid to Russia (in its darkest hour against the Nazis); efforts to save European Jews and to deal with the Holocaust (and interacting directly with Pope Pius XII in those efforts); ensuring that the Vatican did not oppose the Allies' unconditional surrender policy; efforts to block Germany from enlisting the

Vatican to broker a mediation for the European War; helping to godfather the Bretton Woods Agreement and the creation of the United Nations; and helping Italy to recover after the War.

In awarding Taylor the presidential Medal for Merit on December 20, 1948, President Harry S. Truman praised Taylor for having "earned the accolades of his countrymen whom he has served faithfully and well wherever duty called him."[16] And, upon his death on May 6, 1959, the *New York Times*, after reviewing his "extraordinary abilities" and his multifaceted career, employed considerable understatement when it concluded that "[h]is was, indeed, a useful life."[17]

Notes

1. Troy, N.Y. "Record" of May 13, 1959, reproducing an item from the *Washington Evening Star*.

2. This account of the dinner is drawn from Harold Brayman's *The President Speaks Off-the-Record* (Dow Jones Books 1976). The quotation is found at pp. 309-10.

3. *Id.* p. 311.

4. C. Merriam April 12, 1937, letter to M.C. Taylor (Taylor Papers, Cornell University); M. Sullivan April 10, 1937, letter to M.C. Taylor (Taylor Papers, Cornell University). *See also* A. Krock April 15, 1937, letter to M.C. Taylor, reporting that all in attendance "have agreed that your speech was most fitting to the occasion and to the condition of the world today." (Taylor Papers, Cornell University).

5. H. Brayman, *The President Speaks Off-the-Record*, p. 314. FDR subsequently sent a set of his remarks to Taylor with a handwritten note: "What I said at his 'premiere' FDR." *See* F.D. Roosevelt April 10, 1937, letter to M.C. Taylor (Taylor Papers, Cornell University).

6. R.E. Sherwood, *Roosevelt and Hopkins: An Intimate History* (Harper & Bros. 1948), p. 398.

7. *Wartime Correspondence Between President Roosevelt and Pope Pius XII* (Macmillan 1947), p. 19.

8. The historic importance of the *Greer* incident and the "shoot on sight" policy cannot be understated. An insightful analysis of Hitler's decision to declare war on America after Pearl Harbor identifies FDR's policy as provoking Hitler to

believe that it constituted a de facto "state of war" against Germany. B. Simms & C. Laderman, *Hitler's American Gamble: Pearl Harbor and Germany's March to Global War*, pp. 40 & 235 (Basic Books 2021). And FDR's use of the *Greer* incident was recently cited by a prominent diplomatic historian as precedent for President George W. Bush's foreign policy of preemptive/unilateralist initiatives in the aftermath of September 11, 2001. *See* M. Leffler, "9/11 and American Foreign Policy," 29 *Diplomatic History* 395, 398 (June 2005).

9. The text of President Roosevelt's address was printed in *the New York Times* of September 12, 1941, p. 1.

10. S. Rosenman, *Working with Roosevelt* (Harpers & Brothers 1952), pp. 290-93.

11. *Id.* p. 293.

12. Transcript of Meeting of Protestant Clergymen with Myron C. Taylor at Union Club (New York City, October 20, 1947), at p. 27 (Taylor Papers, Cornell University).

13. The account of this meeting is drawn from John G. Winant's *Letter from Grosvenor Square* (Houghton Mifflin 1947), pp. 182-85.

14. C. Hull, *The Memoirs of Cordell Hull* (Macmillan 1948), Vol. II, p. 1563.

15. Winant, J.G. *Letter from Grosvenor Square*, p. 184. *See also* J.G. Winant December 3, 1942, memorandum to C. Hull (Taylor Papers, Cornell University) ("I could not help thinking of General Sherman's statement that 'war is hell' as I sat listening to Mr. Taylor and Mr. Churchill arguing with great sincerity and eloquence their two points of view.").

16. Citation accompanying the award of the Medal for Merit to Myron C. Taylor by President Harry S. Truman on December 20, 1948.

17. *New York Times* editorial dated May 8, 1959.

CHAPTER II

Early Years in Lyons, New York

Lyons is located in upstate New York, midway between Rochester and Syracuse and about 25 miles south of Lake Ontario. It is the county seat of Wayne County, and at the time of Myron Taylor's birth there on January 18, 1874, some 3,000 people resided in the village and the adjoining rural areas. The Erie Canal and the New York Central Railroad served the transportation needs of those who lived there. Although Lyons was predominantly a farming community, it was also the site of a number of small industrial enterprises, among them the Taylor family tannery.

The founder of this business was Myron's grandfather, Elijah Pomeroy Taylor. Elijah, who had previously lived in Northampton, Massachusetts, settled in Lyons in 1822 and became one of Wayne County's first tanners and curriers. The business was subsequently carried on by Elijah's son, Myron's father, William Delling Taylor, who was born in Lyons on July 26, 1844.

The 1870 federal census figures paint an interesting picture of the status of the Taylor family enterprise as of that time:

Capital Investment Value	$8,000
Motive of Power	Steam boiler, 10 horsepower
Average Number of Employees	3 males over 16
Total Amount of Wages Paid During Year	$800

Materials Used: Value: 1,000 Hides, $4,000
400 Skins, 50 Cords Tanbarb
Product—Leather: Value: $7,000[1]

These, then, were the industrial origins of the individual destined some 60 years later to head one of the largest corporations in the world.

Myron's mother was Mary Morgan Underhill Taylor, born in New York City on November 26, 1833. She was a descendant of Captain John Underhill, a noted colonial soldier and leader. Prior to his death in 1672, Captain Underhill had embraced what were then to be heretical views—the Quaker faith; as such, he went into exile from the Massachusetts Bay Colony, and later settled in Locust Valley, Long Island (the property that centuries later would serve as Myron Taylor's country estate). Because of Captain Underhill's notoriety, there would always be frequent public references to Myron Taylor's Quaker background and heritage, notwithstanding his membership and leadership in the Episcopal Church.[2]

In addition to Myron, his parents had two older sons, Willard Underhill Taylor (1868–1940) and Morgan Delling Taylor (1871–1897). Myron Taylor and his brothers grew up in a large, old-fashioned house on Broad Street in Lyons. His parents, although not wealthy, were prosperous and lived in comfortable circumstances. Taylor attended the Lyons Union School, played the guitar, and sang in the choir of the local Presbyterian Church. His contemporaries especially remembered his maturity and his ability to relate well to older persons. In his own words:

> I enjoyed to the fullest the swimming, the boating and the fishing afforded by the extensive waterways of the area.... Possessed of excellent health and strong physique I can, I think, without transgressing the rules of reticence lay claim to some prowess as a swimmer. Hunting was another favored sport and I always felt that I held my own as a wing shot.[3]

Following his graduation from Lyons Union School, Myron left home to study law, returning to open his own office there in 1895. During the summer of 1895, he had an experience that was typical of his earlier boyhood in that upstate New York community.

The episode in question considered of a ten-day canoe trip taken by Taylor and two of his young friends, Fred Leach and Will (Walt) Whitman. During the period July 29–August 8, 1895, the three voyagers traveled from Lyons down the Erie Canal to Cross Lake and then on to Lake Ontario. Myron Taylor was known to his fellow travelers as "Charlie" or sometimes as "Tade." His canoe was the *What the L'Bill*. Walt Whitman kept a detailed log of the journey, and some of the entries provide helpful hints and insights about Taylor's interests and personal traits at this stage of his life.[4]

It is clear, for example, that Taylor enjoyed the out-of-doors for, in addition to his presence on the trip, the log notes that Tade "had made numerous hunting and fishing excursions to this somewhat isolated though picturesque locality."[5]

One entry in the log gives some indication of Taylor's wit and sense of humor: "Today's cruise has been rather uneventful; in fact the only thing at all amusing—that is, to us—was an expression dropped by Tade. When he first woke up and gazed upon the outside world, the stern of his canoe presented a somewhat bespattered appearance … As our legal friend gazed upon his dappled boat he was heard to mutter, in all seriousness: 'Thank God, cows don't fly!'"[6]

At another time, after remarking on a "magical night—the black overhanging bluffs, the white clouds crossing the blue vaults of heaven, the wan light on the lake," the log continues: "As we gazed upon the ineffable stillness of the night, his judicial nibs (Taylor) had an inspiration, and gently murmured:

'Oh ever wet and watery sea
'Could I just write poetry
'I'd rattle off a ode to thee,
'Oh hully gee!'"[7]

There is also an interesting reference to a personal triumph that probably was as important to Taylor at that time as would be any of the industrial or diplomatic achievements of his later years. For several hours the three voyagers had been beset by bad weather, with gusting winds and foam-crested rollers that made any headway virtually impossible and ultimately drive them ashore. "Tade landed first and climbing about forty feet up the face of a bluff swung his hat in the air and yelled: 'The world is mine!' in a way calculated to admit of no dispute."[8]

But there was a deeper, more important side to Taylor that was clear to his childhood friends early on. In the words of Whitman:

> As a boy Myron Taylor always seemed to have a faculty for meeting older people with ease and confidence…. This undoubtedly resulted in a more mature outlook on life than most of his companions of the same age. His father … gave him business responsibility at an early age, and a different business viewpoint than that of most young men.[9]

Taylor's boyhood and teenage years in Lyons were an important formative period in his life. And he would never forget this hometown community and his family roots there. His remembering took various forms. He established a village park in honor of his father. He turned the family homestead into a community center in honor of his mother, and later built a facility for use by the Boy and Girl Scouts organizations in honor of his brothers. Lyons' churches received much-needed new organs. There were substantial capital gifts in support of hospital and library programs in Lyons, as well as neighboring localities. Taylor once said: "Youth may leave Lyons for wider fields, but they do not forget Lyons and Lyons does not forget them."[10] For Myron Taylor, this was clearly the case.

Notes

1. Letter from Marjory Allen Perez, Wayne County Historian, dated August 31, 1990.

2. For genealogical information concerning Myron C. Taylor, *see* A. Pound, *Myron C. Taylor: Lawyer, Industrialist, Diplomat, Humanitarian* (New York Genealogical and Biographical Society 1955), pp. 1-36.

3. *Id.* pp. 47-48.

4. A copy of Will (Walt) Whitman's log is at the Wayne County Department of History in Lyons, New York.

5. *Id.* p. 27.

6. *Id.* p. 13.

7. *Id.* p. 22.

8. *Id.* p. 30.

9. Pound, *supra* note 2, p. 50.

10. Pound, *supra* note 2, p 47.

CHAPTER III

Cornell, the Law, and a Short-Lived Political Career

Myron Taylor's first extended sojourn outside of Lyons was in Washington, DC, as a first-year student at the National University School of Law. His decision to become a lawyer was not unexpected for his growing up in the county seat had stimulated his interest in attending trials in the Wayne County courthouse. In those days a high school education qualified one to enter law school. Following his graduation from Lyons Union School, therefore, Taylor began the study of law in Washington. He remained at National University Law School for only one year, however, thereafter transferring to the Cornell Law School in Ithaca, New York, in the fall of 1893.

Taylor and his classmates studied in Boardman Hall, the recently completed law facility named for the first Dean of the Law School, Judge Douglass Boardman. Boardman Hall would continue to be the home of the School until 1932 when it moved to new quarters bearing Myron Taylor's own name. The cost of his year of law study at Cornell was estimated at $320, with $100 going for tuition, $200 for room and board, and $20 for textbooks.

Taylor's academic record was solid and he was graduated with the degree of Bachelor of Laws on June 21, 1894. His extracurricular activities consisted largely of membership in the Cornell University Glee Club where he sang as a second tenor. The highlight of the year was a concert tour that involved appearances in 17

Myron Taylor 1894, Cornell yearbook picture

different cities, including St. Louis, Chicago, Minneapolis, Milwaukee, and Cleveland. It was customary to close each program with Cornell's Evening Song, an emotionally stirring reminder of campus life to graduates of the university. It is an interesting circumstance that some 65 years later, and pursuant to Myron

Taylor's own request, his memorial service would end with the playing of the Evening Song.

There was one aspect of his law school career that was destined to take on special significances in later years, and that was his coming to know Charles Evans Hughes. Hughes joined the Cornell law faculty in 1891, and at age 29 he was the youngest full professor at the university. He returned to private practice in 1893 but continued his association with the school as a nonresident lecturer until 1895. Hughes and Taylor thus crossed paths in a teacher–student relationship.

Hughes's later career in public service is well known: Governor of New York, Republican Nominee for President of the United States, Secretary of State, and Associate Justice and Chief Justice of the United States. In looking back on his experience as a law professor at Cornell, Chief Justice Hughes many years later was to write: "Whether my efforts were of benefit to the students I cannot say but they were of incalculable benefit to me."[1] The Chief Justice need have had no such doubt about student reaction to his teaching—they were "vastly impressed ... by his extraordinary reasoning power, his amazing memory, and the ease with which he use[d] both."[2] Myron Taylor especially admired Hughes, believing him to be the most exciting and stimulating member of the faculty at that time.[3] And years later that protégé–mentor bond formed in law school would be utilized for an important geopolitical benefit.

Taylor was admitted to the New York State bar on March 26, 1895, at a term of the New York Supreme Court in Rochester. The delay between his acquiring the Cornell law degree in 1894 and his admission to the bar the following year was necessary to enable him to reach the 21-year age of majority required for the practice of law. He spent this 9-month period both working in his father's leather manufacturing business—principally traveling to meet suppliers and customers, but also traveling to Washington, DC, to observe the workings of government and the civil litigation system in action.

Taylor began his career as a practicing lawyer by joining the small firm of DeForest and DeForest in his hometown of Lyons, and he continued there in the general practice of law for the next five years. This fact alone merits some elaboration. Almost without exception, accounts of his professional career report that following his swearing in as a member of the bar he established an office on Wall Street in New York, specializing in the practice of corporate law. A *Fortune* magazine summary of his legal experience, for example, notes that "ambitious and able young lawyer Taylor leaped the years of apprenticeship in law."[4] There is practically no mention whatever of his first few years as a struggling young lawyer in a rural community in upstate New York. This is a troubling omission in light of the fact that Taylor was undoubtedly aware of the biographical material included—or omitted—from at least some of the accounts of his professional career.

There is not a great deal of information available concerning the nature of Taylor's hometown law practice. As set forth in the next chapter, a considerable amount of his time and attention was devoted to matters connected with the family tannery business. There is evidence that he counseled clients to settle rather than to litigate disputes.

An 1896 item in a local Lyons newspaper left no doubt that he was then handling legal cases of a far different magnitude than those that would later characterize his Wall Street practice. "M.C. Taylor," the item stated, "has been retained to prosecute the action for damages against the town of Junius, brought on by Miss Ida Rankert of Dublin, who stepped into a hole in the highway and broke her leg."[5] The legal notice section of the same local paper noted that on February 22, 1896, in a judicial proceeding to sell real property, the New York court had appointed Myron Taylor as a referee to conduct the sale.[6]

Taylor's practice was thus generally comprised of run-of-the-mill cases characteristic of a small rural law practice at the close of the nineteenth century. There was, however, another dimension to his professional life that deserves mention—one he would (again) later not publicize, and has not been referenced in any prior biographical works on Taylor. Myron Taylor aspired to elective office. Although Taylor would later become a registered Republican, he was then a member of the Democratic Party, and he twice ran as a Democratic candidate for public office.

In 1898, the County of Wayne was entitled to one representative in the New York State Assembly, the lower house of the state legislature. The term of office was for one year. In the 1898 election, the Democratic candidate was M. Charles Taylor, who received 4,405 votes compared to the 6,756 votes polled by his victorious Republican opponent.

In 1899, Taylor was again the Democratic candidate for Member of Assembly, but this time was listed on the ballot as Myron C. Taylor, the name by which he would be known for the rest of his life. Nothing exists to explain the shift in his name— perhaps he thought the voters would prefer a candidate who went by his first name. In any event, in 1899 he was the choice of 3,594 Wayne County voters compared to the 4,973 persons who supported the Republican winner, Frederick W. Griffith.[7]

A political item in the November 1, 1899, edition of *The Arcadian* weekly gazette advised the Wayne County electorate that

> [a] vote for Mr. Taylor, the Democratic candidate for Assembly, is a vote for Tammany Hall. A vote for Mr. Griffith, the Republican candidate, is a vote for a man who will back the administration of Gov. [Theodore] Roosevelt. Please remember this election day.[8]

A majority of the voters did "remember this" on election day. Nevertheless, considering his youth, and the fact that Wayne County, then as now, was one of the indisputable Republican strongholds in the state, Myron Taylor's early venture into partisan politics was impressive. His quite respectable runs for the Assembly in 1898 and again in 1899 suggest what might have been a promising political future. This was a career that he would not thereafter pursue, however, nor would he ever publicize it. Indeed, later in his business career he would be cited for being "disgusted with the muddleheadedness of politicians," as well as being "[e]motionally unfitted for the leadership of the masses and inexperienced in the technique of politics."[9] Notwithstanding those negative assessments, in the same later years he was in fact encouraged by others to enter the political arena.

In 1930, for example, the Chairman of the Democratic National Party, and his top political lieutenant, sought to promote a Taylor presidential candidacy, in some measure to check Franklin D. Roosevelt's growing momentum.[10] Eight years later a Burlington, Vermont, newspaper item reported that friends of Taylor had "started a boom for him as a presidential candidate in 1940" and quoted from a letter that they had sent out on his behalf:

> America calls for a Twentieth Century Samaritan. For one who heals wounds. For one who knows and is known by the Siamese Twins, Labor and Capital. And favorably. For one with experience in American and worldwide affairs of magnitude. For one old enough to look back, and young enough to look forward. A driver who holds the accelerator and the brake in equal respect. And knows how and when to use them. Think it over. Why not Myron C. Taylor?[11]

Taylor's reaction to this development was unequivocal. A member of his staff advised one of the sponsors of the movement:

> I find that he [Taylor] would be very much opposed to any activity looking to bringing his name before the country as a possible candidate for any political office.... I feel that you could earn his greater gratitude if you would drop the matter entirely, so definitely is he opposed to having any part in politics.[12]

In 1900, Myron Taylor closed out his law practice in Lyons and moved to New York City, where he became affiliated with the law firm of his brother, Willard Taylor (Cornell AB, Class of 1891). The firm of McFarland, Taylor & Costello had offices at 71 Wall Street, and specialized in corporate and admiralty law. Myron Taylor focused his practice on corporate matters. Soon, however, his interest in the practice of law as such gave way to an increasing involvement in the fields of business and finance. It would be as an industrialist, first in textiles and later in steel, rather than as a lawyer, that his professional career would evolve. However, he never lost sight of the importance of his early training in law. In addressing the graduating class of the Cornell Law School on May 29, 1941, he stated:

> I am speaking from life. For quite recently I ended ten years in directing one of our largest and, I can say unqualifiedly, one of our most useful corporate enterprises. The administration of industrial or financial enterprises requires in part the exercise of many of the functions of the judicial mind. That is, one must separate the relevant from the irrelevant and dispassionately weigh the evidence. Therefore in an ever-increasing degree we find lawyers occupying places in our business and financial life that seem to have nothing at all to do so with the law. That comes about, I think, because only the law provides the broad and unspecialized type of training which in this age of specialization we so greatly need if the specialists are not to run amuck.[13]

Throughout his life, Myron Taylor manifested his steadfast conviction of the importance to society of his chosen profession as well as his personal pride and satisfaction in being a member of the bar. These manifestations took various forms but none was more significant than his continuing relationship with the institution that in 1894 had awarded him his law degree.

Taylor served as a member of the Cornell University Board of Trustees from 1928 to 1953, and thereafter as an emeritus trustee until his death. On December 14, 1928, he announced his intention to make a gift of $1.5 million to be used to construct a new home for the Cornell Law School, noting the "growing need ... for competent and well trained lawyers to guide in the handling of the larger affairs of the country."[14] At the dedication of Myron Taylor Hall (as the new facility would be known) on October 15, 1932, the donor made clear that "[i]f, through greater knowledge of and a growing respect for the law and its enforcement, it inspires increased regard for the rights of others in individual and community life, ... Mrs. Taylor and I shall have achieved an enduring reward."[15]

Myron Taylor Hall was (and is) one of the most beautiful Gothic architectural structures on the Cornell campus, and certainly ranks among the country's outstanding facilities for a law school, its faculty, and its students.

Almost 20 years later, Taylor pledged an additional $1.5 million to Cornell, to build an adjoining, complimentary structure in honor of his wife, Anabel, to serve a unique and then unheard of purpose: providing an interfaith place of worship for all Cornell students and faculty of any and all religions. This was undoubtedly due, in large measure, to his experiences at the Vatican and in his considerable interactions with religious leaders of all faiths throughout the world. It also probably was due to his education at, and lifelong attachment to, Cornell, an institution whose original charter was so boldly nonsectarian in nature that the religious press once attacked it as the "godless university."[16]

As part of the pioneering Anabel Taylor Hall, there was built a revolving altar so that the altar could be used effectively by all faiths. It proved more than a bit tricky, however, because the first set of stained glass windows—designed at significant cost to Taylor—were directly at odds with the Jewish faith's prohibition against worshiping in a place where there are representations of

Study, new law school presented to Cornell University, Ithaca, New York,
by Myron C. Taylor

the human figure. Resolving this problem became a point of significant controversy on campus among those planning the building's
interior space (including Cornell President Edward Ezra Day,
who was fearful of offending the building's benefactor); in the
end, it was resolved only because of Taylor's direct intervention,

Dedication of Myron Taylor Hall, October 1932
from left Frank H. Hiscock (Chair of Cornell's Board of Trustees and
former Chief Judge of the New York Court of Appeals),
Cuthbert W. Pound (Chief Judge of the New York Court of Appeals),
Myron C. Taylor, Livingston Farrand (President, Cornell University), and
Charles K. Burdio (Dean, Cornell Law School)

recommissioning new windows that would depict objects in nature.

Almost four decades after Anabel Taylor Hall was dedicated on October 26, 1952, world-renown Cornell Professor Milton R. Konvitz, who directly participated in the process by which the interfaith mission was implemented, remembered it as if it had just taken place the prior day:

> What I took away from this experience are a number of things: One was the firm conviction of Mr. Taylor that the building must be an interfaith chapel. To him that meant a great deal, expressing his belief that religions, though separate, yet have a great deal in common; that there is a brotherhood that religions need to nurture;

although there probably is no room for such an interfaith chapel in a city, there should be room for it on a university campus, for the university has an educational function. The chapel could demonstrate an ideal that needs to be achieved. This was to the great credit, I think, of Mr. Taylor.

Another aspect of the incident, to his credit, was his willingness to see the Jewish point of view. He was not obstinate, he would not sacrifice the interfaith aspect in order to have the original designs because they were produced by an artist he favored, and because they were congenial to Mr. Taylor's own religious faith and convictions. So, in at least two ways, Mr. Taylor's character made an outstanding contribution to the success of the whole project.[17]

In view of Taylor's later career in diplomacy, it was perhaps prophetic that early on he should have envisioned a growing role for his alma mater in the field of international affairs. Thus, in his December 14, 1928, offer of financial support for a new Law School facility, he encouraged inclusion in the curriculum of courses that would permit "students to equip themselves especially for our Government's foreign service."[18] To the same end, on June 13, 1948, he established the Myron Taylor Lectures on Foreign Affairs. In announcing this lectureship, Cornell's then President Edmund Ezra Day remarked:

> Mr. Taylor's appreciation that world order, and therefore our own security and well-being, is now dependent upon our foreign policy to a degree unparalleled in history, is the inspiration of these lectures on foreign affairs. With recognition of the appropriate force of public opinion in a democracy, it is hoped that this series will stimulate thoughtful consideration of the world situation and its meaning to us.[19]

Among the Myron Taylor Lecturers were Isaiah Bowman, President Emeritus of Johns Hopkins University; Ralph Bunche, at the time Director of the United Nation's Trusteeship Division; and Dean Rusk, then Assistant Secretary of State in Charge of Far Eastern Affairs (and later Secretary of State under Presidents Kennedy and Johnson). An appropriate addition to the list would have been the founder of the lectureship, for by then Myron Taylor had achieved a preeminent position in American diplomacy through his service as the personal representative of Presidents Roosevelt and Truman to the Vatican during the period of World War II.

Notes

1. Statement of Chief Justice Charles Evans Hughes, reprinted in 26 Corn. L. Q. 1, 1 (1940).

2. E.H. Woodruff, "History of the Cornell University School of Law," 4 Corn. L. Q. 91, 130 (1919).

3. W.D. Curtiss, "The Cornell Law School From 1954 to 1963," 56 Corn. L. Rev. 375, 397-99 (1971).

4. *Fortune* (Vol. XIII, No. 6, June 1936), p. 117.

5. *Wayne Democratic Press*, Vol. XL, No. 33, p. 5 (Jan. 1, 1896).

6. *Wayne Democratic Press*, Vol. XL, No. 42, p. 4 (Mar. 4, 1986).

7. *See* Proceedings of the Wayne County Board of Supervisors for 1898 and 1899, respectively, and the official canvass of votes included therein.

8. *The Arcadian* weekly gazette, Nov. 1, 1899, p. 6.

9. *Fortune* (Vol. XIII, No. 6 June 1936), p. 174.

10. M. Morgan, *FDR—A Biography* (Simon & Schuster 1985), p. 325.

11. *Burlington, Vermont Free Press* (September 27, 1938). *See also* May 23, 1936, letter from B. Black to M.C. Taylor, urging him to run for President in 1940 (Taylor Papers, Cornell University).

12. J.C. MacDonald October 4, 1938, letter to W.M. Connelly (Taylor Papers, Cornell University, Olin Library Archives).

13. M.C. Taylor, "The Lawyer's Opportunity," p. 4 (Taylor Papers, Cornell University).

14. Letter from M.C. Taylor to Cornell University Board of Trustees, December 14. 1928, in Day Hall archives.

15. "Dedication of Myron Taylor Hall," 18 Corn. L. Q. 1 (Dec. 1932).

16. M. Bishop, *A History of Cornell* 65 (Cornell University Press 1962).

17. Interview of Milton R. Konvitz by W. David Curtiss, October 25, 1990. To convince Cornell's president (who said he needed it to convince Myron Taylor), Professor Konvitz sought and received an expert legal opinion from a rabbinical scholar on the subject of the windows. For a fairly detailed compendium of the dedication ceremonies for Anabel Taylor Hall, *see* A. Pound, *Myron C. Taylor: Lawyer, Industrialist, Diplomat, Humanitarian* (New York Genealogical and Biographical Society 1955), pp. 56-58.

18. *Supra* note 13.

19. Statement of President Edmund E. Day, June 13, 1948.

CHAPTER IV

Lawyer Turned Businessman

The reason Myron Taylor left the law is emblematic of the vision and insight he applied to challenges throughout his long and varied career. As mentioned earlier, a good chunk of Taylor's legal practice was on behalf of his father's business(es). And it was through some litigation protecting the interests of William D. Taylor's leather-working plant that Myron Taylor saw a unique opportunity.

His father's company had sold a large quantity of leather to an entity that made mail pouches for the U.S. government. A Rochester bank, which stood behind the company, had caused the Taylor company to ship the leather on credit. It turned out that at the time the bank was informing the Taylors that the company was in fine shape, it was in fact insolvent and virtually bankrupt.

Myron Taylor brought suit against the bank. Unfortunately, he was unable to collect damages, notwithstanding several appeals. There was a bright lining, however.

During the course of the various proceedings, Myron Taylor had discovered certain interesting facts, first through trial testimony, and later through a friendship he established with a witness. The government, it turned out, would shortly be contracting out for a huge quantity of mail pouches and related products. Armed with this knowledge, as well as with a thorough grounding in the legal ins and outs of government contracts for such products, Myron Taylor bid for the contract. At the same time, he had one of the Taylor companies begin to focus its efforts on making mail pouches (initially they were a mixture of leather and cotton, later they were all cotton), as well as on the manufacture of government-stamped envelopes and newspaper wrappers.[1]

Having won the contract, Taylor quickly turned to introducing new techniques by which to improve production methods. Included in these innovations were production line assembly, standardization of envelope size, increasing the number of envelopes per blank paper, and establishing nationwide distribution facilities for the stamped envelopes. More familiar to today's readers, Taylor also introduced the use of the "window"—the transparent opening through which the return address is displayed (which eliminates the possibility of handwritten errors).[2]

All of the foregoing innovations were popularly received, reduced operating costs for the government and domestic consumers, and helped to improve service throughout the country. As such, when the initial contract was up for renewal, it was re-awarded without competitive bidding.

On a renewal in 1915, however, an entity named the Middle West Supply Company submitted a bid somewhat lower than that by Taylor's Mercantile Corporation. Middle West Supply had no plant, no machinery, and little capital. Notwithstanding, given that it was a lower bid, as well as the fact that Taylor's presumptuous bid many years before was not from a very much different situation, the U.S. government was leaning toward awarding Middle West Supply the contract.

Taylor would not be defeated that easily, however. With the explicit support of the U.S. Postmaster General, he simply bought out Middle West Supply, and the mail pouch and stamped envelopes continued to be produced as before.[3]

And he did not always need outside assistance in winning these contracts. In 1936, a former superintendent of the Mail Bag Repair Shop in the Post Office Department recalled how Myron Taylor years before had astutely outbid J. Spencer Turner Company, the leading firm in the cotton duck world, for certain contracts on mail sacks and pouches. Thereafter, Taylor had received a rather unhappy telegram from a Turner official; and as the superintendent recalled: "you telegraphed him [back] that he might travel to a superheated climate!" The superintendent also remembered that it was not much later that Myron Taylor bought the Turner Company and became its president.[4]

Taylor's relationship with the Postmaster General must have been very close; indeed, it seems clear that he well understood, early on, the importance of developing business partnerships with the government.[5] About the same time as the Middle Supply Company incident, business interests representing unstamped envelope manufacturers wanted to bar further production of the government's return-card envelopes; the contention was that the government-stamped, return envelopes competed (and unfairly) with the envelope business of the private sector. This was a direct challenge to the government, but also a direct threat to the Taylor business interests.

While the private interests were having bills introduced in Congress, Taylor and the Postmaster struck back. Organizing a counter wave of protest by users of the return-card stamped envelope (trumpeting the time and cost savings of them), a tidal wave of many thousands of letters descended upon the U.S. Senate. Together with congressional hearings that were weighted heavily in favor of the existing status quo, this well-orchestrated counter-protest carried the day, and the more efficient, consumer-friendly process continued on.[6]

It was during this first experience as a business leader that Taylor's set of beliefs as to management's responsibility to labor began to emerge. Besides instituting clubs and organizing social and musical events on a regular basis, Taylor provided insurance for the workers in the stamp envelope factory.[7] While this is quite modest compared to what he would eventually provide for and agree to in subsequent years in the steel industry, for that era this was enlightened and progressive action.

At its peak the business was producing 10 million envelopes a day. By the mid 1920s, however, the rate had declined to between 3 to 4 million a day. At that level, the business was no longer profitable, and it was thus sold to another concern in 1928.[8] As we will see, by that time Myron Taylor had much more on his business plate.

Notes

1. A. Pound, *Myron C. Taylor: Lawyer, Industrialist, Diplomat, Humanitarian* (New York Genealogical and Biographical Society 1955), p. 90.

2. *Id.* p. 91.

3. *Id.* pp. 91-92.

4. *Id.* p. 74.

5. As noted in one admiring biography: "Through his law practice, Mr. Taylor was instrumental in organizing companies especially fitted to produce for urgent requirements of the Government. These companies performed to the complete satisfaction of the Government and with signal credit to Mr. Taylor." R. Blough, Myron C. Taylor: An Appreciation (U.S. Steel 1956), p. 51.

6. Pound, *supra* note 1, pp. 92-93.

7. Pound, *supra* note 1, p. 93.

8. Because the U.S. Post Office developed a policy of having federal convicts produce mail sacks, Taylor had already shut down that business line altogether. Pound, *supra* note 1, p. 75.

CHAPTER V

The Textile Years

Myron Taylor's father and grandfather had both been prosperous tanners. Myron followed in the Taylor family tradition of manufacturing, but cotton rather than leather became his
special field of interest.

It is perhaps misleading to refer to Taylor as a textile "manu-
facturer" as that term is generally understood. His personal focus
was not on the technical processes involved in turning cotton into
cloth. His role, rather, was in acquiring, financing, merging, and
overseeing the operation of textile mills in which those processes
could be efficiently and profitably employed. Taylor's fortes were
corporate finance and reorganization, not engineering or manufacturing. Indeed, it was generally agreed that he was "one of the
greatest financiers" of the twentieth century.[1]

Taylor's involvement in cotton developed principally as a
result of the mail pouch business he initiated with the government. That led him to a study of the cotton markets generally,
and to scout out where good opportunities might be available. His
general practice was to take over a struggling mill that at best was
only marginally successful, and transform it into an expanding and
remunerative one. Time and again, for more than two decades,
he followed this practice throughout New England and into the
South; Taylor was attracted to this latter region because of easier
access to raw materials and lower labor costs. In the textile industry his modus operandi became known as the "Taylor Formula."

One of the first mills to come under Myron Taylor's control was located in LeRoy, New York, not far from his hometown of Lyons. This was a somewhat exceptional case in that it involved the organization of a new company rather than reorganizing an already existing one. The milling operations were located in a collection of buildings that had for some time been primarily occupied by the American Malting Company. In its May 9, 1906, edition, the *LeRoy Gazette* headlined "Cotton Mills For Leroy" and went on to report:

> The promoters of the company include M.C. Taylor, of New York, who has a large factory in Lyons, where he manufactures mail bags and is one of the largest buyers of duck in the country.... Mr. Taylor had visited LeRoy on several occasions and became very favorably impressed with the place and readily saw what an excellent location the malt houses afforded for a manufacturing plant. A short time ago he wrote to Mayor Huysk and told him he thought Eastern capital could be interested in establishing a cotton mill here and thus make use of the vacant malt houses, and asked him to confer with LeRoyans in regard to the matter, saying he would like to meet a delegation in Rochester within a day or two.[2]

With characteristic drive and determination, Taylor pushed ahead with his plan. Within a month, the LeRoy Cotton Mills Company had been incorporated with a capitalization of $450,000 and Myron C. Taylor as one of three directors. By the end of the year the malt house buildings had been rehabilitated, textile machinery had been installed, and some 150 local residents had been employed to carry out the factory's function of manufacturing yarn to be used in making cloth.

From these beginnings, LeRoy Cotton was destined to prosper and grow and to become the hub around which an increasing number of Taylor-controlled textile companies were linked.

These included mills at Lowell and Newburyport in Massachusetts, which Taylor combined with the LeRoy operations to form Bay State Cotton Mills. And to facilitate marketing efforts, he formed the Boston Yarn Company.

In 1910, the Consolidated Cotton Duck Company, a federation of widely scattered mills, was floundering in serious financial difficulty—it had over $5 million in debt, and had lost $1.5 million in the prior year alone. Under these circumstances, the company's bankers invited Myron Taylor to take charge of a thorough-going corporate reorganization. Taylor accepted the challenge, and quickly concluded that a complete rationalization of the industry itself was necessary to deal with antiquated equipment, lack of proper financing, and excess capacity. The ultimate outcome of Taylor's work was the creation of a new business entity called the International Cotton Mills Corporation. A further result of Taylor's role in these developments was the effect on his own professional reputation. As viewed by one commentator: "With International's advent, Myron Taylor became a national figure almost overnight, for the merger was big news on the industrial scene."[3]

The new textile giant was capitalized at $20 million. Its 12,000 employees operated over 20 mills in 8 states and Canada.[4] It had a capacity for producing annually some 75 million pounds of cotton fabric. And International prospered under Taylor's leadership. As reported in the *American Wool and Cotton Reporter*, a leading trade journal of the time, progress was swift and fundamental:

> [Myron] Taylor organized the International Cotton Mills as the successor of the decrepit Consolidated Cotton Duck Company, and it was Mr. Taylor who started the duck trust upon its forward path, taking a company that had lost $1,299,371.15 in 1910, was financially embarrassed and poorly equipped. He put in about $2,000,000 worth of new machinery in 1911 and pushed production from about $8,000,000 a year to $16,000,000

in 1912, with a profit of $635,755 in that year. On this showing the company was re-financed and its debts entirely paid....[5]

Taylor's interest in the South, and openness to new ideas and experiences, directly benefited these efforts. For example, his mills became the largest consumer of Sea Island cotton. Moreover, through a meeting with a British friend, he made contacts with the merchant princes who controlled access to cotton grown in the Delta area of Egypt. This led to the establishment in London of the Egyptian Delta Cotton Company, which produced as much cotton as Taylor's operations needed, with it being shipped directly to the United States.[6]

He also demonstrated his growing conviction that management and labor's interests were not inherently at odds. Observing that he "saw the problem of fixed overhead costs clearly," Taylor did away with the 12 hours "on," 12 hours "off" schedule, replacing it with a 3-shift operation of 8 hours apiece. This increased both productivity and made for a better (and safer) workplace.[7]

Having placed International Cotton Mills on a sound and profitable footing, Taylor, as was his practice in such cases, moved on to new challenges, with his professional reputation enhanced and his personal fortune enlarged. Next, he founded his own textile firm of Taylor, Armitage and Eagles, which he assembled through the mergers and acquisitions of a number of existing companies that made the cotton end product used in car tires (known as combed tire fabric).

With remarkable foresight as to the future consumer use of the then infant automobile industry, Taylor propelled his firm into becoming the leading supplier of combed tire fabric. One of the firm's plants in Massachusetts went from producing 1.5 million pounds of fabric in 1915 to 36 million pounds just 2 years later.[8] In short order the business operations of Myron Taylor's new company grew larger than those of International's. Taylor, Armitage and Eagles dominated this new and burgeoning market in part because of superb equipment, but also because of Taylor's decision not to be tied to the highly speculative commodities markets for cotton. Instead, he made a decision that the plants should be run (night and day) on a service basis for the tire companies, with them setting the price at which cotton would be purchased. This protected his firm from the risk of widely fluctuating markets, and was, in turn, quite an acceptable arrangement for the tire companies.[9]

When World War I came, the plants were promptly converted to war production. And while this was done at a significant disadvantage to the firm because of low prices and the fact that that yarn the machinery was designed to spin out was much finer than that which was being spun out for the government, Myron Taylor's view of his national responsibilities was unwaivable during that period. As one biographer has noted, "those mills became 'a war-necessity' industry almost in themselves."[10]

Throughout his years in the textile industry, Taylor had demonstrated an uncanny sense of timing—a knowledge of just when to take on a particular project and, equally, just when to leave it. This talent again stood him in good stead in the years immediately following World War I. The interest of the major rubber tire companies to become more integrated and supply their own cotton fabric requirements, coupled with what he foresaw as a boom-bust cycle coming in the domestic and international cotton markets, persuaded Taylor that the time had come for him to leave the textile field. This he did with his usual decisiveness, and he did so at or near the peak of earnings. By 1923 he had disposed of his holdings in these specialized mills. The buyers were mainly the tire manufacturers who had been his principal customers, including Firestone, Fisk, Goodrich, and Goodyear.

When Myron Taylor closed out his career in textiles in the 1920s, his reputation as a leading figure in American industry was firmly established.[11] The professional qualities he possessed and the management techniques he employed in achieving this result are, therefore, worthy of note.

Taylor's traditional business approach in dealing with a problem situation in the textile industry was perceptively stated as follows:

> The Taylor [F]ormula, like all sound business formulas, was simple, unspectacular, conservative. A textile mill was not doing well. Taylor appeared or was called into the picture. He analyzed the situation cautiously and thoroughly, first from a financial point of view, then with an eye to efficient production, finally with regard for sales. Then he made his recommendations, led or became one of a group that carried them out. If more money was needed he found it—privately; operations in the stock exchange neither were necessary nor did they appeal to him. Usually he simplified the financial structure and with the craft afloat turned his attentions immediately to the engine room. Mills in which Taylor had a hand were characteristically equipped up to the minute. If he had an operating philosophy beyond the best-equipment-well-managed it was that of continuous production. He saw the problem of fixed overhead costs clearly, was a pioneer in that confused industry in putting factory operation on a three-shift basis. (He is proud to remember that other textile industrialists thought him crazy to increase production amid overproduction; they ate their words when his more efficient plants were able to undersell them with a better product.) His money and his mills in order, he was then able to make stable sales connections and the job was almost done. Not quite, for the Taylor [F]ormula was an equation. Beyond the equal sign lay: his own withdrawal with a profit—a fee for work well done or if he had come to own or control the property, its sale outright.[12]

One of Myron Taylor's associates during his textile years was W.J. Casey, later to become Vice Chairman of the Board of the

Maryland Trust Company in Baltimore. Casey remembered well the Taylor Formula, and its many benefits and beneficiaries:

> In this early chapter of textile manufacturing, as in many other industrial operations of the same era, the wage scale had long been of sub-standard character. In the Taylor regime the relation of per capita cotton goods consumed posed the problem that workers … were receiving wages largely excluding from them purchasing power of a normal share of the products they were making. This was a pioneering recognition of the retarding effort on the national economy and upon social welfare of sub-standard wages with impact on each industry. In this particular industry steps were taken towards solving this problem by lifting the wage scale of the local mills above the then prevailing standards. This had an extending influence not only in the textile field but in many other industries. Initiated by enlightened management, this has long since become a fixed pattern of industrial economy.
>
> * * *
>
> Summarizing the Taylor program in textile manufacturing inaugurated in substitution for managerial practices anchored to traditions of preceding decades, the main facets were: Plant modernization; sales policies as an integral part of mill management; raw material controls related to the trend of sales and the timing of the processing of goods on order; credit upbuilding; diversification of products, and the betterment of the conditions of factory workers.[13]

J.D. Armitage was one of Myron Taylor's partners in Taylor, Armitage and Eagles, and in that capacity had a long and close association with him. Asked to identify some of the basic

principles that characterized Taylor's business management philosophy, Armitage responded:

> Make the best quality of goods that materials,
> machinery, and skill can produce.
> Make work pleasant and profitable for workers by
> keeping everything at the highest pitch of efficiency.
> Arrange things so that our output is equal to the
> best in quality, quantity and price.
> Whatever other employers can afford to pay, we
> must be able to pay no less.
> Make customers satisfied so that you can rely upon
> their repeated demands.
> Always prepare a second line of trenches behind the
> first line.
> Never consider yourself beaten or at the end of your
> physical resources.[14]

As Myron Taylor closed out his career in textiles, he had
every reason to contemplate long and happy retirement years. He
was only in his early fifties and in good health. His wife of three
decades, Anabel—who was truly his partner in all of his endeavors—loved to travel. He liked to play golf and tennis. Collecting
art, enjoying his yacht, listening to music, reading, entertaining
friends—these were all favorite pastimes. And the financial means
necessary to support such an elegant lifestyle were assured by the
$25 million personal fortune he had already amassed.

It was an ironic circumstance, however, that Taylor's impressive business acumen, which made possible his early and affluent
retirement, was the very same reason why this retirement was so
short-lived. His extraordinary success in the textile industry had
not gone unnoticed by the nation's leading financiers of that day.
On September 15, 1925, therefore, and at the urging of such Wall
Street bankers as J.P. Morgan, Thomas W. Lamont, and George
F. Baker, Myron Taylor became a Director of the United States

Steel Corporation and a member of its Finance Committee. However, before turning to Taylor's new career in steel, two intervening chapters in his life deserve attention. One has been labeled the "Goodyear Rescue."[15] The other involved his role in masterminding the merger of two New York banks to become what at that time was the largest financial institution in the country.

Notes

1. R. Blough, Myron C. Taylor: An Appreciation (U.S. Steel 1956), p. 10.

2. *The LeRoy Gazette*, May 9, 1906, p. 1.

3. A. Pound, *Myron C. Taylor: Lawyer, Industrialist, Diplomat, Humanitarian* (New York Genealogical and Biographical Society 1955), p. 76.

4. International had plants in Connecticut, Florida, Georgia, Maryland, Massachusetts, New Hampshire, New York, South Carolina, Nova Scotia, and Ontario.

5. *American Wool and Cotton Reporter*, Vol. XXXI, No. 13, March 29, 1917, p. 521.

6. Pound, *supra* note 3, pp. 79-80.

7. Blough, *supra* note 1, p 11.

8. *American Wool and Cotton Reporter*, Vol. XXXI, No. 13, March 29, 1917, p. 521.

9. *See* April 29, 1936, letter from T.W. Lamont to R. Ingersoll (Lamont Papers, Baker Library, Harvard Business School).

10. Blough, *supra* note 1, p. 12.

11. J.P. Morgan subsequently prevailed upon Taylor to help his son-in-law with respect to the rehabilitation of Dwight Manufacturing Company, an old-line Massachusetts cotton firm that had fallen on hard times. Agreeing to recapitalize one-third of the entity if Morgan would put up the other two-thirds (which he did), Taylor closed down the New England operations in favor of committing the company's resources to its Birmingham, Alabama, plant. This business plan was astute, and proved to be a money-making proposition for both Morgan and Taylor. Pound, *supra* note 3, pp. 83-84.

12. *Fortune* (Vol. XIII, No. 6 June 1936) p. 118.

13. W.J. Casey February 6, 1950, letter to M.C. Taylor, p. 2 (Taylor Papers, Cornell University).

14. Memorandum of J.D. Armitage, reported in Pound, *supra* note 1, p. 83.

15. Pound, *supra* note 3, p. 94.

CHAPTER VI

The Goodyear Rescue and the Guaranty Trust Merger

The end of World War I ushered in a nationwide depression. The time was 1920-21. Although short-lived, the economic hard times were severe and took their toll on businesses, large and small, across the country. This included the Goodyear Tire and Rubber Company of Akron, Ohio, then the largest rubber manufacturing company in the country.

Goodyear, founded in 1898, grew by leaps and bounds under the leadership of Frank Seiberling, and by 1920 owned capital assets of some $90 million and did an annual business of more than $200 million. Then the bubble burst. The company's large inventories of rubber and cotton plummeted as much as 40% in value. March 1920 sales of $20 million dropped to $4.5 million in November. Despite deep cuts in the workforce, the ability to meet even the reduced payrolls was often in doubt. Merchandise suppliers pressed for payment of past due bills. Banks called existing loans and refused to make new ones. The market price of Goodyear stock fell from a level as high as $400 per share to a low of $5.

With debts totaling $100 million, it appeared highly likely that the Goodyear Tire and Rubber Company would be forced into receivership. This drastic result was avoided, however, as the result of the successful completion of a plan of corporate refinancing and reorganization of major importance in the annals of American industry.

It is enough to note here the broad outlines of this so-called "Goodyear Rescue." A merchandise creditors' committee was established. This was followed by the formation of a bank creditors' committee, made up of representatives of major financial institutions in New York, Chicago, Cleveland, and Akron. There were countless meetings and prolonged negotiations among the members of these committees as well as Goodyear officials and shareholders. Complicated financial and legal decisions regarding how to raise the enormous sums necessary to keep the company afloat had to be made and were made. The board of directors was reconstituted and new top management was installed. By May 1921 the reorganization was essentially complete. It was, however, not only complete but, more importantly, it was highly successful.

The Goodyear Tire and Rubber Company had indeed been rescued. Furthermore, it was destined soon to have regained its status as one of the country's preeminent manufacturing enterprises.

This summary of the Goodyear reorganization deserves a place in this book because of Myron C. Taylor's role in bringing it about. It is difficult, however, to define that role with any precision and certainty. The reason for this lies in conflicting accounts of the real nature of Taylor's participation in the venture.

One point of view paints Myron Taylor as the recognized leader who masterminded the dramatic, company-saving reorganization. Thus, "Mr. Taylor carried out one of his greatest of economic undertakings.... There is no statue of Myron C. Taylor among the congeries of rubber plants in Akron, Ohio. But, metaphorically at least, one will always stand there."[1] To the same effect: "Switching from the grudging Goodyear bankers to the general creditors of the company, he [Taylor] prepared another plan for the rescue of Goodyear.... Mr. Taylor saw the reorganization through, and then pulled out. Saving Goodyear involved no personal reward for the man that did it."[2] And yet again to the same effect: "Its [Goodyear's] perilous position spurred Taylor into action. To protect himself [Taylor had sold Goodyear one

of his cotton mills], he brought his fellow creditors together, ral-
lied the banks, and by reorganizing it saved the company from a
receivership that might have been costly to all."[3]

There is another point of view that assigns a much more
modest role to Myron Taylor in achieving the Goodyear rescue. A
number of historical accounts of the reorganization, some describing it in considerable detail, make no specific reference to Taylor's
participation.[4] Among the individuals singled out for mention of
their respective contributions to the project are the lawyer, Paul
D. Cravath; the banker, Clarence Dillon; and the industrialist,
Owen D. Young. The history of the Cravath law firm gives Taylor
passing reference in reorganizing the company, noting: "A merchandise creditors' committee was formed: Myron C. Taylor and
Frederick L. Jenckes represented the cotton suppliers...."[5]

The truth likely is between the two extremes. What can
be reconstructed is that Frank Seiberling had a long-standing
business relationship with Taylor, which also grew into a strong
personal bond. Seiberling had engineered the purchase of Taylor's New Bedford, Massachusetts, tire fabric plant prior to the
collapse of the bubble, and now sought out Taylor's good counsel
on how to deal with the imbroglio in which he found Goodyear.
Taylor agreed to study the company's operations, and found them
fundamentally sound.[6]

This convinced Taylor to propose a plan to a consortium
of bank creditors. To his astonishment, however, it was rejected
because of some personal antagonism on the part of one of the
bankers. It was then left to the entire group of creditors to tackle
the issue of whether to force Goodyear into receivership (and dis-
mantlement), or to restructure its debt to allow the company to
go forward. Here, Taylor's leadership in convincing a number of
skeptical and recalcitrant creditors to forestall their particular
interests in favor of the bigger picture and greater good seems to
have been his most important contribution; in achieving that aim,
his "prime stipulation of the reorganization effort [was] that no

Myron Taylor formal portrait

member of any committee of creditors should receive any compensation out of Goodyear's adversity."[7] In the end, receivership was in fact rejected as an option, the banks ended up infusing $32 million into Goodyear's operations, the rights of the company's creditors were ultimately validated, and the company itself revived and thrived.[8]

That Myron Taylor was one of the most influential participants in the process of saving Goodyear from financial disaster seems clear, even if it represents a modification of the point of view that he was the universally recognized leader who masterminded and dominated the company's reorganization. The available objective evidence, as well as a professional understanding of how such complex reorganizations are effected, supports this somewhat more limited description of the role he played.

The 1920s also allowed Taylor to display the financial and leadership skills he had perfected during his textile years (and used to good advantage in the Goodyear Rescue) in another arena—the banking industry. In 1920, Taylor formally entered that arena upon election as a director of the Guaranty Trust Company in New York City; undoubtedly, this was because of his close relationship with J.P. Morgan.

Guaranty Trust was then the fourth largest U.S. bank. Next door in an adjoining building was the National Bank of Commerce, then ranked ninth in size. As noted at the time, "[s]hould a ghost with the gift of flitting through walls flit through the rear wall of Guaranty Trust and continue flitting, it would flit through the rear wall of National Bank of Commerce. For these two great U.S. banks [stood] back-to-back."[9]

For reasons far more weighty than their geographical proximity, there were long-standing rumors of a Guaranty Trust–National Bank of Commerce merger. Prior efforts at merging the two had failed; in the eyes of the Bank of Commerce officials, failure had been because of the way J.P. Morgan's chief lieutenant, Thomas W. Lamont, had handled the Guaranty side of the negotiations. In 1928, with Morgan and Lamont off in Europe restructuring Germany's World War I reparations, Myron Taylor stepped in.[10]

Reducing "his formula for this giant consolidation on a single sheet of paper," Taylor first checked with his long-time friend, mentor, and Long Island neighbor, George F. Baker Sr. Baker was the president of First National Bank of New York and together with J.P. Morgan dominated American banking in that era. With Baker's blessing,[11] Taylor then set up a meeting with another old friend, James Alexander, the president of Commerce Bank. Initially, Alexander was reluctant to bite because of opposition interposed by one of his lawyers. Taylor's "usual quiet persistence" eviscerated those concerns,[12] however, with the entire negotiation process taking just three weeks. When it was over the combined, new bank, with total assets of approximately $2 billion, was for a time the largest bank in the country. In essence the investment banker on the transaction, Myron Taylor asked for and received no compensation, notwithstanding that it was publicly reported that "a bill for $1 million might not have been out of order."[13]

In addition to his membership on the Guaranty Trust board, Taylor was also a director of the First National Bank from 1922 to 1953. Upon his relinquishment of that post, the First National Bank recognized the importance of the Taylor–Baker bond, resolving that "[h]e stood high in the confidence of [Mr.] Baker; over the years the board came to share Mr. Baker's affection and admiration."[14]

In view of his proven record for sound business and financial judgment, it is not surprising that Taylor was invited to join the governing boards of a number of other, prominent American business enterprises. These included directorships of the American Telephone and Telegraph Co.; Atchison, Topeka and Santa Fe Railway Co.; Erie Railroad Co.; Mutual Life Insurance Company of New York; and New York Central Railroad Co.

It was at the United States Steel Corporation, however, where Myron Taylor firmly established his reputation as one of the nation's preeminent industrial leaders. We now turn to Taylor's steel years.

Notes

1. R. Blough, Myron C. Taylor: An Appreciation (U.S. Steel 1956), pp. 13-14. *See also* Brian Apelt, *The Corporation: A Centennial Biography of United States Steel Corporation* (U. Pittsburgh 2000), p. 152.

2. A. Pound, *Myron C. Taylor: Lawyer, Industrialist, Diplomat, Humanitarian* (New York Genealogical and Biographical Society 1955), pp. 97-98.

3. *Fortune* (Vol. XIII, No. 6, June 1936), p. 120.

4. *See* H. Allen, *The House of Goodyear* (Corday & Gross 1936); N. Beasley, *Men Working: A Story of The Goodyear Tire and Rubber Co.* (Harper & Brothers 1936); P. Litchfield, *Industrial Voyage: My Life as an Industrial Lieutenant* (Doubleday 1954); M. O'Reilly, *The Goodyear Story* (Benjamin Company Book 1983).

5. R. Swaine, *The Cravath Firm and Its Predecessors 1819-1948* (Vols. I & II) (New York 1948).

6. Pound, *supra* note 2, p. 95.

7. Blough, *supra* note 1, p. 13. Receivership would have been a "calamity," both for Goodyear and the entire tire industry. *See* T.W. Lamont April 21, 1936, letter to R. Ingersoll (Lamont Papers, Baker Library, Harvard Business School).

8. Pound, *supra* note 2, pp. 96-97.

9. *Time*, March 4, 1929, p. 55.

10. Pound, *supra* note 2, pp. 101-02.

11. Pound, *supra* note 2, p. 101.

12. One can only imagine government regulators and antitrust enforcers in today's world reacting to such an "old boy" network of doing mergers and acquisitions.

13. *Fortune* (Vol. XIII, No. 6, June 1936), p. 120.

14. Pound, *supra* note 2, pp. 103-04.

CHAPTER VII

Ten Years of Steel

The United States Steel Corporation was founded in 1901 when the nation's leading investment banker, J. Pierpont Morgan, engineered the merger of several steel-producing companies into the world's largest industrial enterprise. The "Corporation" (as it will hereafter be referred) employed tens of thousands of workers in subsidiary companies scattered throughout the country; owned huge deposits of iron ore, coal, and limestone; and operated far-flung railroad and shipping networks. At that time it accounted for 65% of the nation's steel-making capacity.

The Corporation prospered from the outset under the leadership of Judge Elbert H. Gary, a corporate lawyer who in 1903 became the chairman of the Board of Directors. Gary ruled U.S. Steel with a heavy hand until his death in 1927. About two years earlier, however, two prominent members of the Board, J.P. Morgan (son of the founder) and George F. Baker Sr. (president of the First National Bank of New York) had given some thought to Gary's successor. As Morgan would later recall:

> The way it began was this: Back in 1924 and '25 the elder George F. Baker and I had a very heart-to-heart conversation on the subject of the position of the Steel Corporation. As Judge Elbert H. Gary was nearly eighty, it was becoming important to think of someone to succeed him.... Mr. Baker and I agreed that, in spite of what

the Judge felt, we ought to introduce additional strength somehow.

Mr. Baker said, "All right, how, but whom do you think we ought to have? The board is getting to be too much composed of officers of subsidiary companies. Whom can we get?" And, as far as I can remember, Mr. Baker and I both thought of Mr. Taylor at the same time.

Our whole course was certainly justified, because within two years of that time Judge Gary passed on, and without Mr. Taylor there we should have been out of luck.[1]

Initially reluctant to make the commitment, Taylor's resolve was strengthened when J.P. Morgan told him he would break a long-standing rule of not holding office in a corporation, and become Chairman of U.S. Steel; but only on the condition that Taylor would sign on as well. With that, Taylor's answer was a simple one: "I'll do it."[2]

Thus began Myron C. Taylor's career in steel. On September 15, 1925, he was elected to membership on the Board of Directors, as well as on the all-powerful Finance Committee of the United States Steel Corporation. On December 27, 1927, he assumed the chairmanship of the Finance Committee and served in the capacity until January 1, 1934. From March 29, 1932, to April 5, 1938, he was Chairman of the Board and Chief Executive Officer of the Corporation. On January 12, 1956, he retired as a Director and member of the Finance Committee.

Taylor's connection with U.S. Steel thus spanned a period of more than 30 years. But it was during the 10-year period from 1927 to 1938 that he dominated the affairs of the Corporation, and left his mark on its history. His stay for even this short time was longer than he had anticipated; as he later noted, he had succeeded Judge Gary "with an understanding that I would remain only until a new management could be set up."[3] This expectation proved to be overly optimistic, for it failed to take into account the advent of the great Depression. These Depression years brought with them problems that required Taylor to remain at the corporate helm for the duration. And the duration for Taylor in this case would be until 1938, when he moved onto the international stage at the behest of President Roosevelt.

Upon taking up his posts at the Corporation, Taylor—originally dubbed "the man nobody knows," the "sphinx of Wall Street"—became a reluctant media target. Feature and cover articles soon appeared in such leading periodicals as *Time*, *Fortune*, *Business Week*, *The New Yorker*, and the *Saturday Evening Post*. Not all were completely flattering. In *Fortune*, for example, Taylor's overly serious side was depicted as the man bearing responsibility for "the destiny of the greatest industrial enterprise in America and the welfare of the 200,000 human beings who work[ed] for it":

> He is a tall, heavy-shouldered man, handsome. He can be very impressive. He talks in a low, well-modulated voice and the life in his face is in his eyes. The lines in his face are pugnacious, determined. Reading, he wears a tortoise-shell pince-nez. He invariably dresses in very high stiff collars, double breasted dark blue suits, dark ties. In pictures of him taken when he was younger, the set of his features was more aggressive. Nowadays he often looks tired.
>
> All Myron Taylor's adult life has been lived as a rich man. He has done the things rich men do, lived their life. But just as nothing he ever did in business caught and held him emotionally, nothing in his personal life seems to have caught or held him. The life of Riley never took with Myron Taylor; there's no evidence he ever got any fun out of it. He has shot on the moors of Scotland a season or two. He has lived in Newport, in Palm Beach in rented villas. He has cruised on chartered yachts. He belongs to many clubs he never visits. When, just before the War, he felt himself growing too stale he turned to

walking, twenty-five miles a day for thirty days in the Swiss Alps. He has collected a little art—a few tapestries, an Italian primitive or two. Italy has interested him a little. He owns a villa outside Florence that once belonged to the Medici, spends a little time there each year.

. . .

Mr. Taylor is not a hard worker, as American executives like to think of themselves as hard workers. His hours are not long, he is never feverish, he has always taken vacations when it pleased him. Yet he is strangely a man who gives the impression of never relaxing. Perhaps it is because he gets so little enjoyment out of idleness, perhaps because as a responsible man he can never leave his responsibilities alone. Perhaps it is because he has always placed such a very great premium on dignity. He is very close to his wife, a handsome, kindly woman who is always with him. They have no children.[4]

An earlier cover story in *Time*, however, presented a somewhat different picture. Believing they were unlikely to be even able to get a glimpse of the great man, the *Time* reporters were surprised when their request for an interview was met with a "courteous" yes. *Time*'s first impression was of Taylor's "good looks," and found him with "gentleness and humor," "surprisingly human," "a man of great personal charm and geniality," and that "no one could doubt the sincerity of his dislike for anything resembling self exploitation." The article closed by quoting an evaluation of Taylor by a prominent New York banker: [H]is main characteristic is justice, coupled with a high sense of honor.... To a greater extent than any other big business figure I know of, he has risen by the sheer power of his own intellect—clear reasoning and resolute acting."[5]

Taylor's initial goal at U.S. Steel was to acquire a firsthand, working knowledge of all aspects of the company's operations. He spent almost two years in achieving this result. In the course of

Taylor on the cover of *Time* magazine when he became chairman of
U.S. Steel's Finance Committee in 1927

doing so he read and digested huge quantities of written reports
and materials, made personal visits to all the major U.S. Steel
plants and facilities, and interviewed a wide array of corporate
employees, ranging from senior executives to rank-and-file workers. As he surveyed it, the Corporation had "experienced 'a slide
from leadership', a slip into a rigid pattern of complacent maturity,
and [it was] anchored a bit too firmly in the past."[6]

His period of orientation over, Taylor assumed the important responsibilities of Chairman of the Finance Committee. The

first major problem he faced related to the Corporation's existing indebtedness, which totaled $400 million. The year was 1929, but the October 29 stock market crash and the great Depression that followed were still to come. Taylor foresaw the troubled economic conditions that lay ahead for the country, and was therefore especially concerned about the impact on the Corporation's future of the burdensome ongoing interest charges required to finance its outstanding indebtedness.

"Perhaps I'm a little old-fashioned," Taylor said at the time. "I don't like to see a mortgage on U.S. Steel." Recalling his concern about the state of the nation's economy, he later conceded: "No one paid any attention to me. But nevertheless I was convinced that the Corporation should begin to clear the decks and get ready."[7]

Taylor's solution was to alter the Corporation's financial structure in a fundamental and critical way. Bonds of a value of some $340 million were retired. The funds necessary to achieve this result were raised through the sale of 1,016,605 additional shares of common stock, supplemented by recourse to available surplus reserves. The savings in interest charges resulting from these transactions alone totaled about $31 million per annum.

Myron Taylor evaluated the outcome of this venture with characteristic understatement. "It is fortunately not necessary to speculate," he said later in 1938, "as to what would be the condition of the Corporation today, had it been required to pay this heavy interest charge during the depression years."[8] A few years earlier the *New York Herald Tribune* in 1933 was not so restrained: "If it had not been for [the Taylor-directed] bond retirements and maintenance of the dividend rate, it is believed that economic pressures of the last three years might have forced defaults."[9]

In 1938, J.P. Morgan assessed what Taylor had accomplished in even starker terms: "There are three things that Mr. Taylor has done which are of supreme importance to the Company. One of them, and the first one, was the extinguishment of the bonded debt, which was really entirely due to him. That was the most

important thing that ever happened. That was done in 1928 and
'29, and we should now be 'busted' permanently if it hadn't been
for that. There is no doubt about it. And we are not now close to
being 'busted'—not by a long shot."[10]

At the same time he was engaged in revising the Corporation's financial structure and ensuring that it would be in a position to survive what lay ahead in the Depression years, Taylor's
attention was also focused on the state of its far-flung physical
plants and properties. One of his first moves in this connection
was to develop a comprehensive survey of all of those resources.

U.S. Steel was an extraordinarily complex entity, owning
approximately 200 subsidiary companies. Many of these units
were engaged directly in making steel and their plants and mills
were located in four main steel-making districts. These districts,
in turn, were centered in Pittsburgh, Pennsylvania; Chicago, Illinois; Youngstown, Ohio; and Birmingham, Alabama.

Other subsidiary companies were engaged in providing raw
materials and services essential to the production of steel. The
Corporation, for example, controlled one-half of the country's iron
ore reserves.[11] It had "enough coal in sight to last a century."[12] And
it owned and operated a transportation and warehousing system
capable of carrying the coal and iron ore from the mines to the
mills and then moving the finished steel products on to their designated markets. U.S. Steel's railway system included 1,190 loco-
motives pulling 41,700 freight cars on some 4,000 miles of track.
Seventy-eight ore-carrying boats ultimately plied the Great Lakes,
including the later-christened *Myron C. Taylor*, which became the
flagship of the U.S. Steel fleet with an iron ore capacity of 11,600
gross tons. Twenty-eight ocean-going freighters rounded out the
Corporation's naval resources.[13]

And while these assets were mighty and formidable, there
was no doubt that the Corporation was losing ground to its competitors. It was no longer a leader in industrial efficiency, new
consumer demands had changed the economy away from heavy
industrial needs to lighter, consumer-oriented goods (e.g., cars,

kitchen stoves, etc.), its plant locations no longer made much sense, its internal structure(s) hindered quick and nimble economic adjustments to customer needs, etc. As a result, when Myron Taylor acceded to the pressure to become U.S. Steel's Chairman and CEO, he knew that he had taken on "the toughest industrial job in the world."[14] And in taking that job on, he knew the stakes involved:

> The Corporation is much more than a commercial enterprise. It is a national institution and its pulse throbs with that of the Nation. And so it cannot be successfully managed solely and restrictedly as a commercial enterprise. But, at the same time, it is a private institution, in that it must stand on its own feet. It has the three-fold obligation of keeping its policies in consonance with the public interest and with the interest of the more than two hundred thousand men and women whose savings have been entrusted to it, and with the interest of the two hundred fifty thousand employees who depend upon the Corporation for a living.[15]

Applying the Taylor Formula to Steel

Within four months of his taking over the reigns, the *New York World-Telegram* breathlessly reported:

> Coming into steel and iron a stranger … Mr. Taylor has … simplified the financial structure of the largest industrial enterprise in the world; revamped, reconditioned and expanded the plants and equipment of the company, made broad changes in the personnel that involved the entire plant family of approximately 210,000 employees from the president down to the lowest mill-yard worker.[16]

In so effecting these changes, Taylor appears to have reengi-neered his famous "Formula" to a different industry. For example, he closed or sold 34 plants that specialized in the heavy indus-trial steel products or were too far from the Corporation's cli-ents. Taylor recognized that iron and steel were, at heart, merely commodities, and "a large part of their cost to the consumer is transportation. The ideal plant location is one where the cost of getting raw materials into the plant and getting the finished prod-ucts out to the customers at a minimum."[17] Plants therefore had to be (and were thereafter) grouped in and around major hubs of transportation. He also sold off U.S. Steel's Canadian subsidiaries because tariffs and other problems had reduced their ability to be competitive.

Modern equipment had to be the order of the day. Under Taylor's leadership, some $643 million was spent to upgrade the Corporation's operations. Fully a third of that was committed during the nadir of the Depression (1930-33). And the Corpo-ration converted to continuous strip mills, and into alloys and stainless steel, as well as improving and expanding its facilities for flat hot and cold rolled products. In the words of an independent study, the Corporation became "the last word in modernity of wire, rails, and structural shapes."[18]

Taylor merged two of the Corporation's principal subsid-iaries—Carnegie Steel Company and Illinois Steel Company—to create Carnegie-Illinois Corporation. This led to dramatic cost savings, the elimination of redundancies, and brought on improved productivity. Recruiting Benjamin Fairless away from Republic Steel to head the new entity not only reenergized those operations but also served notice to complacent U.S. Steel exec-utives that promotions would not always come from within; the move further served to please Wall Street.[19] As noted by *Fortune*, Carnegie-Illinois became, standing alone, a most formidable oper-ation, making "as much steel as England and Germany together produced in 1934."[20]

MAN OF THE WEEK IN FINANCE

Evening Journal, April 18, 1931

Acquisitions and investments demonstrated Taylor's business plan for the Corporation. Columbia Steel Corporation was acquired for $41 million, financed by U.S. Steel common stock. This acquisition gave the Corporation direct access to the important (and expanding) West Coast markets. Oil Well Supply Company was bought to expand U.S. Steel's reach and diversification. Taylor reached down to the South, expanding and diversifying further Tennessee Coal & Iron's product lines. And the Corporation's traditional operations in Pittsburgh and Chicago were also upgraded.

The Man of the Week in Finance

New York Evening Journal, April 4, 1932

The year 1938 brought two new major initiatives. First, Myron Taylor implemented his decision that Pittsburgh, not New York City, was to be the headquarters of U.S. Steel. For a city that had always been the center of the steel universe, that might seem not to be very meaningful. But during the depths of the Depression, with capacity at disastrous levels and things seeming to point westward (e.g., the Columbia Steel purchase), Taylor had had to make a major public address in 1935, assuring Pittsburgh that its status would remain unchallenged. As such, when the news was announced in December of 1937, Pittsburgh declared December 20 as "United States Steel Day," and staged a gala reception to welcome Benjamin Fairless, the newly elected president of the Corporation.[21]

The other major initiative was the Irwin Works, named for William A. Irwin, former president of the Corporation. This model plant, located on the Monongahela River near Pittsburgh, cost $47 million and was able to produce 600,000 tons of steel a year. The Irwin Works were dedicated on December 15, 1938. Myron Taylor was not present for the occasion because he was in London at the time. He had gone to England at the request of President Roosevelt to address the problem of political refugees fleeing from Nazi Germany.

It was arranged, however, for Taylor to make a radio address to those who had assembled in Pittsburgh for the dedication ceremony. This he did, entitling his comments: "The Importance of Our New Steel Works."

Taylor's remarks must have required some 20 minutes to complete in the measured style of delivery he invariably used. A sampling of those remarks follows:

> Its [the new Irwin plant] purpose is ever better to serve the community and the world of today and of tomorrow. It is not just a steel works, it is not just an assembly of mortar and metal. It is a contribution towards making life fuller and better.
>
> ...
>
> This greatest and most modern of all the steel works of the world was conceived and created to contribute to human occupation and human happiness. To repeat, it is not only a great mill—it is an example of the cooperative use of the savings of the public and of the ingenuity of the human mind in a freedom of action possible only in a free country. It is a symbol reared to the glory of the unfettered human achievement—to the glory of free enterprise.
>
> ...

As men come and go through the corridors of the
years, each lending his hand to the task of his day and age,
this plant will long stand as a beacon of inspiration and of
courage displayed in a time of depression.[22]

Although Myron Taylor could be engaging when involved
in one-on-one or small-group conversation, his manner of public discourse was often ponderous. Indeed, *Fortune* magazine
noted his "record of platitudinous public pronouncements."[23] His
remarks at the dedication of the Irwin Works clearly fell into this
latter category.

Another problem requiring Taylor's attention related to the
manner in which the Corporation marketed its finished products.
In short, the existing sales program was inefficient and costly. The
various subsidiary companies had independent, poorly coordinated, and sometimes even competing sales departments and personnel. Taylor's solution was to consolidate sales offices, streamline
merchandising procedures, and allow for quicker decision making
at these "lower levels." He also convened meetings in both New
York and Pittsburgh of the Corporation's sales managers to plan
specific counterattacks against its more pesky competitors.[24] Taylor also changed the Corporation's relationship to the media, man-
dating that it become more purposeful and offensive-minded in
getting out affirmative news; and in 1936 he christened a new
publication to that end: *U.S. Steel News.*

From the time he first became associated with U.S. Steel,
Taylor made clear that the stimulation of corporate research was
one of his priorities. It is appropriate to ask, therefore, how successful he was in achieving this objective.

Taylor had no doubt on this score and was proud of the result.
In his 1938 valedictory report to shareholders he stated:

There must be an inquiry into the nature of things,
in order that the output of the Corporation may be of
a constantly increasing usefulness. In other words, there

must be both pure and applied research—the pure research to extend our horizons and the applied to make better that which we already know. Ten years ago we set up a central research laboratory at Kearny, New Jersey. Since then metallurgy and research have been elevated into a major division of the Corporation; that is, metallurgy and research now rank with production, sales and finance.[25]

In responding to Taylor's conclusion that "metallurgy and research now rank with production, sales and finance," one critic has written: "To the continuing detriment of the firm and its industry, Taylor was wrong."[26] This critic is Professor Paul A. Tiffany of the University of Pennsylvania. It is Tiffany's contention that any attempt to build a strong, centralized research department at U.S. Steel necessarily encountered two basic obstacles: "a fear that the centralization of the function would diminish the power of the subsidiaries and their managers, and a belief that research not directly related to short-term commercialization was an unnecessary expense."[27] And he maintains that these formidable obstacles were never wholly overcome, at least during Myron Taylor's years at the helm. At the same time, Tiffany does acknowledge that the Corporation's centralized research program grew in size and achieved important scientific results.

Regardless of one's assessment of the strength of the Corporation's commitment to research under Myron Taylor's leadership, there is another aspect of the matter that is worthy of note. This has nothing to do with research, per se. Rather, it looks to Taylor's use of the Corporation's research capabilities as an indication of his own personal makeup. There were often times when his curiosity had been piqued by something he had heard or read, and he simply wanted to know more about the subject. On such occasions it was not unusual for the research division to receive a note or a newspaper clipping from the Chairman requesting further information on a particular topic. A typical scenario of this sort found Taylor interested in the pros and cons of steel shingles as well as in developing a process whereby supersonic waves might be used to dispel fog. In short, he had a searching and inquiring mind.

The bottom line of Taylor's various efforts demonstrates the efficacy of his leadership. At the lowest point of the Depression steel production was at 245 pounds per capita. Taylor vowed to bring it to between 800 and 900 pounds, and by 1937 he had done so: steel production that year stood at 879 pounds per capita. And although he had eliminated approximately 2 million tons in inefficient production capacity, U.S. Steel's ingot capacity dwarfed where it had been before Taylor began his tenure—by January of 1938 it stood at 29 million net tons.

Finally, in responding to changed markets and client needs, by 1938 "scarcely one-fourth of U.S. Steel's product was of the same composition, or made in the same way, as in 1928."[28]

An Innovative Approach to Labor in a Period of Extremis

Although Myron Taylor's efforts to reorganize and strengthen U.S. Steel affected every aspect of its corporate life, it was his personnel policies that provide special insights about him both as a public figure and a private individual.

When Taylor became head of the Finance Committee in 1927, there were 231,549 men and women employed by the Corporation. In 1937, his last full year as Chairman of the Board, the corresponding number was 261,293. In addition to these U.S. Steel employees, there were thousands of other workers indirectly affected by the Corporation's labor policies and practices because of their ripple effect throughout the industry and the country.

As indicated earlier, the decade of the 1930s began with the country in its history's worst economic calamity. Closed banks, failing businesses, long unemployment lines, and swollen welfare

The *Myron C. Taylor* was launched in 1929 for the
Pittsburgh Steamship Company (the private fleet of U.S. Steel).
The *Taylor* remains an active, versatile member of the
USS Great Lakes Fleet in the limestone, coal, and aggregates trades.

rolls were hallmarks of the day. U.S. Steel Corporation was faced
with a falling demand for its product and the related necessity of
cutting costs of production. A wholesale reduction in the work
force was, of course, one possible solution—and one that corporate executives today would reflexively invoke. Taylor, however,
chose an innovative, alternative course of action—he decided to
inaugurate a share-the-work program.

Under this plan, the work at hand was divided among current employees in as fair and equitable a manner as possible. As
a result, no person lost his or her job, but rather continued to be
employed at his or her regular rate of pay, although for a shorter
working day and correspondingly less total compensation. In
1932, when the company was operating at an average of 17.7% of
ingot capacity (hitting a low of 11.8% in July of 1932) and at 18.3%
of finished steel capacity, this share-the-work program provided
an income to some 75,000 more individuals than would otherwise
have been required to handle the decreased workload; looked at
another way, the Corporation had only one full-time worker for

each seven part-time workers that year. The satisfaction Taylor took in having established this policy as a means of combating the hardships of unemployment was evident in his conviction that it "turned out to be the most important single contribution to the human side of the [D]epression."[29]

Taylor must have found painful an independent appraisal of his role in creating the share-the-work program. While pronouncing his labor policies as "consistently thoughtful, sometimes progressive," *Fortune* magazine further described them as "always detached," and went on to say:

> Myron Taylor at his desk studies figures, issues orders to share what work there is among all those who are dependent upon his enterprise for their food and shelter. That there is great hardship in the sharing of work that, unshared, did little more than keep one alive, he knows only because someone has told him so.[30]

This harsh conclusion, to the extent it implied a lack of compassion and concern for the Corporation's rank-and-file workers, seems both unfair and unfounded.[31]

As the Depression continued and worsened, Taylor's sensitivity to the welfare of the Corporation's employees took other, compelling turns. One was in the form of a program that encouraged the planting and cultivation of home vegetable gardens and harvesting the resulting produce. An employee who wished to participate in this project was provided with an individual plot of land located near his place of work together with essential seed, fertilizer, and equipment. In 1933, for example, participants in this program of community gardens produced fruits and vegetables with a total estimated value of $1.8 million on 85,915 separate plots covering 16,506 acres of land.[32] Another program addressed employees who had debt and/or mortgage problems; they were extended low-interest loans of more than $7 million between 1930 and 1935. And in the bleakest year of the Depression, the

Corporation spent over $16 million in direct relief to compensate employees for wages lost while they were only partially employed.

These share-the-work, home garden, and credit and subsidy programs—all designed to address the miseries created by the Depression—provide an important insight into how Myron Taylor viewed his responsibility toward the thousands of employees of U.S. Steel. In a conversation with Clarence Pickett, then secretary of the American Friends Service Committee, Taylor made a revealing comment about his striving to keep in proper balance his obligations to workers and stockholders alike. In Pickett's words: "One day when Myron Taylor and I were sitting together in his office, he revealed to me something of his own inner struggle when he said, 'It is not easy to be a kind of St. Francis and at the same time an effective chairman of a great corporation; and I should like to be both.'"[33]

During the Taylor years a variety of additional employee benefit programs were initiated or, if already in place, were strengthened and improved. These included plans designed to help employees finance the acquisition of their own homes and to provide pensions to those reaching retirement. Apprentice and vocational training programs offered educational opportunities ranging from elementary courses open to foreign-born workers to instruction in the more advanced technology of steel making. Group life and health insurance coverage was increased, and a vacation plan instituted.

Myron Taylor truly believed that there was not "a brighter page in the history of a company than the one which your Corporation wrote with respect to the treatment of its employees during the entire [D]epression."[34]

Taylor Encounters the New Deal

All of the foregoing took place upon the initiative of Myron Taylor and the Corporation. He found it more difficult to adjust to initiatives brought on by the New Deal, however, believing (at least at first) that comprehensive governmental interference and directives would hinder industrial recovery.[35]

One of the major new pieces of legislation enacted in the "First One Hundred Days" was the National Industrial Recovery Act. Widely publicized as the NRA, the law was designed to improve working conditions by allowing for the creation of industrial "codes," which would regulate working hours, minimum wages, etc., in specific industries.

When Frances Perkins, President Roosevelt's Secretary of Labor, embarked on her attempt to work up a code for the steel industry, one of her first calls was to Myron Taylor. Perkins asked for his cooperation, and said that she wanted to speak with employees without management present. As she writes, Taylor "politely agreed, whether reluctantly or not I shall never know." She later met with William Irwin at U.S. Steel's plant at McKeesport, and found him "courteous, frank, and vigorous in his co-operation."[36] According to Perkins, the same reception was not always forthcoming at other steel mills.

Some weeks later, the Labor Department was drafting the final provisions for the steel code, and Secretary Perkins invited the leaders of the steel companies to Washington to meet with her. Unbeknownst to those leaders, Perkins had also invited William Green, president of the American Federation of Labor, to attend; although Green did not technically represent steel workers (they were not unionized), Perkins thought his presence would facilitate an agreement on the code.

Unfortunately, the opposite occurred. When the steel executives (including Taylor) entered the meeting room, they were startled to see Green there. In the words of Secretary Perkins:

> Most of them did not permit themselves to be introduced to Mr. Green. They backed away into a corner, like frightened boys. It was the most embarrassing social experience of my life. I had never met people who did not

know how, with hypocrisy perhaps but with an outward
surface of correct politeness, to say how-to-you-do even
to people they detested. I had been engaged in conversation with Green and went right back to him, thinking
perhaps he would not notice the coldness. After a while,
at the invitation of the steel executives' lawyers, I went
over to the corner where they were having their huddle
to see what ailed them. I found that they had expected to
see only me and economists of the Department of Labor.
They did not see how they could meet with the president
of the AF of L. I was a little shocked, unable to believe
that grown men could be so timid. But their faces were
long, their eyes were solemn, and they were the picture
of men with no self-assurance whatsoever.

I still could not see why anybody should be afraid of
William Green, mildest and most polite of men. The steel
executives explained to me privately that if it were known
that they had sat down in the same room with William
Green and talked with him, it would ruin their long-time
position against labor organization in their industry.

"But," I argued with them, "Mr. Green doesn't represent the steel workers. He is not a steel worker. I will tell
you what he is going to say."

I gave them a copy of his prepared remarks. He was
to make a laudatory statement regarding the NRA and to
give his full approval to the proposed steel code.

No, that would not do. They were still afraid that it
would become known in the steel industry towns that they
had spoken to Mr. Green of the AF of L. This backing and
filling went on for almost three quarters of an hour. The
difficulty penetrated to Green. I apologized to him. He
was courtesy itself. In the end, however, he left in a huff.

As the great barons of steel filed out, still looking
solemn and sorrowful, I could not resist the temptation

to tell them that their behavior had surprised me and that I felt as though I had entertained eleven-year-old boys at their first party rather than men to whom the most important industry in the United States had been committed.[37]

Distressed and upset, Perkins went to report on this incident to FDR. Roosevelt, however, laughed heartily at the image conjured up by the Secretary of Labor, and she ultimately joined in his reaction. In her memoirs Perkins added two other interesting vignettes. The first was the fact that FDR "never forgot … [t]his episode. He often referred to it years later, and even after Myron Taylor had become one of his best friends he would say, 'You know, Myron has learned a lot from us. He is a better man than he was that day he wouldn't talk with William Green. And I think he is happier.'"[38]

Taylor's reaction may, in fact, have been caused by the group dynamics at the Labor Department. As Perkins next recounted:

A few weeks later I was having a dinner party of twelve or fifteen guests and Green was among them. During the dinner a member of my family was called to the telephone and I heard her say, "Oh, how nice! Do come over. We're having a few people in to dinner. Do join us for coffee."

I didn't think to ask who it might be. But we had no sooner left the dining-room and I was standing with Green near the door of the living-room when the door opened and in came Mr. and Mrs. Myron Taylor. This time everyone's manners were equal to the occasion. After a little chat about nothing Taylor and Green sat down on a small sofa and with one other gentleman engaged in a long and apparently absorbing conversation. It was broken up only when Mrs. Taylor went over and said, "Myron, can't I talk to Mr. Green too?"[39]

While Roosevelt had laughed about Taylor's discomfort at the Labor Department, the President had had two prior incidents with Myron Taylor that suggest they were by no means the best of friends at first sight. The first involved a confrontation in August of 1933 between FDR and Taylor and his counterpart at Bethlehem Steel, Charles M. Schwab. As FDR recounted the incident to his chief political adviser, James A. Farley, the Postmaster General, he had met with both men to read them the "riot act" in response to their claims that they were paying their employees a fair wage:

> I told them quite bluntly that they were not paying a living wage.... Furthermore, I said that the miners had to live in "coke ovens" under very unsatisfactory conditions. And then I told Schwab that it would be unwise for him to appear in some mining sections because the miners are much incensed against such things as paying million dollar bonuses as had been done in the past. I looked him in the eye and went on to say hereafter the employees would receive a living wage and there would be no more million dollar bonuses paid to the top out of stockholders' money. They didn't like it, but they had to listen.[40]

Shortly thereafter, FDR had another confrontation with Myron Taylor. Describing Taylor as "a man of the world who shot grouse in Scotland and had autographed pictures of Mussolini and FDR in his office," Roosevelt biographer, Ted Morgan, recounts the President ripping into U.S. Steel's reluctance to accept the coal code under the NRA. FDR reminded Taylor that "the old doctrine 'pigs is pigs' applies—coal mining is coal mining whether the coal is sold to some commercial plant ... or whether the coal goes to a steel plant." He went on to observe: "I am getting a bit fed up and if I am I guess the coal miners are."[41]

During this period of direct governmental intervention, Taylor felt compelled to spend the better part of two years shuttling back and forth to Washington. And through his increasing contacts with FDR, a friendship began to blossom. As was reported back circuitously to the head of U.S. Steel, Roosevelt had said that he had "been seeing a lot of Myron since he had been down here, and he certainly is a peach."[42] And it probably helped some that Eleanor Roosevelt found Taylor to be interesting and charming.[43]

But why did FDR (who had few personal friendships—in fact, near the end of his life his "closest companion" was an old-maid cousin who termed him "the loneliest man in the world"[44]) ultimately bond with Taylor on such a personal level? Quite likely because of the social strata similarities between the two men, as well as the fact that Taylor asked for and wanted nothing from the President, a person who spent most of every day fending off (in a most charming way) highly ambitious and ego-charged individuals. FDR also undoubtedly valued Taylor's thoughtful, constructive, and nonconfrontational approach to solving problems. As Thomas Lamont (J.P. Morgan's partner, a U.S. Steel director, and Taylor's closest friend) remarked to FDR in 1941:

> I know how quick you were, with your acute perceptions, to take advantage of [Taylor's] support almost from the day of your first inauguration, and how since then he has continued to help in many constructive fields. You have undoubtedly found that he has his own views and expresses them in a quiet and helpful and cooperative way. I do not assume to say that he is always in agreement with all others, but if he is not, he makes it known, not in a belligerent fashion, but in a clear and helpful way. He does not hesitate to change his views, but always maintains an even mind. That is why he can get on in negotiations with men like [John L.] Lewis.[45]

From Taylor's perspective, FDR "was always outspoken, friendly and completely loyal to me." And in "heated battle when patience was under severe heat ... he was at all times a gentleman, but in my case he was much more than that."[46]

"All America Gasped"

Whatever Roosevelt's particular complaints with Taylor and U.S. Steel on a business level early on in the New Deal, as well as the specific issues involved with NRA industry codes, they became mooted when the Supreme Court struck down the NRA as unconstitutional by a 9-0 vote in May of 1935. No sooner did that legislation die, however, than the Wagner Act (the National Labor Relations Act) rose in its place. Myron Taylor's reaction to this governmental initiative proved to be dramatically different.

With the passage of the Wagner Act, J.P. Morgan remarked to Myron Taylor that he knew no one in favor of collective bargaining, which was the central tenet of the legislation.[47] Morgan was wrong, however.

There is an apocryphal story of Myron and Anabel Taylor in the dining room of their favorite Washington, DC, hotel—the Mayflower—in December 1936. Spying the wildly distinctive John L. Lewis, with his great, bushy eyebrows and unique mannerisms, Mrs. Taylor supposedly changed U.S. labor-management history with these words: "Myron, I want to meet that man. Bring him over here."[48] Although that never happened, the real story is more interesting.

Lewis was then the head of two of the country's most powerful unions, the United Mine Workers of America (UMW) and the Committee for Industrial Organization (CIO). He was also the dominant force in the Steel Workers Organizing Committee, a subsidiary of the CIO. Lewis was, in short, the nation's preeminent labor leader at that time.

Early in 1937 Myron C. Taylor and John L. Lewis reached a historic agreement. The United States Steel Corporation would recognize the Steel Workers Organizing Committee as the collective bargaining agent for those employees who were members of that union.

According to one labor historian, the Taylor–Lewis agreement "must surely rank as one of the critical junctures in American

Mr. and Mrs. Taylor arriving in Washington, DC

economic history."'[49] A second analyst viewed it as leading directly to "the most important single document in the history of the American labor movement."[50] Another labor historian's take was that "all America gasped as United States Steel surrendered without a struggle."[51]

From outside appearances alone, Taylor and Lewis were an unlikely source of agreement on common goals. As is evident from the earlier review of his professional career in the textile and steel industries, negotiation and compromise characterized Myron Taylor's style of corporate management.

Taylor meeting with John L. Lewis, the head of the Committee for
Industrial Organization, regarding organizing U.S. Steel's workers

If Taylor favored diplomacy, however, John Llewellyn Lewis
was given to confrontation. The son of an immigrant Welsh coal
miner, Lewis' entire life, beginning at age 12, was spent working in
the mines or for the United Mine Workers union. Those who saw
him were struck by his red shaggy eyebrows, his protruding jaw,
and a scowl that he once described to Secretary of Labor Frances
Perkins as "worth a million dollars" to him.[52] And those who heard
him speak remembered his sonorous voice, causing one listener to
recall that "the native eloquence of the Welsh has flowered in all
its spell-weaving pomposity."[53]

Taylor and Lewis first crossed paths in a labor dispute in 1933
in connection with the settlement of a strike by the workers in a
captive coal mine. The mine, described as "captive" because, owned
by U.S. Steel, produced coal for the Corporation's mills rather than

for sale in the open market. The confrontation involved issues of wages, hours, and collective bargaining, and reflected the widespread unrest and turmoil that characterized the labor scene at that time.[54]

The Amalgamated Association of Iron, Steel, and Tin Workers of North America, the steel workers union at that time, claimed only a small minority of those eligible for membership. U.S. Steel, in turn, established a "Plan of Employee Representation" under which its employees selected their own representatives to bargain collectively with the company's management on matters of wages, hours, and other conditions of employment.[55]

This was the state of affairs in November 1935 when John L. Lewis founded the Committee for Industrial Organization (and in June 1936 when he formed the Steel Workers' Organizing Committee (SWOC)). The CIO was designed to promote the unionization of unorganized workers throughout the mass production industries, and the goal of the SWOC was to achieve this result in the particular case of steel workers.[56]

In a real sense, the nature and outcome of the drive to organize the employees in the steel industry came to be personalized in the relationship between Taylor and Lewis. *Fortune* magazine, in its May 1937 issue, wrote that the deal's origins sprang from a chance meeting in the dining room of the Mayflower Hotel, on Saturday, January 9, 1937.[57] The luncheon guests that day included Mr. and Mrs. Myron C. Taylor and, at nearby table, John L. Lewis and Senator Joseph F. Guffey of Pennsylvania. Earlier, upon entering the dining room, Taylor had exchanged pleasantries with Lewis and Guffey, who later reciprocated this gesture as they left the room. Lewis tarried at the Taylor table for a friendly exchange that ended in the two men agreeing to meet again the next day in Taylor's Mayflower suite.

While this meeting did in fact occur (unlike the apocryphal story), a labor historian with direct access to Lewis has put their first meeting on the subject of collective bargaining back in

October of 1936.[58] Thereafter, Taylor and Lewis met on several occasions, sometimes in Washington, at other times in Taylor's town house in New York City, but always in private, off-the-record sessions. The secrecy of their negotiations, however, was threatened on February 27, 1937, when a Washington reporter called Taylor and informed him that the existence of the ongoing negotiations had been discovered and a story about them was soon to be published. It was only when the editor of the paper was persuaded that such disclosure would ruin any chance of a successful settlement that he decided not to prematurely break the story.[59] The Taylor–Lewis conversations thus continued, and their agenda was clear: to reach a settlement that would prevent the threatened strike by the steel workers against the U.S. Steel Corporation. A crucial part of any such settlement would, of course, have to resolve the status of the Steel Workers Organizing Committee as the recognized bargaining agent for the company's employees.

In this context, it is important to remember the U.S. Steel Corporation's long history of opposition to outside unionism. Indeed, as late as June 29, 1936, the Corporation had joined other steel manufacturers in presenting a united front of resistance to Lewis' proposed campaign to organize the employees of the industry. A public statement issued by the American Iron and Steel Institute proclaimed that the steel industry would "oppose any attempt to compel its employees to join a union" and would help them "in maintaining collective bargaining free from interference from any source."[60]

As Taylor and Lewis continued to meet in their search for industrial peace in the steel mills, the time came when Taylor put on the table for discussion a proposition subsequently known as the "Myron Taylor Labor Formula." Taylor had not developed this proposal during the give-and-take of his ongoing negotiations with Lewis. Rather, it was the result of a summer's (the summer of 1936) reflection at his Italian residence, Villa Schifanoia, located near Florence. Taylor's formula was just 100 words long:

The Company recognizes the right of its employees to bargain collectively through representatives freely chosen by them without dictation, coercion or intimidation in any form or from any source. It will negotiate and contract with the representatives of any group of its employees so chosen and with any organization as the representative of its members, subject to the recognition of the principle that the right to work is not dependent on membership or non-membership in any organization and subject to the right of every employee freely to bargain in such manner and through such representatives, if any, as he chooses.[61]

This proposal became the cornerstone of a Taylor–Lewis accord. Other elements of the agreement thereafter fell readily into place: $5.00 minimum daily wage; 8-hour day, 40-hour week; time and one-half overtime pay; a procedure for handling grievances.

The agreement was announced on March 2, 1937, with initial public reaction swift and varied. "Steel Bows to Lewis' Union," headlined the *New York Daily News*.[62] The *New York Times*, however, in its editorial comments noted the "significant fact that this agreement does not provide for an 'exclusive' bargaining agency, or give the union the right to speak for anyone save its own members."[63]

The evaluation of Taylor's personal role in reaching the agreement with Lewis was likewise varied. He was caustically criticized as a traitor to his cause (and class) by some and praised as an industrial statesman by others.

Tom M. Girdler, then president of Republic Steel, wrote: "I was bitter about this. So were a vast majority of the steel men of the nation.... [W]e were convinced that a surrender to C.I.O. was a bad thing for our companies, for our employees; indeed for the United States of America."[64] Thus convinced, Girdler and Republic

Steel chose the alternative and were left with massive and bloody labor riots in 1937, which severely hurt that company's business.

There was, on the other hand, an outpouring of public support for the agreement that averted a dreaded steel strike and for Myron Taylor's pivotal role in achieving this result. John L. Lewis, who had invested so much of his professional standing in the accord, could, of course, be expected to praise it. Yet his appraisal of Taylor's part in their joint venture was hardly perfunctory. At the time Lewis told him that "your name will be remembered and revered by labor for generations as the man who turned the whole scale of labor relations. You are the most far-seeing man in American industry and have done the greatest service to the country."[65] Lewis' enthusiastic view of the agreement never diminished over the years; as late as August 23, 1955, he reminded Taylor of the "great settlement negotiated by you and me for the Steel Industry in 1937" and continued, "In many ways, I consider that settlement to be one of the outstanding landmarks in the industrial history of our country."[66]

Another labor leader who well understood the stakes was Lee Pressman, the CIO's general counsel. In his view, Taylor's statesmanlike agreement was essential because the union "couldn't have gone through the NLRB [National Labor Relation Board] for an election and didn't have the strength among U.S. Steel workers to have won an election by itself."[67]

Former President Hoover reflected the national consensus on the agreement when he wrote to Taylor: "That was a wise move. It is statesmanship of a high order."[68] J.P. Morgan's analysis was more praiseworthy and parochial: "That was the finest performance I have ever known. No one else in the whole industry could have done that.... [It gave U.S. Steel] eight to ten months of complete [labor] peace."[69]

It is interesting to speculate about the reasons that may have led Taylor to an agreement that, in the eyes of at least some, marked an unwise and unnecessary capitulation to the demands of labor. There are a number of possible reasons that deserve mention.

The first is the economic cost of a strike. In Taylor's view, the damage "to the Corporation, to the public and to the men—would have been incalculable."[70] After several years of operating in the red, corporate profits were on the upswing. Further, a strike would have jeopardized the company's chances of being selected to supply the steel for England's then emerging several billion dollar rearmament program.

Second, even conceding U.S. Steel's ability to withstand a prolonged strike, there were nevertheless a variety of circumstances that might have put the ultimate outcome in doubt. The political climate in the country, as reflected in President Roosevelt's New Deal programs, was clearly pro union. Notwithstanding Lee Pressman's realistic assessment, the CIO, fresh from its success in organizing the workers in the automobile industry, might well have been able to mount an equally impressive drive to unionize the steel workers.

Third, it is possible that Taylor's growing friendship with FDR—who, after all, was the most charming and persuasive political salesman of his era—may have swayed and shaped Taylor's political views on this subject.[71]

Another likely reason was articulated by the former governor of New York, Nathan L. Miller (now the Corporation's general counsel), who lavishly praised Taylor's negotiating performance as merely giving up to Lewis those matters that the Wagner Act explicitly guaranteed him anyway, but ceding nothing more: "[M]ake no mistake about it. No one but Myron Taylor could have conducted that difficult negotiation to a successful conclusion, and I think it is very unlikely that Mr. Lewis did not appraise all that he had to start with."[72]

Perhaps it is best to let Taylor's words express the most reasonable explanation:

I felt that it was my duty as a trustee for our stock-holders and as a citizen to make an honorable settlement that would ensure a continuation of work, wages, and profits.[73]

Whatever the underlying reasons for reaching it may have been, the Taylor–Lewis agreement indisputably represented the most dramatic development in the labor relations field during the 1930s.

There was one last personnel-related achievement in which Taylor took special pride. This involved the selection of the senior officers and executive staff of the Corporation. Taylor stated his objective in these terms: "[A] well-balanced organization should have an ample number of mature men of judgment and experience and an ample number of younger men gaining judgment and experience."[74] To gain this balance, he was insistent that whenever practicable an executive replacement should be younger than his predecessor.

Taylor's emphasis on the importance of attracting younger persons to positions of responsibility was successful. The average age of the members of the Board of Directors was 64 in 1927 and 59 in 1937. In 1927 the average age of the principal executive officers of the Corporation was 65 and in 1937 it had dropped to 55.[75] And, in an even more striking example of this trend, when Taylor retired as Chairman of the Board at age 64, he was succeeded by Edward R. Stettinius Jr., then 37, who Taylor had recruited from General Motors.

At Myron Taylor's retirement dinner, J.P. Morgan gave colorful recognition to Taylor's success in lowering the age level of the Corporation's executive staff, saying: "When I first came to these dinners, there were none but white heads all around the table. And now there are only a few. Those of us who are on the point of retiring are a little gray on the head, but all the rest of you are young chaps, and you are doing splendidly."[76]

Notes

1. Remarks at 37th Annual Dinner of U.S. Steel Corporation on January 11, 1938, at the Waldorf Astoria hotel in New York; reprinted in A. Pound, *Myron C. Taylor: Lawyer, Industrialist, Diplomat, Humanitarian* (New York Genealogical and Biographical Society 1955) at pp. 197-98. Thomas Lamont, Morgan's partner and a U.S. Steel director, remembered it a bit differently, taking the lion's share of the credit for putting the "Taylor idea" in the heads of Messrs. Morgan and Baker. Lamont, who had been in touch with Taylor on various business matters dating back to 1907 (and who considered himself Taylor's closest friend), had argued that while "[c]otton mills are very different from steel mills, ... the principles are the same." September 25, 1935, T.W. Lamont Memorandum for Partners: U.S. Steel (Lamont Papers, Baker Library, Harvard Business School).

2. R. Blough, Myron C. Taylor: An Appreciation (U.S. Steel 1956), p. 16. Taylor was undoubtedly influenced in his decision by his high regard for George Baker, his mentor and model who he regarded "as the greatest business thinker of [his] time." *Time* (April 22, 1929).

3. *U.S. Steel News*, Vol. 3, No. 4 (April 1938), p. 1.

4. *Fortune* (Vol. XIII, No. 6, June 1936), pp. 120-21. The austere and formal personality depicted by this article is underscored by the fact that in preparing for his remarks at the January 1938 dinner marking Taylor's "Ten Years of Steel," Lamont (Taylor's "warmest friend") had an outside consultant prepare a 15-page précis on Taylor's endearing qualities for use in his remarks at the dinner. January 4, 1938, "Reflections upon Myron Taylor, the Man, by George Bacus for Thomas W. Lamont" (Lamont Papers, Baker Library, Harvard Business School).

5. *Time* (April 22, 1929), pp. 29-73. Several years later, the *New York Times Magazine* was almost giddy in its description of Myron Taylor: "His eyes are not simply clear; they are young and warm with life, they are the green of Spring. His voice is not merely firm; it is quiet, even, pleasant, persuasive, because it speaks both of a strong will and a warm heart.... His manner is not simply self-controlled; it is gentle." (August 21, 1938).

6. Blough, *supra* note 2, p. 18. At the time, Taylor reported to Lamont that he had found it "vastly entertaining to review the Company's activities for the past 25 years." M.C. Taylor April 2, 1929, letter to T.W. Lamont (Lamont Papers, Baker Library, Harvard Business School).

7. Blough, *supra* note 2, pp. 19-20.

8. M. Taylor, *Ten Years of Steel* (Hoboken, NJ 1938), p. 9.

9. Blough, *supra* note 2, p. 20.

10. Pound, *supra* note 1, p. 198.

11. *Fortune* (Vol. XIII, No. 3, March 1936), p. 63

12. *Fortune* (Vol. XIII, No. 3, March 1936), p. 192.

13. *Fortune* (Vol. XIII, No. 3, March 1936), p. 63.

14. Blough, *supra* note 2, p. 18

15. Blough, *supra* note 2, p. 16.

16. Blough, *supra* note 2, p. 21. *See also* "Taylor, in 5 years, Alters Capital, Plant, Personnel of Gigantic Steel Combine," *N.Y. World Telegram* (April 19, 1932).

17. Brian Apelt, *The Corporation: A Centennial Biography of United States Steel Corporation* (Univ. Pittsburgh 2000), p. 148.

18. Blough, *supra* note 2, p. 24.

19. Apelt, *supra* note 17, p. 149.

20. *Fortune* (Vol. XIII, No. 3, March 1936), p. 200.

21. *Pittsburgh Sun-Telegram* (December 20, 1937), p. 1.

22. Pound, *supra* note 1, pp. 158-160.

23. *Fortune* (Vol. XIII, No. 6 June 1936), p. 174.

24. Apelt, *supra* note 17, p. 149.

25. Taylor, *Ten Years of Steel*, p. 21.

26. Professor Paul A. Tiffany of the Wharton School at the University of Pennsylvania presented a paper entitled "Corporate Culture and Corporate Change: The Origins of Industrial Research at the United States Steel Corporation, 1901-1929" at a meeting of the Society for the History of Technology in Pittsburgh, Pennsylvania, on October 25, 1986, at p. 31.

27. Apelt, *supra* note 17, p. 52.

28. Blough, *supra* note 2, pp. 23-27.

29. *Ten Years of Steel*, p. 25. This had been one of Taylor's principal objectives at the outset of the Depression. *See* "Employers Urged to Prorate Work," *New York World* (January 28, 1931) ("We are confident that when the final chapter of this depression is written, the United States Steel Corporation's record in providing work and in extending relief to its employees will be one of its outstanding achievements."). *See also* "Thirty-Five Years of United States Steel," *U.S. Steel News*, June 1936, p. 9, *and* "The Steel Corporation's Employment Plan," *Review of Reviews*, March 1931, p. 61.

30. *Fortune* (Vol. XIII, No. 6 June 1936), p. 174.

31. That this conclusion, as well as other less than flattering observations, came out about Taylor in that and various other *Fortune* articles during this time period is somewhat surprising given that Thomas Lamont (Taylor's closest friend) was allowed to screen them prepublication. Lamont gave detailed feedback on a whole variety of inaccuracies, but clearly was unable to warm the editors of *Fortune* up to Taylor's "informal" side. *See* January 29, 1936, T.W. Lamont Memorandum for M.C.T.: Fortune Article; April 21, 1936, T.W. Lamont Memorandum for Mr. Ingersoll; March 29, 1937, T.W. Lamont Memorandum for Mr. Ingersoll

(Lamont Papers, Baker Library, Harvard Business School). This was not the only area where Lamont interceded on Taylor's behalf. He also dressed down a Philco radio commentator for misrepresenting Taylor's actions vis-à-vis organized labor (*see* June 30, 1937, letter from T.W. Lamont to B. Carter), as well as critiquing for Taylor a draft of his final remarks upon stepping down as the Corporation's CEO (*see* October 26, 1937, T.W. Lamont Memorandum for M.C. Taylor) (Lamont Papers, Baker Library, Harvard Business School).

32. R.S. Craig, "History of the United States Steel Corporation and Predecessor Companies" (unpublished manuscript, Cornell Law Library) (April 1966), p. 297; *Ten Years of Steel*, pp. 26-27.

33. Pound, *supra* note 1, p. 140. Taylor's complex motives with respect to labor are well explicated in an April 18, 1935, memorandum he wrote to his U.S. Steel colleague William Filbert, who succeeded him as Chairman of the Finance Committee. In the memorandum Taylor proposes that the Corporation support a Pennsylvania-based unemployment plan not only for "the welfare of these men" but also to help ensure that "public attitude" not "turn antagonistic to the Corporation as a whole." (Lamont Papers, Baker Library, Harvard Business School).

34. Pound, *supra* note 1, p. 37.

35. Taylor's contemporaneous public pronouncements on policy matters did not line him up well with New Deal orthodoxy. *See, e.g.,* "Taylor Blames Rise in Taxation for Slow Trade," *N.Y. Evening Post* (March 24, 1932); "Balance Budget and Leave Money Alone, Says Taylor," *N.Y. Evening Post* (February 15, 1933). Interestingly, Taylor's first written communication with Roosevelt, as president, was a congratulatory letter, reporting that "industry is solidly behind you." May 16, 1933, letter from M.C. Taylor to F.D. Roosevelt (Taylor Papers, Cornell University). And several months later, Taylor publicly urged support of FDR as the "plain duty" of every citizen. "Steel Head Hails New Era on Way," *New York Times* (October 21, 1933). That supportive tone changed, however, when FDR got down to specifics in the early New Deal. Years later, even after Taylor had become extremely good friends with FDR, Taylor described this period as "a new economy that [was] reached after a substitute for competition." *Ten Years of Steel*, p. 4. Lamont believed that the time Taylor was forced to spend in Washington dealing with the NRA and other aspects of the early New Deal clearly "slowed down" Taylor's efforts to reorganize and modernize the Corporation. September 25, 1935, T.W. Lamont Memorandum for Partners: U.S. Steel (Lamont Papers, Baker Library, Harvard Business School).

36. F. Perkins, *The Roosevelt I Knew* (Viking Press 1946), p. 217.

37. Perkins, *supra* note 36, pp. 221-23.

38. Perkins, *supra* note 36, p. 223.

39. Perkins, *supra* note 36, p. 223. Francis Perkins elaborated on this critical, ice-breaking session between the Taylors and Green at her home in Georgetown in her oral history. Mrs. Taylor, according to Perkins, reported later: "You know, William Green's a very interesting man, and quite a gentleman, isn't he?" Oral History of Francis Perkins, p. 165 (Columbia University). Given the importance that both Taylors put on manners (*see*, for example, note 64, *infra*), such an impression undoubtedly improved the dynamic between Taylor and Green significantly.

Mrs. Taylor's propensity for introducing herself at important points in her husband's career was well known. Another example took place early on in the New Deal during the social security and collective bargaining struggles. Sitting next to Robert Jackson (a key Justice Department official and later a famed Supreme Court Justice) at dinner one evening, Mrs. Taylor turned to Jackson as the dinner was breaking up and said, "in utter sincerity: 'I don't think you're so bad a person.'" Oral History of Robert H. Jackson, p. 601 (Columbia University).

40. J.A. Farley, *Jim Farley's Story* (McGraw Hill 1948), p. 42.

41. T. Morgan, *FDR: A Biography* (Simon & Schuster 1985), p. 403. Besides shooting grouse in Scotland, Taylor had little interest or skill in competitive sports. In a July 31, 1930, letter to Lamont, Taylor wrote: "Since my wretched performance at golf in Southampton, I have taken up a little tennis, which is also pretty bad, but has the advantage in that the disappointments are sooner over." (Lamont Papers, Baker Library, Harvard Business School).

42. December 13, 1933, letter from J.B. Carse to L. Fraser (Taylor Papers, Cornell University).

43. B.W. Cook, *Eleanor Roosevelt—The Defining Years* (Penguin 1999), p. 220.

44. G.C. Ward, *Closest Companion* (Houghton Mifflin 1995), p. 201. (Harry Hopkins, FDR's closest aide, is later cited, observing that in the White House "evening after evening … Franklin was left entirely alone, but for [Hopkins]." ibid. p. 353).

45. T.W. Lamont November 3, 1941, memorandum to F.D. Roosevelt (Lamont Papers, Baker Library, Harvard Business School).

46. M.C. Taylor April 18, 1945, letter to T.W. Lamont (Lamont Papers, Baker Library, Harvard Business School). Taylor then added: "Not that I ever sought anything at his hands." After FDR's death, Harry Hopkins (FDR's closest advisor and also a good friend of Taylor's) echoed much of Lamont's and Taylor's observations about this bond: "It seems about impossible to realize that … the President has died. I know how devoted you were to him and his purposes and what implicit confidences he had in yours." H. Hopkins April 28, 1945, letter to M.C. Taylor (Taylor Papers, Cornell University). Taylor was also generous with

thoughtful presents to FDR, including portraits by Taylor's favorite British artist; Taylor also hosted the President's mother and his son, James, at Schifanoia in 1937.

47. R. Chernow, *The House of Morgan* (Atlantic Monthly Press 1990), p. 409.

48. S. Alinsky, *John L. Lewis* (Putnam 1949), p. 148. For some of Mrs. Taylor's actual off-the-cuff bon mots, see note 39.

49. W. Galenson, *The CIO Challenge to the AFL: A History of the American Labor Movement 1935-1941* (Harvard University Press 1960), p. 93.

50. R. Brooks, *As Steel Goes: Unionism in a Basic Industry* (Johnson Reprint Corp. 1970), p. 108. For the viewpoint that this represents an overstatement of the importance of the Taylor–Lewis accord, see M. Dubofsky and W. Van Tine, *John L. Lewis, A Biography* (Quadrangle 1977), pp. 194-96.

51. Alinsky, *supra* note 48, p. 148.

52. M. Reutter, *Sparrows Point: Making Steel—The Rise and Ruin of American Industrial Might* (Summit Books 1988), p. 249.

53. *Fortune* (Vol. XIV, No. 4 October 1936), p. 152.

54. *Ten Years of Steel*, pp. 29-30.

55. *Ten Years of Steel*, p. 30; Apelt, *supra* note 17, pp. 158-59.

56. *Ten Years of Steel*, p. 30; Apelt, *supra* note 17, pp. 159-60.

57. *Fortune* (Vol. XV, No. 5, May 1937), p. 94.

58. Alinsky, *supra* note 48, p. 158.

59. Pound, supra note 1pp. 174-75.

60. *Fortune* (Vol. XV, No. 5, May 1937), p. 91.

61. Blough, *supra* note 2, pp. 31-32

62. *Fortune* (Vol. XV, No. 5 May 1937), p. 91; "Taylor's Steel Surrender to Lewis Amazes," *N.Y. Evening Journal* (July 21, 1937).

63. *New York Times* (March 3, 1937), p. 22.

64. Galenson, *supra* note 49, p. 96. Other industrial leaders also did not follow Taylor's lead in lockstep. In her oral history, Francis Perkins recreated Taylor's attempts to counsel Alfred Sloan of General Motors on how to address these same issues facing his company and the automotive industry generally. After having prompted Sloan to call Taylor, Perkins then reported the following:

> Mr. Taylor said, "I thought I would like to tell you that a most extraordinary thing has happened. Mr. Sloan called me up earlier this afternoon. He, of course, had a great deal to say about the strike they've got on. I certainly do sympathize with him. He's having a very difficult time. He asked my opinion—that's very interesting—about what I thought of a formula for meeting the union which

would be practically the same thing as Stettinius talked to you about a few days ago. That is the formula of recognizing the union's power to bargain for their members who worked for the company, but not a general representation. He had some little extra slants in it, but it was very much like the thing that we talked about the other day. I thought that was very interesting."

I said, "that is interesting, very interesting, Mr. Taylor. What did you say to him?"

He said, "I said to him about what I said to you, that it was a possible thing. It was tolerable. We could think in terms like that. Sloan asked my advice as to whether I thought that General Motors could safely proceed in that way. I told him I thought that they could, that none of this was safe for any of us. We had to realize that. But it was at least fair."

They were all bogged down because they thought it was unfair to deal with a union representing men that didn't belong to it. It was unfair to the men that didn't belong to it. I think they were honest in that feeling, because they had made such a point for twenty years of their open shop policy—"nobody needs to belong to a union," which really means, "no one can belong to a union"—that they knew they had brought many men to work for them who couldn't get into a union, who never had belonged to a union, who didn't want to belong to a union. They had made it a part of their propaganda. They had educated the men against it. They knew that. They had a certain sense of the incongruity of a change of front on the matter. Therefore, they felt it was unfair.

We talked for a while over the telephone. He said, "Why don't you call up Sloan now?"

I said that I would. I called him up and asked him if he'd had any opportunity to think it over any further. He said that yes he had, that he had talked to Myron Taylor, that Taylor had told him he thought it was all right. He said, "Now, Taylor, of course, has more experience in these things than I have." He hadn't had, but it was Sloan's way of looking up to the older statesman. "Taylor's had more experience. I should think that if they can endure it, we can endure it. I think that might be a good thing."

...

I've only told this to one other person. This was the circumstance. The person to whom I told it was Myron Taylor. I told him several years later. I met Myron Taylor somewhere or other socially,

accidentally. We were pleased to see each other and had many things
to reminisce about and talk about, with all these troubles over—no
steel trouble, no strike in the automobile industry, big union, big contract, competition between Ford, Chrysler and General Motors to
see who can give the union the mostest the firstest and so get ahead
with the new season's production. Myron by that time had been
asked to be the President's envoy. We were just reminiscing and having pleasant conversation. In the course of the conversation, I said to
him, "Do you ever see Alfred Sloan, Mr. Taylor?"

"Well," he said, "I don't see him very often."

I said, "Don't you really? I remember the day that you intervened with him."

"Well," he said, "I have intervened more than that too. You
don't know the degree to which I went on intervention, because you
know only of one afternoon when I intervened. As a matter of fact,
I intervened again when I understood that negotiations were off for
the second time. I intervened again, but since that time I have not
seen Alfred Sloan much." Mr. Taylor, who is a very solemn person,
cleared his throat and said, "As a matter of fact, I don't like to see
Alfred Sloan now. I feel very nervous and uneasy. Alfred Sloan said
something to me on that afternoon. I went to his apartment really
to give him my best advice, to offer him my help as an older man,
to share with him some of my own philosophical thinking, which
I admit has changed a good deal in the last few years. I want you to
believe me, Miss Perkins. I went with the kindest and most Christian
feeling to try and talk with Alfred and to perhaps help him to see his
way through this situation. He said some things to me, Miss Perkins,
that I can never forget, and that shouldn't be said."

I said, "Really, Mr. Taylor? He said some things to me, Mr.
Taylor, that shouldn't be said."

"Did he really, Miss Perkins? Did he really?"

I said, "Yes, he did. I could hardly believe that anybody would
say them and I have never repeated them, Mr. Taylor, because it was
so humiliating, so disgusting for a grown man to say these things. The
human race was humiliated by his mere saying what he said to me."

"Really? That was just the way I felt."

I said, "Mr. Taylor, I'm going to tell you, if you'll swear to me
that you'll never repeat it, what he said to me. I told him that he
was breaking his word to me, breaking his word to other people and
that he couldn't change his mind between one train and the next

train, that what he had agreed to at four o'clock was equally good at eight o'clock, that he could not change his mind after I, acting on his agreement, had taken certain steps, and other people, who were his opponents in the matter, had been led to believe they could take certain steps with their principals. You know what he said to me? He didn't defend himself, or make any argument about it. He just said, 'I'm worth seventy million dollars and you can't talk to me like that.'"

"Oh, Miss Perkins," said Myron, "that's exactly what he said to me. Why, I didn't suppose he would ever think of saying it to anybody else! Isn't that awful! Isn't that awful!"

Myron Taylor acted as though he and I had seen a man commit murder, and only we two knew it. "Isn't it awful!" he said.

By this time, or course, two or three years had passed. I had forgiven Alfred Sloan as far as I was concerned. I had begun to think of it as more comic than awful.

Then we both looked at each other and he said, "It must be that that's in his mind all the time. That idea must be in the back of his mind all the time, or he couldn't have said it to me and said it to you also. Isn't that a horrible thought?"

I said, "Oh well, Mr. Taylor, you and I will have to pray for Alfred, that sometime, somehow, before the day of his passing over into eternal life, he will have some understanding of the situation and that idea will pass out of his mind and will cease to seem important to him. Because, of course, it's not going to be important to him after he's crossed the great divide. It would be wonderful, wouldn't it, if he could really come to an inner recognition that it's of no consequence."

Then Myron said, "You and I will never tell it."

Oral History of Francis Perkins, pp. 188-89 and 214-18 (Columbia University).

65. In his papers housed at Cornell, Taylor handwrote this on a piece of paper as representing what Lewis had said verbatim to him on December 6, 1937. This is the only document of that type in the papers, so clearly Taylor valued these words and wanted them to be remembered posthumously. For a somewhat more restrained contemporaneous Lewis quotation, *see* Galenson, *supra* note 49, p. 96.

66. J.L. Lewis August 23, 1955, memorandum to M.C. Taylor (Taylor Papers, Cornell University).

67. Alinsky, *supra* note 48, p. 149.

68. Pound, *supra* note 1, p. 179.

69. Pound, *supra* note 1, p. 198.

70. *Ten Years of Steel*, p. 44. Taylor had made substantial efforts to obtain business from European nations preparing for war. *See U.S. Investor* (September 11, 1937).

71. This was a subject of speculation in the press at that time. "Taylor Under Fire," *Waterbury Republican* (July 19, 1937) (further speculating that this might lead to Taylor's appointment to the Court of St. James).

72. Pound, *supra* note 1, p. 201 (comments of the Honorable Nathan L. Miller).

73. Blough, *supra* note 2, p. 32.

74. *Ten Years of Steel*, p. 44.

75. Pound, *supra* note 1, p. 183.

76. Pound, *supra* note 1, p. 198.

CHAPTER VIII

Political Refugees

April 1938 was an especially important month in Myron Taylor's life, for it marked both the end of his industrial career and the beginning of his career in international diplomacy.

On April 5, 1938, Taylor resigned as Chairman of the Board and Chief Executive Officer of the United States Steel Corporation. He hoped to enter what he called a "sabbatical period of life," where he and Mrs. Taylor could spend part of the year at their villa (Schifanoia) in Florence, and the remainder traveling around the world. That was not to be, however, for later that same month he received a call from President Roosevelt requesting him to assume a position of leadership in helping to solve the deepening crisis of Jewish refugees fleeing from persecution in Adolf Hitler's Nazi Germany. Taylor promptly accepted this challenge, and FDR appointed him "Ambassador Extraordinary and Plenipotentiary."

Hitler's initial goal was to force all Jews to leave Germany. He would later seek to exterminate Jews throughout Europe by means of systematic mass execution. The measures Hitler initially employed to drive the Jews from their homeland ranged in intensity from economic harassment to personal violence. A Jew could not hold a public position or practice as a doctor or lawyer. He could not own a private business or even be employed in one in any significant way. These restrictions, however, paled in comparison with the brutal physical violence to which Jews were increasingly subject at the hands of the Nazi authorities.

Shortly after Germany's annexation of Austria in March 1938, an on-the-scene observer wrote:

> Demoralization is pursued by constant arrest of the Jewish population. No specific charge is made, but men and women, young and old, are taken each day and each night from their houses or in the streets and carried off, the more fortunate to Austrian prisons, and the rest to Dachau and other concentration camps in Germany. These raids are not restricted to the rich; they include doctors, lawyers, merchants, employees, poor artisans and peasants. There can be no Jewish family in the country which has not one or more of its members under arrest. The state of hopelessness and panic which is engendered can be imagined.... The authorities demand rapid and impossible emigration. The Jews would welcome evacuation, but for most it is impossible. Only a few still own any considerable property and they cannot take out even the tithe that hitherto Jews leaving Germany have been able to save. Thousands turn in despair to relatives and friends abroad, beseeching them to obtain permanent or temporary visas. Thousands stand outside the consulates of America, England and other countries, waiting through the night for admission so that they may register their names.[1]

Franklin Roosevelt's initial attempt to rouse America out of its isolationistic sleep and recognize the growing threats of both Germany and Japan was in his famous "Quarantine" speech, which he delivered in Chicago—the epicenter of American isolationism—on October 5, 1937. Unfortunately, it did not work as planned. Secretary of State Cordell Hull later wrote that the reaction was "quick and violent" and set back "for at least six months" the administration's attempts "to create and strengthen public opinion toward international cooperation."[2] Samuel Rosenman,

FDR's principal speechwriter and counsel, recalled a forlorn Roosevelt turning to him afterward and saying: "It's a terrible thing to look over your shoulder when you are trying to lead— and to find no one there."[3]

FDR's reaction to the Austrian annexation in 1938 and resulting exacerbation of the refugee problem was more visceral. At a March 18 cabinet meeting he sputtered that "something has to be done."[4] When Treasury Secretary Henry Morgenthau followed up with the President, he was told to meet with Sumner Welles, the Undersecretary of State. Welles came up with a proposal for an international conference on refugee issues. Roosevelt immediately agreed, and 32 countries were issued invitations on March 22 (Germany and Russia were not on the list of invitees; Italy refused to attend). Taylor's first task in his new post was to represent the United States at the conference.

Roosevelt's charge to Taylor was somewhat glib: "All you need do is get these people together ... All you will need to do is to organize them in the form of a conference and undertake to find a solution of the matter."[5] Taylor recognized that statement for what it was, however, and he took on the job without any illusions. As viewed by one Roosevelt biographer: "[Taylor] was a man of ability who was sincerely committed to the rescue of the victims of Nazi persecution. But he knew, when he accepted his post, that any considerable resettlement of refugees in his own country was out of the question."[6] Why? Because America was a strongly anti-Semitic country—so much so, that FDR always publicly referred to the refugees as "political" and not "racial" or "religious."[7] Another reason was that pervasive anti-immigration biases in this country (which had only been heightened by the economic miseries of the Depression) restricted German/Austrian immigration to a relatively modest number of people a year; Congress was not only highly unlikely to change those numbers, it had enacted a law in 1934 that no immigrant could become a public charge— and because Hitler's regime reduced the money an emigrating

Jew could take out of Germany to 10 reichsmarks ($4.00), that provided another almost insuperable barrier to entry. On the eve of the international conference, this point was hammered home when the New York Veterans of Foreign Wars resolved to bar all refugees from coming to the United States, as well as any immigration whatever for 10 years.[8]

The refugee conference was held in Evian, France (because the Swiss declined to hold it across the lake in Geneva for fear of upsetting Germany). Beginning on July 6, the delegates met for 10 days. The first order of business was to elect a chairman of the conference. Although a novice at diplomacy, Myron Taylor was quickly designated; and he became a popular figure with the delegates.

Once procedural matters were out of the way, the Evian Conference floundered on substance. The reason lay in its basic, and flawed, structural design. One of the ground rules set out in the invitation was that no country was expected or would be asked to receive a greater number of immigrants than was permitted under its own national law. As the Conference went on, and as each country's delegates espoused platitudes of various sorts, it became more and more obvious that no country was planning to deviate from the prepared script. Indeed, some nations were extraordinarily blunt. Britain, for example, forbade any mention of Palestine in connection with refugee relocation. Australia took the view that it had no "racial problem" and was "not desirous of importing one." Several Central American nations issued a joint statement that they would accept "no traders or intellectuals." In the end, there was a lot of hot air, but no constructive proposals emerged to help the refugees.[9]

Even Myron Taylor's optimistic opening remarks at the Evian Conference were shadowed by the political realities at home. America "prides itself upon the liberality of its existing [immigration] laws and practices ... I might point out that the American government has taken steps to consolidate the German and former Austrian quotas so that a total of 27,370 immigrants may enter the United States on the German quota in one year."[10] But this tinkering with the quotas (which had been the idea of Sumner Welles[11]), in reality, offered nothing more than the prior status quo.

Anne O'Hare McCormick, the *New York Times* foreign affairs essayist, articulated well not only the moral issues at stake but also the Evian Conference's failure to even attempt to address them:

> It is heart breaking to think of the queues of des-
> perate human beings around our consulates in Vienna
> and in other cities waiting in suspense for what happens
> at Evian. But the question they underline is not simply
> humanitarian. It is not a question of how many unem-
> ployed this country can safely add to its own unemployed
> millions. It is a test of civilization. Can America live with
> itself if it lets Germany get away with this policy of exter-
> mination, allows the fanaticism of one man to triumph
> over reason, refuses to take up this gage of battle against
> barbarism?[12]

Newsweek's ultimate view of the Conference was that the participating nations had "slam[med] their doors against Jewish refugees."[13] FDR's odd epitaph was that the nations had been "overly cautious."[14]

One concrete achievement did come from the Evian Con-
ference, however. Because of Taylor's leadership, the attending nation-states agreed to the establishment of an ongoing, interna-
tional mechanism to address the refugee issue. Taylor had urged that a "fresh approach" was needed, and the delegates signed off on the creation of the Intergovernmental Committee on Refugees (ICR). Even this was not done easily; the British opposed the concept, wishing to leave permanent jurisdiction in the hands of the toothless League of Nations. Taylor "overc[a]me British lassitude" to the ICR, however, and was even able to have the Committee

centered in London by his personal intervention with Lord Hali-fax.[15] Myron Taylor was subsequently named as the United States' delegate to the Committee and vice chairman of the ICR (Lord Winterton of Great Britain was the chairman); it was also arranged for George Rublee, a senior partner of the Covington & Burling law firm in Washington, DC, to act as its director.[16]

The Committee, Taylor, and Rublee faced two challenges right off the bat: attempting to negotiate with Hitler's government a rational method by which to allow emigration; and to find an appropriate place or places for resettlement of the refugees. Taylor was optimistic at the outset, at least publicly. In an address before the Council on Foreign Relations in New York on October 3, 1938, he voiced the view that he expected a positive outcome of the Committee's work: "It is unthinkable that the emigration of these unwanted people from Germany cannot be accomplished in a more orderly and humane manner. Despite the difficulties involved, I am confident that means can be found which will be acceptable both to the German Government and to the govern-ments of the countries of refuge whereby a considerable portion of [the refugees' wealth estimated at between $2 and $6 billion] can be saved for the emigrants to enable them to find, each and establish themselves in new homes."[17] Unfortunately, that opti-mism was misplaced.

With respect to dealing with the German government, ini-tial feelers at first looked to be promising, as Rublee was all set to travel to Berlin to meet with Herman Goering, Hitler's principal aide, and Walter Frank, Germany's Minister for National Econ-omy. That trip was cancelled, however, after a young Polish Jew assassinated a German diplomat in Paris in November of 1938, an action that set off a frenzy of violent Nazi reprisals (later known as *Kristallnacht*—the "Night of Broken Glass") against the Jews who remained trapped in Germany.[18]

FDR recalled the U.S. Ambassador to Germany in protest, but ordered that efforts be continued to try to reach some form of accommodation. Those efforts bore fruit insofar as Goering, who had been given responsibility by Hitler for the Jewish expulsion, committed to sending Hajalmar Schacht, president of the Reichsbank and also head of the German Ministry of Economics, to meet with Rublee in London. Schacht reported that Germany planned to expel 150,000 Jews over the next 3 years—but in an "orderly" fashion. The expulsion would be paid for by confiscated Jewish property, and through the financial wherewithal of "international Jewry."[19]

Sumner Welles, writing on behalf of the State Department, cabled back to Taylor and Rublee that "[t]he plan is generally considered as asking the world to pay a ransom for the release of hostages in Germany and to barter human misery for increased exports.... On the other hand, we ... must proceed with care lest, by summary rejection, the plight of the Jews in Germany be made even more serious."[20] At the same time, FDR directed Taylor to make a "special effort" to achieve a breakthrough, also making clear that America's policy toward refugee immigration would not (and could not) change.[21] Needless to say, this directive did not give Taylor a whole lot with which to work.[22]

Out of the blue, Joseph P. Kennedy, the U.S. Ambassador to England (and father of the future President), injected himself into the process. Kennedy, as a general matter, had not been helpful to the Taylor–Rublee effort, thinking "it was impossible to succeed."[23] But, in an attempt to resuscitate his battered public image after the disastrous Trafalgar Day speech (in which he called on the "democracies" and the "dictators" to find common ground to avoid war), Kennedy launched what was quickly dubbed the "Kennedy Plan."[24] Under this vague and undefined "plan," massive numbers of German Jews would somehow be transported to unspecified, underpopulated parts of the world, presumably somewhere in Africa and South America. That Kennedy may well have thought this possible is evidenced by a November 18, 1938, cable he sent to Secretary of State Hull, reporting that Taylor had been told by

Bernard Beruch that "[i]f [we] had a good place to put the Jews, the Jews in the United States could raise one hundred million dollars."[25] And it was not just Kennedy who was of this mind-set. FDR himself said to Henry Morgenthau, his Treasury Secretary, that if Morgenthau "would give him a list of the thousand richest Jews in the United States, he was prepared to tell each how much money he should contribute."[26]

The Kennedy Plan was praised in the *New York Times* and other media.[27] Going overboard, *Life* magazine wrote that: "if [Kennedy's] plan ... succeeds, it will add new luster to a reputation which may very well carry Joseph Patrick Kennedy to the White House."[28]

That type of publicity won Kennedy no fans in FDR's White House; moreover, it converted no one at the unadvised State Department, and was not well received by Taylor and Rublee. Kennedy, who viewed this as a "simple" issue involving money (as he did most things), perceived no moral issue at stake in the refugee problem.[29] As recorded by his son, Joe Junior, the Ambassador was "alarmed that the country should get so worked up by the treatment of the Jews, for if they can be roused to fever heat on this question, there doesn't seem to be much possibility of keeping them out of the war."[30] The "Kennedy Plan" with no moral underpinnings, no substance, and no support, thus simply faded away.

Taylor decided to focus his efforts in other spheres. Responding to Benito Mussolini's decree to expel all Jews from Italy, Taylor traveled to Rome in early 1939 to meet with church officials (including the future Pope Pius XII, then Cardinal Pacelli), as well as political figures (including Mussolini and his son-in-law, Count Ciano). As later described by Taylor:

> I enquired if influence could be brought to bear in some way on the Italian Government—not to cancel the decrees in expelling the Jews, not to retreat, which is a difficult thing for a politician to do, but to so modify the decree that each such case would be determined on its

merits, and avoid a mass exodus by bringing about a personal and individual study of each case, following gener-
ously in deciding these cases and disturbing the Jewish
people as little as possible. The result was that they were
never expelled from Italy. With that influence brought to
bear on Ciano and the influence on Mussolini, whom I
had known during his best period when he used to come
to Florence and I dined with him, the decree was so mod-
ified and was never enforced at all.[31]

On that same trip, an Italian neighbor of Taylor's, Princess
Helene (the Queen Mother of the King of Romania and daughter of the former King of Greece) contacted Taylor. The Princess
knew that Taylor had previously gotten a number of Italian Jews
she knew out of Italy and to America, and told Taylor that she and
her family were "all very much interested in this refugee problem
you are working on." Visiting at her villa was Hitler's doctor, and
she arranged for Taylor to meet with him. Taylor laid out for him a
précis for how the orderly emigration of German Jews could work
and gave him a copy of the ICR's plan.[32] Hitler' s doctor encouraged Taylor to "get your plan to Goering," who was on vacation
with his wife at San Remo, just over the French border.

Mr. and Mrs. Taylor drove up to Monte Carlo with Hitler's
doctor and his wife, and then invited Mr. and Mrs. Goering over
to a nearby estate (the Villa Anabel—named after Mrs. Taylor)
that they had donated to graduates of the music department of the
American Academy in Rome. Goering agreed to meet Taylor at
the border—"he did not want to go into France." The night before,
Taylor received a telephone message that Goering had received
the ICR's "informal memorandum [presumably from Hitler's doc-
tor] and was going back to Berlin," and that while Goering "was
rather agreeable to [the plan, he] had to discuss it with Hitler."[33]

This then led to an invitation for Rublee to meet Goering
in Berlin. Goering at that point offered to moderate the terms
of the deal Schacht had previously proposed—he was willing to

forgo the cash barter; the Jews permitted to leave could take one-third of their resources with them, with one-third for the German government, and the remainder to be put in trust for those emigres with no resources. Goering also proposed that once the 150,000 "able-bodied" Jews had been emigrated, their dependents would be allowed to join them; moreover, the Nazi regime would be amenable to working with international organizations to facilitate the process.[34]

That development seemed to justify Taylor's original optimism. He later recollected that everything "was all ready and agreed upon by both Goering and Hitler," and Welles wrote to FDR that it was "better than we hoped for."[35] But these were false hopes, and for two fundamental reasons. The first was the onrush of World War II in Europe. In March, Hitler took over Czechoslovakia; and in September, Poland was invaded, which triggered the outbreak of formal hostilities. In Taylor's words, "we failed because of the war coming on just at the moment of success."[36]

But there was an even more fundamental problem that Taylor perhaps did not fully appreciate—U.S. policymakers had never figured out the answer to the ICR's first challenge: to find a home for the refugees. As Treasury Secretary Morgenthau had cogently put it, in cutting off FDR's ruminating about "the thousand richest Jews in the United States"—"Mr. President, before you talk about money you have to have a plan [where to put them]."[37]

As to a "place," the history of what was being considered is of some interest. Palestine was the logical place for the refugees to resettle. But an insurmountable obstacle lay in the way—Great Britain. Although the British government had committed itself to a Jewish homeland in Palestine during World War I, by the 1920s the importance of Middle East oil and having unfettered access to India supplanted that commitment.[38] As FDR expressed to Morgenthau, "[t]he whole problem is England."[39]

With Palestine unworkable as a solution, overtures were made to nations in Latin and South America, as well as Africa. Those proved either unworkable or were rejected out of hand.

FDR initially thought he might persuade Portugal to commit one of its African colonies, but ultimately the Portuguese Foreign Minister to the United States persuaded the State Department from even formally raising the subject with his government.[40]

In desperation, Sumner Welles had suggested that Mindanao, the second largest island in the Philippines archipelago, be considered. Surprisingly, both FDR and Manuel Quezon, the Philippine president, approved that proposal in concept.[41] With the 1941 Japanese attack on Pearl Harbor, the Philippines, and other strategic U.S. possessions throughout the Pacific and Southeast Asia, however, this idea became stillborn. It is interesting to contemplate how different geopolitical issues would be today if the Mindanao plan had reached fruition.[42]

With World War II having commenced and the Nazi curtain drawn over virtually all of the European continent, any substantial or substantive progress by the ICR in effectuating the emigration of political refugees effectively came to a halt. As Sumner Welles later wrote, "notwithstanding the tireless work of … Myron Taylor, the final results amounted to little more than zero."[43] And while the Committee continued in existence (albeit with no real or achievable accomplishments),[44] Taylor's role thereafter in attempting to help European Jews, as well as assisting refugees in Italy during and after the war, is well documented in a different post—that of the President's "Ambassador Extraordinary" to Pope Pius XII.[45]

Notes

1. A.D. Morse, *While Six Million Died: A Chronicle of American Apathy* (Overlook Press 1983), pp. 209-10. An informative (and relatively brief) explication of the evolution of Hitler's anti-Jewish policies is set forth in John Lukacs' *The Last European War* (Yale University Press 1976), pp. 427-53.

2. C. Hull, *The Memoirs of Cordell Hull* (Macmillan 1948), p. 545.

3. S. Rosenman, *Working with Roosevelt* (Harper & Brothers 1952), p. 167.

4. B. Welles, *Sumner Welles: FDR's Global Strategist* (St. Martin's Press 1997), p. 220.

5. Transcript of meeting of Protestant Clergymen with Myron C. Taylor at Union Club (October 20, 1947), p. 3 (Taylor Papers, Cornell University). FDR's more formal charge to Taylor came in a letter dated April 26, 1938 (Taylor Papers, Cornell University).

6. K.S. Davis, *FDR: Into the Storm (1937-1940)* (Random House 1993), p. 268.

7. Welles, *supra* note 4, p. 220.

8. Morse, *supra* note 1, p. 218. A *Fortune* magazine poll in April of 1939 showed that 83% of the American people were opposed to any change in immigration laws or policies. H.L. Feingold, *The Politics of Rescue* (Rutgers University 1970), p. 42.

9. Davis, *supra* note 6, p. 269. Some State Department officials later tried to argue that a settlement in the Dominican Republic constituted a significant achievement of the Evian Conference and the efforts of the ICG. *See* October 12, 1946, letter from R. Pell to M.C. Taylor (Taylor Papers, Cornell University). In fact, however, the Dominican Republic limited its refugee immigration to "agricultural" labor—a category that explicably excluded virtually all of the refugees seeking asylum. Davis, *supra* note 6, p. 269. *See also infra* note 42. Archival movie footage of the Evian Conference has been assembled by the UCLA Film and Television Archives, and can be accessed on the United States Holocaust Memorial Museum website at www.ushmm.org.

10. Davis, *supra* note 6, p. 269. *See also* July 6, 1938, State Department Press Release, p. 3. Taylor's subsequent, extemporaneous speech to his colleagues "changed the atmosphere and remain[ed] the remembered speech of the session." "Bewildered Refugees Find a Friend in Taylor," *New York Times Magazine* (August 21, 1938) (One Latin-American diplomat called it a "very moving speech," and "something new in my diplomatic experience. This man is so straightforward, speaks with such sincerity and feeling. We were all stirred. There is something of a crusader in him.").

11. Welles, *supra* note 4, p. 220.

12. *New York Times* (July 13, 1938). Germany monitored the Evian Conference closely. When nothing substantive came from it, those who supported the Third Reich's policies were very pleased. As one Berlin newspaper put forth as a headline: "Jews for Sale: Who Wants Them? No One." P. Wyden, *Stella* (Simon & Schuster 1992), p. 63.

A German professor, Dr. Heinrich von Neumann, arrived in Evian "as part of the Nazi campaign to cash in on the proceedings." After swearing one correspondent to secrecy, von Neumann boasted: "You know, I'm here to sell the Jews of Austria." He further reported he had been instructed to ask for individual ransoms of $400 per person, but that, if pressed, he would drop the price to $200.

According to this story, von Neumann gained a private audience with Myron Taylor, "who offered no encouragement toward the deal." Wyden, *supra* note 12, pp. 61-64.

13. D.S. Wyman, *Paper Walls: America and the Refugee Crisis 1938-1941* (Pantheon Books 1985), p. 50.

14. *Id.* p. 51. Taylor's reputation, however, received a large boost. *See* "Bewildered Refugees Find a Friend in Taylor," *New York Times Magazine* (August 21, 1938) (Taylor's debut at Evian was termed a "remarkably successful one … He came out … with a reputation for sincerity and for kindliness."").

15. Morse, *supra* note 1, p. 213. In selling his approach, Taylor used business tactics, stating: "I have to, for these are the only methods I know." He also found the diplomatic world little different from his business experience: "There is much diplomacy in business, especially in selling. In both business and diplomacy you have something to sell, and you have to make it palatable, attractive, to the other man." "Bewildered Refugees Find a Friend in Taylor," *New York Times Magazine* (August 21, 1938).

16. H. Westwood, *Covington & Burling: 1919-1984* (Covington & Burling 1986), pp. 72-73. Mr. Rublee was recruited to assist Myron Taylor by Thomas Lamont of J.P. Morgan. Oral History of George Rublee p. 281 (Columbia University). In this same period it was speculated in the media that Taylor would become a "roving ambassador" on behalf of the United States, "if he shows any bent for diplomatic work in the international field anywhere near the same standard … he demonstrated [in negotiating with John L. Lewis]." ABC Radio Broadcast of Boake Carter (May 18, 1938; 6:30 p.m.).

17. October 1, 1938, State Department Press Release, pp. 5 & 7. In his address to the Council on Foreign Relations, Taylor identified the delegates from England, France, Brazil, and Argentina as being important in ensuring the "success" of the Evian Conference, and expressed "confiden[ce] that the German Government will recognize that extreme persecution is unnecessary to accomplish the emigration of those unwanted people …" Ibid. at 8.

18. Davis, *supra* note 6, pp. 364-67.

19. Welles, *supra* note 4, p. 223.

20. Welles, *supra* note 4, p. 224.

21. November 23, 1938, letter from F.D. Roosevelt to M.C. Taylor (Taylor Papers, Cornell University); FDR also opined on the need to figure out a mechanism to structure the financing of the emigration, because "much of the burden … will fall upon private individuals and organizations in the United States and England." That same day Lamont wrote to Taylor, reminiscing about the day in April Taylor first agreed to take on this task: "We all agreed, including yourself, that the refugees would give you a headache more than once, but that under the

circumstances, it was a public duty you could hardly decline. New developments have been such as to make the whole situation more difficult. You are such a philosopher that I know you won't worry unduly about it but will carry it through with your extraordinary amiability and sense of humor." (Lamont Papers, Baker Library, Harvard Business School).

22. Morse, *supra* note 1, pp. 246-47.

23. Oral History of George Rublee, pp. 284-85 (Columbia University).

24. Davis, *supra* note 6, pp. 368-69; D.K. Goodwin, *The Fitzgeralds and the Kennedys: An American Saga* (Simon & Schuster 1987), pp. 569-70.

25. A. Smith, *Hostage to Fortune: The Letters of Joseph P. Kennedy* (Viking 2001), pp. 302-03.

26. J.M. Blum, *The Morgenthau Diaries: Years of War (1941-1945)* (Houghtin Mifflin 1967), p. 208.

27. *New York Times* (November 11, 1938) (Sunday, Section 4, p. 3); *New York Times* (November 15, 1938), pp. 1, 5; *New York Times* (November 16, 1938), pp. 1, 9.

28. *Life* (November 28, 1938), p. 24.

29. Goodwin, *supra* note 24, pp. 569-70.

30. Smith, *supra* note 25, pp. 305-06. Ambassador Kennedy had previously criticized the Evian Conference, telling Lord Halifax that it created "a very delicate problem" in America because "anti-Semitic feelings might easily become activated and take shape in Ku Klux Klan activities." D.E. Koskoff, *Joseph P. Kennedy* (Prentice Hall 1974), pp. 175-76.

31. Transcript of Meeting of Protestant Clergymen with Myron C. Taylor at Union Club (New York City, October 20, 1947), at p. 7 (Taylor Papers, Cornell University). Taylor estimated that this action saved 90,000 Orthodox Jews from being expelled from Italy.

At the same time Taylor was engaged in these endeavors, Ambassador Kennedy and his family were representing the United States at the coronation of Pope Pius XII on March 12, 1939. The pomp and ceremony of the coronation is described in Kennedy's diary. Smith, *supra* note 25, pp. 316-19. As an indication of how out of the loop Kennedy was from FDR's diplomacy, when the Pope asked the Ambassador about U.S. recognition of the Vatican, Kennedy said he "would help" but thought the U.S. Church Hierarchy was "against it." Smith, *supra* note 24, pp. 317-18.

32. The ICR plan, as "agreed upon by both Goering and Hitler" [Taylor's words], was as follows:

It has been ascertained that Germany is disposed to adopt a policy which will in every way facilitate and encourage the organized emigration of Jews. A program along the lines hereinafter outlined will be put into effect when Germany is satisfied that countries of immigration are disposed to receive currently Jews from Germany in conformity with this program. If the program is put into effect—and its implementation will be greatly facilitated by an improvement in the international atmosphere—the emigration will take place in a uniform and orderly manner.

I.

Organization of Emigration

ONE. This program relates exclusively to Jews of German nationality or stateless Jews in Germany. The term "Jew" where used in this memorandum as provided by the Nuremberg laws means the following:

(1) A Jew is a person who has three of four Jewish grandparents. A grandparent is deemed to be a Jew if he or she embraced the Jewish faith;

(2) A person is also deemed to be a Jew who has two Jewish grandparents and who on September 16, 1935, was of the Jewish faith or thereafter embraced the Jewish faith; or who has two Jewish grandparents and on September 16, 1935, was married to a Jew or thereafter married a Jew.

TWO. There are approximately 600,000 Jews remaining in Germany, including Austria and the Sudetenland, at the present time. Of this number, 150,000 are classed as wage earners; the remainder are primarily the old and infirm who for that reason are not included in this program of emigration.

THREE. The wage earner category shall consist of all men and single women between the ages of 15 and 45, who are individually capable of earning a living and are otherwise fit for emigration.

FOUR. The dependent category shall consist of the immediate families of the wage earners, excluding the old (persons over 45 years of age) and the unfit.

FIVE. The wage earner category shall emigrate first, in annual contingents over a period of three years not to exceed a maximum of five years.

SIX. All persons from the wage earner category as defined above shall be admitted by the receiving governments in accordance with their established immigration laws and practices.

SEVEN. The practical work of organizing emigration shall be carried out with the participation of Bureaus representing the Jewish organizations of Germany under the control of a Commissioner designated by the German Government.

EIGHT. The Bureau organizing the work of emigration may be assisted by foreign experts representing outside private organizations concerned with immigration and enjoying the confidence of receiving governments, on condition that these experts are agreeable to the German Government.

NINE. Passports shall be furnished to persons emigrating from Germany under this arrangement. Stateless persons in Germany shall be furnished with suitable papers for emigration.

TEN. Conditions which have led to the retention of Jews, other than persons detained for reasons of public safety, in camps should automatically disappear if a program of organized emigration is put into effect.

ELEVEN. Facilities shall be granted for the retraining of wage earners for emigration, notably in agricultural retraining centers but also in artisan schools. Retraining shall be encouraged.

TWELVE. Emigration of persons in the dependent category shall take place when the wage earners are established and able to receive them.

II.
Position of Persons Remaining in Germany and of Those Awaiting Emigration

THIRTEEN. A definite method has not as yet been found for caring for old persons and persons unfit for emigration, who are not included in this program and who will be allowed to finish their days in Germany. It is the intention on Germany's part to assure that these persons and persons awaiting emigration may live tranquilly, unless some extraordinary circumstance should occur. There is no intention to segregate the Jews. They may circulate freely. Persons fit for work shall be given the opportunity of employment so as to earn their living; Jews employed in the same establishment as Aryans will, however, be separated from Aryan workers. Generally, in order to provide for adequate administration of the program, centralization of control over Jewish affairs is contemplated.

FOURTEEN. The support and maintenance of the persons referred to in paragraph thirteen above, who are not able to earn their own living, will be financed in the first instance from Jewish property in Germany apart from that portion thereof to be set aside in the trust fund (hereinafter described), and from the income from this trust fund. If the above resources do not suffice, there will be provided for these persons decent conditions of existence from the material standpoint in accordance with prevailing practices relating to the public relief of destitute persons generally. There will be no recourse to sources outside Germany for the support and maintenance of these persons.

III.

Financing of Emigration

FIFTEEN. In order to finance the emigration contemplated by the program, a trust fund shall be established in a specific amount to be ascertained but at all events in an amount not less than 25% of the existing Jewish wealth in Germany, which, if transfer possibilities are found, will represent a material increase over the present rates of transfer. At the present time the remaining Jewish wealth in Germany is in the hands of its individual owners; it has not yet been decided how the requisite amount thereof will be set aside in the trust fund.

SIXTEEN. The trust properties shall be held by a corporation administered by three trustees. Two of the trustees shall be of German nationality. The third trustee shall be of foreign nationality and recognized standing.

SEVENTEEN. The principal of the trust may be used to purchase equipment for emigrants of the wage earner category and (subject to cartel agreements) capital goods for the development of settlement projects and for traveling and freight expenses of the emigrants in Germany and on German boats, all in connection with this program of emigration. It is contemplated that an outside purchasing agency will be established to effect all purchases out of the fund, to maintain contact with the German authorities and generally to handle all problems arising outside of Germany in connection with the transfer of the fund. The types of goods which, in accordance with prevailing practice in Germany, are computed to contain no imported raw material or a relatively small percentage thereof; or, alternatively, no restrictions will be imposed if arrangements can be made to pay to Germany in foreign exchange a portion of the aggregate price of goods purchased which represents the computed value (on an over-all percentage basis to be agreed upon) of the imported raw material content of such goods. Arrangements shall be made to secure the exemption of goods purchased out of the fund from the scope of clearing, compensation and payment arrangements in force between Germany and the respective countries into which such goods are imported. Assurances shall be required of the purchasing agency that the goods purchased will not be disposed of otherwise than for the purpose of equipping emigrants or for the development of settlement projects. It is the intention to facilitate the purchase out of the fund of such goods of the requisite types and in adequate volume to meet the current emigration needs. The prices to be paid shall not be in excess of inland prices for goods or services of a similar character and quality.

EIGHTEEN. The Haavarah method of transfer shall be permitted to operate within its traditional sphere. The Haavarah purchases are to be paid for out of the trust fund.

NINETEEN. The principal of the trust fund, except to the extent that it is used for the purposes above referred to, shall be eligible for transfer whenever a change in conditions may render transfer possible or whenever arrangements to that end can be made, whether by way of agreed schemes for additional exports or otherwise.

TWENTY. Goods purchased out of the trust fund may be exported free of all taxes or other payments, and emigrants may take with them, free of all taxes, levies, contributions or similar exactions, their personal effects (with the exception of jewelry, precious metals, objets d'art, and with the exception of goods of special value recently acquired with a view to emigration, household goods, tools and equipment for use in their trades or professions, owned or which may be acquired by them in a reasonable amount for personal use.

TWENTY-ONE. No flight tax or exaction of a similar nature shall be levied against Jews emigrating in accordance with this program.

Taylor Papers, Library of Congress (Container 5A).

33. *Supra* note 31 at 8. Princess Helene subsequently followed up with an inquiry to Taylor: "I trust you had good news from Berlin." S. Riche January 18, 1939, letter to M.C. Taylor (Taylor Papers, Cornell University). Included among the group of distinguished individuals recruited by Taylor to coordinate the ICR plan (once agreed to) was John W. Davis, the former Democratic Candidate for President in 1924 (and former Ambassador to the Court of St. James, former

Congressman from West Virginia, and founder of the Davis, Polk & Wardwell law firm). *See also* March 6, 1939, memorandum from W. Bullitt to C. Hull (FDR Library, Box 51); July 28, 1939, memorandum of a July 21, 1939, conversation between M.C. Taylor and Herr Wohlthat (Taylor Papers, Library of Congress, Container 5A, Annex A).

34. Welles, supra note 4, p. 224. As Rublee later recalled, his negotiations with Schacht came to an early termination when Schacht confronted one of Rublee's colleagues and reported "that the Gestapo had reported that 'Mr. Rublee and you have stated that I'm disloyal to the regime. Can this be denied?'" Rublee, who knew that their rooms in Berlin were bugged and that they were being watched carefully, had never said anything of the sort. But it was too late—by the next day, Schacht and every Schacht person at the Ministry of Economics had been replaced. Oral History of George Rublee, p. 293 (Columbia University). Goering thereafter assured Rublee: "I ... know exactly what is being done and I assure you that we are interested in this negotiation ... [Y]ou can be sure of my interest and support." Oral History of George Rublee, pp. 297-98 (Columbia University).

35. Welles, supra note 4, p. 224. Rublee later recounted: "I went back quite happy over the results we had got. There was a great surprise in London when they'd learned what had happened.... Ambassador Kennedy had returned from a winter vacation in the United States. He called me up and in an entirely new tone expressed great surprise: 'How could it happen? Why hadn't they done something like this before if they were willing to do such things?' He thought it was quite extraordinary." Oral History of George Rublee, p. 304 (Columbia University). FDR also wrote directly to Taylor, reporting that he was "delighted" at the "progress" being made. *See* F.D. Roosevelt May 22, 1939, letter to M.C. Taylor (Taylor Papers, Cornell University). *See also* July 29, 1939, memorandum of conversation between M.C. Taylor and Herr Wohlthat (Taylor Papers, Library of Congress, Container 5A, Annex A).

36. Taylor October 20, 1947, Transcript, at p. 9; Oral History of George Rublee, p. 306 (Columbia University). In between those two events, President Roosevelt was writing to Taylor, expressing hope of achieving a financial arrangement by which a large number of German Jews would be permitted to emigrate; at the same time Welles was writing to Taylor, reporting on FDR's concern about an "increasing defeatist psychology with regard to the whole refugee problem." *See* May 22, 1939, and June 8, 1939, letters from F.D. Roosevelt to M.C. Taylor; June 22, 1939, letter from S. Welles to M.C. Taylor (Welles also was concerned that Germans "can sit back and smile and say that the people who are most vocal in their protests against the German treatment of the Jews have been entirely

unwilling to do anything of a practical nature to assist the Jewish refugees."). (Taylor Papers, Cornell University).

37. Blum, *supra* note 26, p. 208. There was an additional reason: opposition within the State Department bureaucracy, particularly lead by Assistant Secretary of State Breckinridge Long. Welles, *supra* note 4, p. 225. *See also* October 12, 1946, letter of R. Pell to M.C. Taylor (Taylor Papers, Cornell University) (citing Cordell Hull's criticism of "Mr. Welles' ill advised initiative," and accusing Hull of placing Long and others in positions within the State Department to stop that "initiative").

38. Welles, *supra* note 4, p. 223.

39. Blum, *supra* note 26, p. 208.

40. Welles, *supra* note 4, p. 223.

41. Feingold, *supra* note 8, pp. 97-99; Welles, supra note 4, p. 223.

42. In a memorandum Taylor wrote to President Truman on May 15, 1947, he recorded in detail his efforts in the 1938-39 period to provide for the emigration of German Jews. Besides the stillborn Mindanao plan was also the 1941 effort to settle European refugees in the Dominican Republic; most of the 600 people who were resettled there came from England, France, and the Low Countries. (Taylor Papers, Library of Congress, Container SA).

43. S. Welles, *Where Are We Heading?* (Harper & Brothers 1946), p. 280. In his memoirs, Cordell Hull credits Taylor's efforts as having "facilitated the emigration of scores of thousands of Jews from Germany to new and happier homes, ... even after the outbreak of war on September 1, 1939." Hull, *supra* note 2, p. 578. Unfortunately, Welles' conclusion, and not Hull's, was the accurate one. As Rublee later observed: "[O]nly a few got out." Oral History of George Rublee, p. 306 (Columbia University).

44. Cordell Hull wrote to President Roosevelt that "[w]hen the war broke out the principal justification for the continued existence of [the ICR] ceased." And, while FDR disagreed ("I am not yet ready to 'put the Intergovernmental Committee quietly to sleep."), no real progress was made in 1940 or thereafter. March 7, 1940, memorandum from F.D. Roosevelt to C. Hull, *reprinted in* E. Roosevelt, *FDR, His Personal Letters, 1928-45* (Duell, Sloan and Pearce 1950). Notwithstanding, Taylor retained his title of Vice Chairman of the ICR until July of 1944, when he convinced FDR to allow him to relinquish the position.

45. During the period Taylor served as FDR's personal representative to the Vatican, he also played key roles in postwar planning efforts by the State Department. One of those efforts was undertaken by the Subcommittee on Territorial Problems, under the leadership of Dr. Isaiah Bowman (the president of Johns Hopkins University). That group focused on the massive refugee population (approximately 20 million) that was being created as a result of the

war's devastation. Its principal work product was the so-called "M" program. *See* L. Farago, "Refugees: The Solution As F.D.R. Saw It," *United Nations World* (June 1947).

A major focus of the Bowman group was what to do vis-à-vis Palestine. While the group was struggling with that issue, Taylor wrote to Secretary of State Hull of his concern about efforts "to encourage a consolidation of the Arab world," stating that such a plan "is filled with dangers of many sorts." Among Taylor's worries was the fact that "we in this country know all too little about [the Arab world]." He added, with ominous prescience: "Perhaps one thing the world has to fear in the future is that strong aggregation of people bound by ties of blood and religion, especially those who are almost fanatical, now separated into groups and tribes and states, may join themselves together to oppose … the relatively smaller numbers of the Anglo-Saxon world." March 14, 1944, letter from M.C. Taylor to C. Hull (Taylor Papers, Library of Congress, Container SA, Annex A).

Three years later, in a May 15, 1947, memorandum to President Truman, Taylor expanded on his concerns as to that region of the world:

> From my close scrutiny of the Jewish tragedy during the years I participated in the Intergovernmental Committee, I am convinced that a way out must be found through (1) a common effort on the part of all governments of good will; (2) a broad international program providing many solid alternatives to Palestine, chiefly by admission of immigration and for the rest, settlement; (3) a deflation of the common Jewish attitude that Palestine is the sole destination for the Jews leaving Eastern Europe; and (4) a truce period during which every effort should be made to allow the arouse nationalism of the Arab world to subside.
>
> Day by day, Mr. President, my conviction grows stronger that the conflict over Palestine has implanted in it the seeds of wider conflagration. The overriding compulsion on all our national decisions is the safety and well-being of our country in these days on tightening crisis. The Eastern Mediterranean, in the strategy and circumstances as they have come to exist, directly and indirectly involves the safety and well-being of ourselves and the other nations of the West. Passions in the whole Near Eastern Area are being exploited and used to serve designs in power politics which may lead to fatal collision. We cannot argue uncomfortable or disturbing facts away. But we *can* place Palestine in the wider context of the Jewish migrant as a whole for which no *one* place can offer a solution.

Taylor's proposed solution was to have a series of places for resettlement, and not to have Palestine as the sole local point:

> It is clear that the effort can be made, and must be made, to introduce order into this migratory movement. The exodus from Europe must be directed in systematic fashion into permanent places,—I put heavy emphasis on the plural, *places,*—where settlement will offer reasonable living conditions and congenial homes. Dispersion provides the only possibility of a full solution. We should continue to support emigration to a democratic Palestine but only for a reasonable number of convinced Zionist—a number that conforms to the limited resources of Palestine as they now exist and as they are gradually developed hereafter.
>
> We should insist in our policy that Palestine is only part of the problem: that in itself Palestine physically can not, and will never be able to constitute a final settlement for the Jewish migrants as a whole. It could not do, so if it were clear of all Arabs and were larger than it is and better endowed with resources than nature blessed it. The stark principal fact as to both Jewish and non-Jewish refugees and displaced persons today is that even if the Palestine Problem were peaceably settled by an adjustment satisfactory to Jew and Arab alike, *the Jewish problem* of Europe would not have been solved, and the problem of the remaining displaced peoples of Europe still would remain unsolved. This is a sobering fact which world opinion, especially our own public opinion, is largely overlooking. But it is the greatest challenge in this tragedy."

Taylor Papers, Library of Congress (Container SA).

Ultimately, the geopolitical concerns voiced by Taylor, and others (e.g., Secretary of State George Marshall, Undersecretary of State Robert Lovell), were overruled (after a bitter intra-administration debate) by Truman, buttressed by his principal domestic advisor, Clark Clifford; Truman resolved this debate by recognizing the state of Israel upon its creation in 1948. *See* C. Clifford & R. Holbrooke, *Counsel to the President* (Anchor Books 1991), pp. 3-25.

CHAPTER IX

Appointment to the Vatican

On December 22, 1939, Myron Taylor lay recuperating at his extravagant town house on East 70th Street, steps from Fifth Avenue. Having had two gallstone operations and been in the hospital for four weeks, Taylor's focus was on recovering his health so that he and Anabel would soon be able to travel to their palazzo in Florence. Then the telephone rang.

The White House was calling. Could Mr. Taylor take a phone call from the President? FDR came on the line and asked: "Are you well enough to take on a special mission for me? All of our people are going to be withdrawn from Europe. We will have no diplomatic representation in Europe, except probably in France. There must be someone there who can keep in touch with European events. I would very much like you to go [and be my personal representative to the Pope]." Taylor replied: "I could not go now, so soon after leaving the hospital. But, if you wish to postpone my leaving for a little while, I will go if you want me to do so." FDR assured him that that would "be all right, but I [FDR] want to make the announcement at Christmas time."[1] And so FDR did— but not before calling back Anabel "to make sure there would be no back-sliding on [Taylor's] part."[2]

Taylor's appointment was later described by Eleanor Roosevelt as one of the "wise preliminary steps in our preparation for war."[3] Yet that appointment was made for a multitude of reasons: because of numerous domestic political concerns, as well as international diplomatic reasons. But to understand fully this historic

117

action, one must first look to the years just after the American Civil War.

In 1867 Congress shut down America's official relationship with the Vatican because of long-standing religious and ethno-cultural conflicts that had raged on and off for many years (e.g., the Know Nothing Party of the 1850s),[4] as well as the unpopularity generated by Pius IX's antidemocratic "Syllabus of Error." By 1870 the U.S. government was of the view that the Pope had lost any constitutional basis for diplomatic relations (Italy, not the Vatican, had become the only appropriate entity entitled to that status). That changed, however, when the Lateran Treaty was enacted in 1929; the Treaty reestablished the Vatican as a nation-state for diplomatic purposes.[5]

Notwithstanding the Lateran Treaty, the American domestic political landscape had not changed much since the end of the Civil War. Indeed, World War I had led to increased fissures between the U.S. government and the Vatican, and the 1920s resurgence of the Ku Klux Klan and 1928 presidential campaign of Alfred E. Smith (the country's first Catholic major party candidate) had stirred up a terrible hornet's nest of religious bigotry and hatred in America.[6] By 1936 FDR had nonetheless begun to give serious consideration to resuming diplomatic relations with the Vatican.[7] At that point it appears that his principal motivation was domestic politics.

Catholics were a key constituency of the New Deal coalition.[8] And Roosevelt had a few close friends in the Catholic religious hierarchy. Cardinal George Mundelein of Chicago, the most influential Church official in the United States and a powerful figure in mid-western politics, was a strong supporter of FDR,[9] as were Cardinal Patrick Hayes and Monsignor Robert Keagan of New York; Joseph P. Kennedy had been one of Roosevelt's principal financial backers in 1932, and had helped broker a compromise at the Democratic Convention, which led to FDR's nomination.

But not all prominent Catholics were supporters of FDR. Most notable of the nonsupportive was the "Radio Priest" Father

Charles Coughlin. Coughlin, who initially began as a New Deal supporter, quickly turned against the President (as had the "King-fish," Huey Long).[10] Coughlin's immensely popular and influential weekly radio broadcast became a drumbeat of vitriolic and ad hominem attacks against FDR personally, and his administration's policies generally. Coughlin even sponsored a political movement in opposition to FDR's 1936 reelection bid. FDR and his political lieutenants (e.g., Harold Ickes, the Secretary of the Interior), in response, reached out to Coughlin's superiors in the Church in an effort to shut up/shut down Coughlin, with mixed success. The President even reached out to the Vatican.

Initially, FDR utilized the then auxiliary bishop of Boston, Francis Spellman, to visit with the Church's apostolic delegate in Washington, Archbishop Amelto Cicognani. Cicognani, however, told Spellman that so long as Coughlin retained the support of his local Bishop, he could do nothing.[11] The following day (September 28, 1936), Spellman reported on this disappointing news to Roosevelt at Hyde Park. Spellman also reported to FDR that his mentor, Cardinal Eugenio Pacelli (the Vatican's Secretary of State), would be visiting the United States that fall and set the stage for a meeting between the president and the future Pope Pius XII.

That meeting, which Spellman orchestrated outside the normal bureaucratic Church channels, was purposefully arranged to take place two days after the U.S. election. On November 5, both Pacelli and Spellman traveled to Hyde Park to meet with the reelected president. While there appears to be no record extant of what was discussed, there can be little doubt that the items included FDR's concerns about Father Coughlin, and from the Church's perspective the desire to reestablish diplomatic relations between America and the Holy See.[12]

During Cardinal Pacelli's U.S. trip, he traveled widely and met with a number of leading Americans (Joseph P. Kennedy, for example, had Cardinal Pacelli for tea at his home in Bronxville, New York). One of those prominent Americans was Myron

Taylor, who first met the future Pope at a dinner in New York and then hosted him in his Manhattan home. Years later, Taylor recalled that he and Cardinal Pacelli broke away for a private conversation in his town house and the future Pope said to him: "Mr. Taylor, the time is coming, and it is not far off, when all religious people regardless of denomination will have to stand together to fight communism and atheism." As Taylor further recalled: those words "made a very great impression on me, and I always remembered [them] as a far-sighted prophesy."[13]

Four days after the Spellman–Pacelli meeting, FDR met with Cardinal Mundelein at the White House; there is no record of what they discussed. But a year later, when the president traveled to Chicago in October of 1937 to deliver his famous (but not well received) "Quarantine" speech (*see* Chapter VIII, pp. 96-97), he stayed at Cardinal Mundelein's residence. Cardinal Mundelein later reported to the apostolic delegate that, subject to the Holy See's approval, the president had told him that he intended "to send a special envoy to the Vatican ... of ambassadorial rank."[14] What FDR meant by "special envoy," and in what time frame, were not specified.

From late 1937 until early 1939 there were frequent communications and contacts between Church officials and FDR's administration regarding diplomatic details, but with little concrete progress.[15] Besides the diplomatic issues was the delicate political balancing act FDR was attempting in advance of trying for an unprecedented third term: solidifying his Catholic base by means of a Vatican appointment, without antagonizing Protestant voters by such a step.

Pius XI's death on February 10, 1939, seemed to shake things a bit loose. First off, Cardinal Pacelli (to whom FDR started to refer as his "old friend") was elected as the new Pope—Pius XII.[16] That prompted FDR to take the unprecedented step of having Ambassador Joseph P. Kennedy (and his family) represent the U.S. government at the papal coronation in Rome on March 12, 1939. One month later, Spellman (the new Pope's protégé and key proponent of U.S. diplomatic relations) was named Archbishop of New York.

These events seemed to jump-start both diplomacy and politics. The U.S. Catholic Church began to become more overt in its support of a Roosevelt third term,[17] and the administration began to get more specific on the diplomatic front.

On June 19, 1939, for example, the U.S. Ambassador to Italy, William Phillips, responded to an inquiry from Undersecretary of State Sumner Welles as to the possible benefits of renewed relations, recommending such an action and suggesting that a Protestant be named as the U.S. representative. Five days later, on June 24, 1939, Brooklyn Congressman Emanuel Cellar wrote a lengthy letter to Secretary of State Cordell Hull, urging the reestablishment of diplomatic ties. On August 1 and 2, Welles sent both documents on to the president, adding that both he and Hull had been speaking "some weeks ago" about the advantage of renewed relations, given that "it is unquestionable that the Vatican has many sources of information, particularly with regard to what is actually going on in Germany, Italy and Spain, which we do not possess." As a terse response, FDR fired back a one line memo to Welles on August 6: "Will you speak to me about this?"[18] In separate sessions with the president, Welles and Hull both pressed on the diplomatic benefits of going forward; they also endorsed Phillips' idea of naming a Protestant.

Then on October 2, the same day that Cardinal Mundelein was found dead at his Chicago residence, FDR wrote a memorandum to Hull on the subject of a representative to the Vatican. Incredibly (although perhaps not so when one considers FDR's political style), the document's topic sentence is as follows: "This is a wholly original thought with me and I have discussed it with no one else."[19] In the text of his memo, FDR cited the important work being done by "the Myron Taylor committee" on behalf of refugees as being of particular relevance to the work to be done by a U.S. representative at the Vatican.[20]

FDR asked Spellman to visit him at the White House on October 24, 1939. The next day Spellman reported on his visit to the Vatican's new Secretary of State, Luigi Maglione. FDR had told Spellman the following: (1) the sending of Ambassador Kennedy to the papal coronation had demonstrated the president's "favorable attitude" toward the Vatican; (2) at the same time, FDR did not believe he had the votes in Congress either to establish formal diplomatic relations or to have funds appropriated; (3) while Congress was on recess (until January 3, 1940), FDR planned to "name a special mission to the Holy See"; and (4) FDR was thinking of naming as his representative either Myron Taylor or Breckenridge Long, former ambassador to Italy (and currently Assistant Secretary of State).[21]

Having started to take care of the diplomatic side of the equation, FDR turned to the domestic side of things. In the midst of trying to influence the appointment (ultimately unsuccessfully) of Cardinal Mundelein's successor, FDR and his Interior Secretary, Harold Ickes, discussed on November 3, 1939, the import and impact of the fact that FDR was "considering seriously sending a representative to the Vatican, although not with full diplomatic standing." At that meeting, and at a follow-up days later, Ickes told FDR not only that he was a more powerful president than even his cousin (Theodore Roosevelt) but that he was "on top of the world"—thus giving him a free hand to try to influence Church appointments in the United States, as well as to undertake whatever course FDR deemed advisable and necessary vis-à-vis diplomatic relations with the Vatican.[22]

On November 28, 1939, the Vatican notified Spellman that "[t]he Holy Father has learned of the report with pleasure and hopes that your Excellency as well as I will make opportune overtures to the President, that he may carry out his proposal."[23] In response, Spellman then scheduled a lunch at the White House for December 7, at which he learned to his joy that the president planned to make the announcement at or before Christmas.[24]

THE WHITE HOUSE
WASHINGTON

My dear Mr. Taylor:

    Reposing special faith and confidence in you
I am asking you to proceed at your early convenience
to Italy, there to act as my personal representative,
with the rank of ambassador, to His Holiness, Pope
Pius XII. My purpose in entrusting you with this
mission was set forth in my letter of December 23,
1939 to the Pope, a copy of which is enclosed. I am
also asking you personally to convey a further communication to His Holiness.

    I may from time to time request you to serve as
the channel of communication for any views I may wish
to exchange with the Pope. You will, of course, com-
municate to this Government any matters which may come
to your attention in the performance of your mission
which you may feel will serve the best interest of the
United States.

    With all best wishes for the success of your
mission, I am,

                Very sincerely yours,

Enclosure:
  As stated.

The Honorable
  Myron C. Taylor,
    71 Broadway,
      New York, New York.

President Roosevelt's letter to Taylor appointing him as
FDR's personal representative to Pope Pius XII

On December 22, the same day FDR convinced a sick, but
recovering, Myron Taylor to take on the job of his personal representative to the Vatican, the president was still testing out
the domestic politics of the appointment. He called Postmaster

General (and Democratic National Chairman) James Farley to discuss Vice President John Garner's announcement that day that he would be a candidate for president (in opposition to a third term by FDR). In the course of the call, FDR told Farley of Taylor's imminent appointment. Farley replied that it "was satisfactory in every way ... and bound to be well received."[25]

The following day, December 23, Spellman was again called to the White House. Once there, FDR gave him a handwritten letter to be delivered to the Pope, announcing Taylor's appointment, the text of which put Taylor's appointment in the context of a broad non-secular attempt to find answers to the world's situation and bring about a lasting peace. FDR's letter was also cabled to the Vatican and made public the following day. In order to "soften" the anticipated religious firestorm of bigotry anticipated in response to the Taylor appointment, FDR sent similar "peace letters" to Dr. George A. Buttrick (President of the Federal Council of Churches of Christ in America) and Rabbi Cyrus Adler (President of the Jewish Theological Seminary, New York).[26]

Taylor's appointment was big news and attracted various reactions. In a lead article in the *New York Times*, Taylor said he was "greatly honored" by the president's asking him to serve "in the cause of world peace and good will.... No cause could find any one of us more willing to serve to the utmost of his ability."[27] A number of prominent Catholic and Jewish leaders also praised Taylor's appointment, as well as FDR's letters to Buttrick and Adler.[28] The Pope, who announced this development on Christmas Eve to the College of Cardinals, hailed the news and expressed "gratitude for this noble and generous act of President Roosevelt."[29]

America's leading political columnist, Walter Lippmann, pooh-poohed the notion that Taylor's appointment had anything to do with domestic politics: "[such an explanation] ... is no explanation at all." Lippmann instead applauded the president's action because (1) the Pope had "better sources of information ... than our own diplomatic and consular officials can hope to [have]," and

(2) given the military status quo in Europe at the end of 1939, the only avenue for peace seemed to go through the Vatican and be based on the Pope's articulation of a possible means to avoid a worldwide conflagration. As such, "it is evident Mr. Myron Taylor is going to Vatican City, not to seek peace where there is no peace, but to prepare the ground for the great task of post-war reconstruction."[30]

In the face of such important concerns, however, came the anticipated anti-Catholic reaction. Eleanor Roosevelt, after the war, tepidly noted that Taylor's appointment "created a certain amount of difficulty among some of our Protestant groups."[31] In fact, a coordinated response came within days on behalf of over 10 million Baptists (Southern, Northern, and African American), attacking the president and his appointee.[32]

This led to FDR calling Baptist representatives to the White House in the hopes of defusing the issue. According to one of the Baptist attendees, FDR launched into a 25-minute monologue, defending Taylor's appointment as "unofficial, temporary, and concerned primarily with the protection of world peace."[33] Three days later, on January 12, 1940, FDR wrote a letter to Senator Josiah Bailey (D-NC), responding to the Senator's own protest letter, and observing: "I wish you could have been here the other day when I talked with some of the leading Baptists . . . in regard to Mr. Taylor's going to the Vatican." FDR went on with some gusto to defend the appointment of Taylor as his "messenger":

> In the conduct of foreign relations, which is, of course, my responsibility, it is necessary for me to observe certain amenities of life. Whether we like it or not mere messenger boys, even when they are messenger boys, sent by the President of the United States, eat in the servants' hall in foreign countries—and I could have hesitated to put Myron Taylor, who, after all, is a very great American, into such a position. If you were President you would not do it either.

Again, whether we like it or not there are certain titles which carry with them the right to sit at the supper table above the salt. Whether an American who is essentially acting as a messenger boy is called an Ambassador or by some other title ought to make very little practical difference in this country, including, for example, Afghanistan, Tibet, London, Paris and Rome!

I am perhaps being a bit facetious but if some of my good Baptist brethren in Georgia had done a little preaching from the pulpit against the K.K.K. in the '20s, I would have a little more genuine American respect for their Christianity!

The protest is due, of course, to a lack of appreciation of the difficulties and niceties of conducting foreign affairs, and I am wholly charitable toward them—and, furthermore, I think the result of our conference was 100% good and that we shall hear little or nothing more of it.[34]

Unfortunately, religious opposition did not really die down (or go underground) until the Japanese attacked Pearl Harbor and the United States became a full participant in World War II. By that time, however, Myron Taylor's Vatican mission had been well underway and had already tackled a number of critical geopolitical issues.[35]

Notes

1. Transcript of Meeting of Protestant Clergymen with Myron C. Taylor at Union Club (New York City, October 20, 1947), at pp. 9-10 (Taylor Papers, Cornell University).

2. M.C. Taylor December 26, 1939, letter to Capt. H.H. Hier-Davis (Taylor Papers, Cornell University). FDR's follow-up to Mrs. Taylor went something like this: FDR opened his call by saying he had another job for "them." Mrs. Taylor asked: "What is it?" FDR responded: "I want Myron to go to Rome to represent me with the Pope." Mrs. Taylor objected that her husband was "not in very

good health. I don't think he could stand up to it." FDR was not rebuffed: "You have a villa in Florence. You can live there. The contacts with the Pope , will be occasional. You can accept it." Mrs. Taylor's arm was easily twisted: "All right, I'll see Myron. I think we'll go." T. Morgan, *The Listening Post* (G.P. Putnam & Sons 1944), pp. 189-90.

3. E. Roosevelt, *This I Remember* 209 (Harper 1949).

4. *See* T. Anbinder, *Nativism & Slavery: The Northern Know Nothings & the Politics of the 1850s* (Oxford University Press 1992); J. Mulkern, *The Know Nothing Party in Massachusetts* (Northeastern University Press 1990); M. Summers, *Rum, Romanism & Rebellion: The Making of a President 1884* (University of North Carolina Press 2000); M. Voss-Hubbard, *Beyond Party: Cultures of Antipartisanship in Northern Politics Before the Civil War* (Johns Hopkins University Press 2002).

5. Technically, in the words of Secretary of State William H. Seward, Congress' 1867 refusal to fund the U.S. Mission to the Vatican legally left it "still existing, but without compensation." E. Celler July 24, 1939, letter to C. Hull (www.fdrlibrary.marist.edu/psf/box51/a464c02.html). *See generally* R. Graham, *Vatican Diplomacy* (Princeton University Press 1959), pp. 326, 333-45; A. Manhattan, *The Vatican in World Politics* (Gaer Associates 1949), p. 389; L. Pfeffer, *Church, State, and Freedom* (Beacon Press 1953), p. 260.

6. The World War I tensions between the U.S. government and the Vatican are well documented in G. Fogarty's "Roosevelt and the American Catholic Hierarchy," *FDR, the Vatican, and the Roman Catholic Church in America, 1933-1945* (Palgrave Macmillan 2003) (eds. D. Woolner & R. Kurial), pp. 12-15. For a good explication of the bigoted landscape of American politics in the 1920s, *see* C. Firan, *Alfred E. Smith: The Happy Warrior* (Hill & Wang 2002); R. Slayton, *Empire Statesman: The Rise and Redemption of Al Smith* (Simon & Schuster 2001).

7. Taylor's ultimate appointment was as the President's "personal representative" to Pope Pius XII, not to the Vatican, the Holy See, or the Catholic Church. The Vatican is a nation-state, created as a result of negotiations between Pius XII's predecessor and the Italian government. The Holy See is the religious organization of which the Pope is the head; it is to the Holy See that other nations designated ambassadors. The Church itself is technically a separate organization, although the Pope (as head of the Holy See) is also head of the Church. *See* Graham, *supra* note 5, p. 346, n.11.

8. *See* M. Barone, "Franklin D. Roosevelt: A Protestant Patrician in a Catholic Party," *FDR, the Vatican and the Roman Catholic Church in America, 1933-1945* (Palgrave Macmillan 2003) (eds. D. Woolner & R. Kurial). In 1933, the leading Catholic magazine *Commonwealth* opined that "All Catholics who desire to give practical effect to the principles of social justice laid down by Pope Pius XI will see that … Roosevelt's opportunity to lead … is likewise the Catholic

opportunity to make the teachings of Christ apply to the benefit of all." G. Flynn, *American Catholics & the Roosevelt Presidency, 1932-1936* (University of Kentucky Press 1968), pp. 37-38, 42.

9. Cardinal Mundelein's political influence and sway are well illustrated in FDR's Postmaster General (and Democratic National Chairman) James Farley's political memoir: *Jim Farley's Story: The Roosevelt Years* (McGraw Hill 1948), pp. 173-79. Farley devoted an entire chapter to a July 12, 1939, meeting he had with the Cardinal at the Vanderbilt Hotel in New York City. Cardinal Mundelein told Farley: "I am satisfied [FDR] is going to run [for a third term]," and urged Farley not to launch his own bid, but to support FDR instead. Later in that same memoir (at p. 194), Farley recounted an audience in August 1939 he had with Pope Pius XII. After discussing the deteriorating world situation, the Pope "astonished" Farley by asking about the likelihood of FDR seeking a third term:

> "Will the President run again?" he asked. "I do not know," was my reply. "It will all depend on circumstances. Personally, I do not think he would want to run and, if he does, he would be breaking unwritten law, because no one has ever done so within our party system." The Pope laughed quietly and then said, "You know, I am the first Italian Papal Secretary of State to be elected Pope." I have often thought since that day he was a far better political prophet than I was.

See also J. Blum, *The Secret Diary of Harold L. Ickes: The Lowering Clouds (1939-1941)* (Simon & Schuster 1959), pp. 28-29, 55, 110; R. Tugwell, *The Democratic Roosevelt* (Doubleday, 1957), p. 513. For an excellent overview of Cardinal Mundelein's relationship with FDR, *see* G. Flynn, *Roosevelt and Romanism: Catholic and American Diplomacy: 1932-1945* (Greenwood Press 1976) *and* Fogarty, *supra* note 6. In September 1936, for example, Cardinal Mundelein gave an interview to the *Chicago Times* in which he called Roosevelt "his friend," and tacitly endorsed him, opining that the country should be grateful "for the prosperity, the happiness, and the freedom now abroad in our land." Fogarty, *supra* note 6, p. 18.

10. A. Brinkley, *Voices of Protest: Huey Long, Father Coughlin & The Great Depression* (Random House 1982); M. Sheldon, *Father Coughlin: The Tumultuous Life of the Priest of the Little Flower* (Little Brown 1973).

11. Part of the "political" problem within the Church stemmed from the fact that Coughlin retained the support of the Bishop of Detroit, Michael Gallagher. And part stemmed from the fact that many other Catholic clergy agreed with much of what Coughlin had to say, at least initially. Brinkley, *supra* note 10, pp. 128-33. According to one historian of this period, aiding the pro-Coughlin forces within the Vatican was the fact that the Church official put in charge

of administering the "Coughlin situation" was Joseph Patrick Hurley, a blatant anti-Semite. *See* C. Gallagher, "A Peculiar Brand of Patriotism," *FDR, the Vatican, and the Roman Catholic Church in America, 1933-1945* (Palgrave Macmillan 2003) (eds. D. Woolner & R. Kurial).

12. For greater details of Cardinal Pacelli's trip and his visit to Hyde Park, *see* O. Halecki, *Eugenio Pacelli: Pope of Peace* (Creative Age Press 1951), pp. 156-58. Some have written that an explicit quid pro quo was entered into during this meeting: "gagging" Father Coughlin in exchange for diplomatic relations. *See* J. Cornwell, *Hitler's Pope: The Secret History of Pius XII* (Penguin 1999), pp. 176-77. That seems highly doubtful, for at least two reasons. First, Father Coughlin was not "gagged" and (as reflected in FDR's first diplomatic instructions to Taylor in his role at the Vatican) continued as an irritant to the President for another four years. Second, and as set forth more fully in the text, domestic politics from FDR's perspective required that it would take several years before he could fulfill any pledge (whether concrete—which was never Roosevelt's style—or something he suggested more ephemerally). From the Church's perspective, it would appear that Archbishop Spellman had been laying the groundwork on reestablishing relations beginning in 1935. Fogarty, *supra* note 6, p. 19.

13. Transcript of Meeting of Protestant Clergymen with Myron C. Taylor at Union Club (New York City, October 20, 1947) at pp. 5-6 (Taylor Papers, Cornell University). Two years later (July 18, 1938), James Roosevelt wrote Taylor that "Pacelli asked ... to be remembered to you and that I tell you he was looking forward to meeting you in Rome." (Taylor Papers, Cornell University).

14. Fogarty, *supra* note 6, p. 20.

15. *Id*. pp. 21-22.

16. FDR wrote to Pope Pius XII upon his election: "It is with true happiness that I have learned of your election as Supreme Pontiff. Recalling with pleasure our meeting on the occasion of your recent visit to the United States I wish to take this occasion to send you a personal message of felicitations and good wishes." Morgan, *supra* note 2, pp. 188-89.

17. *See supra* note 9.

18. These documents are at the FDR Presidential Library and can be accessed at http://www.fdrlibrary.marist.edu/psf/box51. FDR and his advisors knew that the Vatican had representatives in 72 nations, and that 38 countries had diplomatic corps accredited to the Holy See. They also believed that the Pope had enormous influence in the world beyond just the members of the Church. *See* J. Lukacs, *The Last European War* (Yale University Press 2001), p. 367. Ambassador Phillips pointed out an additional advantage to such an appointment—it would enhance the geopolitical prestige of the Pope: "At present, the Pope is living in the shadow of a dominant personality, and he may well hesitate at times to take

any action that might incur the displeasure of Mussolini." *Id.* On May 16, 1939, Undersecretary of State Sumner Welles had written to FDR regarding the Pope's message to him (via the apostolic delegate), detailing the Vatican's efforts to head off total war in Europe. *Id.* And on June 29, 1939, the Church's apostolic delegate had lunch with Welles at which diplomatic issues were discussed in great detail; a complete report of this meeting was then directly sent to the Church's Secretary of State in Rome. *See* Memorandum of A. Cicognani to L. Maglione, which is reprinted in full in *The Holy See and the War in Europe: March 1939–August 1940* (Clonmore and Reynolds 1968) (eds. P. Blet, A. Martini, & B. Schneider), pp. 194-97. For an excellent overview of the role of the apostolic delegate during this period, *see* R. Trisco, "The Department of State and the Apostolic Delegation in Washington During World War II," *FDR, the Vatican, and the Roman Catholic Church in America, 1933-1945* (Palgrave Macmillan 2003) (eds. D. Woolner & R. Kurial). *See* J. Lukacs, *The Last European War* (Yale University Press 2001), p. 367.

19. In his memoir, Hull quotes this sentence and then FDR's memorandum liberally without any ironic comment. *The Memoirs of Cordell Hull* (Macmillan 1998), pp. 713-14. Perhaps, given Hull's lengthy political relationship with FDR, he was not surprised by the president asserting that this was all "his idea."

20. FDR thought that it might be possible to address the refugee problem more effectively in the context of, and under the aura of, the Vatican; he believed that the effort would be less vulnerable to anti-Semitic attack.

21. Fogarty, *supra* note 6, pp. 23-24. Archbishop Spellman's memorandum to Cardinal Maglioni detailing the White House visit is reprinted in full in *The Holy See and the War in Europe*, pp. 302-05. After a meeting with FDR on December 7, 1939, Archbishop Spellman wrote in his diary that the president was going to "send either Myron Taylor or Harry Woodring as Ambassador." G. Fogarty, *The Vatican and the American Hierarchy From 1870 to 1965* (Anton Hiersemann 1982), p. 262. In his oral history, Henry Wallace remembered James Farley reporting on a conversation he witnessed between Harry Woodring, the Secretary of War, and FDR. The president told Woodring that his name (along with Taylor's, and others) had been submitted to the Pope, "and that the Pope had indicated that Woodring's was first on the list. Jim said: 'Of course, you and I know the Pope never heard of Woodring, or the name of anyone else in the Cabinet, except possibly Hull's and my own (Farley).' Harry, of course, knew this and said, 'Mr. President, if you want me to resign I will be delighted to do so, but I am not in the slightest interest[ed] in going to Rome. Neither is Mrs. Woodring. Rather than go there I would, of course, resign.' The President replied, 'Why of course I don't want you to resign. Just forget the whole matter.'" (Columbia Oral History Project).

Long would have been a poor choice, if for no other reason(s) than he had a well-known anti-Semitic bias and had used his powerful post in the State Department to oppose any meaningful efforts to deal with the European refugee problem. See www.holocaustchronicle.org/staticpages/442.html. Taylor, on the other hand, not only had met with the Pope before (FDR, in fact, believed that the Pope would consider Taylor to be a "persona gratissima"), (1) he had unique refugee experience, (2) he was one of FDR's few personal friends and had the president's trust and confidence, (3) he was a prominent Episcopalian (an important fact, given the anticipated Protestant reaction), (4) he had independent means (because FDR felt he could not get Congress to appropriate funds, this was not insignificant; later, ICR funds were used to underwrite some of the Taylor mission), and (5) he had a long-standing acquaintance with Mussolini (they had hunted grouse together, and Taylor had publicly applauded his leadership of Italy in the 1930s). See A. Manhattan, *The Vatican in World Politics* (Gaer Associates 1949), p. 389; Morgan, *supra* note 2, pp. 189 & 191; O. Chadwick, *Britain and the Vatican During the Second World War* (Cambridge University Press 1986), p. 101. As to this last point, on November 5, 1936, at a New York City dinner welcoming the new Italian Ambassador to the United States, Taylor lauded Mussolini as not only having made "great advances" in "disciplin[ing] the [Italian] nation," but also for expanding the Italian empire into Ethiopia and "tak[ing] up its responsibilities as the guardian and administrator of an alien backward nation of 10,000,000 souls." "Steel Head Hails Mussolini's Rule," *New York Times* 14 (November 6, 1936). Taylor had also sat right behind Mussolini on the Palazzo Vecchio when he gave his "rattling the saber" speech. Transcript of Meeting of Protestant Clergymen with Myron C. Taylor at Union Club (New York City, October 25, 1947), p. 17 (Taylor Papers, Cornell University). Taylor's prior relationship with Il Duce was not unimportant as it related to one of Taylor's first tasks: to prevail upon Mussolini not to commit Italy to entering World War II on the side of Hitler's Germany.

   22. H. Ickes, *The Secret Diaries of Harold L. Ickes, Volume III, The Lowering Clouds, 1939-41* (Simon & Schuster 1954), pp. 28-29, 55-56, 65. FDR was not completely taken in by this sycophancy, telling Ickes: "But just wait and see the nose dive that I will take about next March." *Id.* p. 65 (anticipating negative public reaction as a decision regarding a third term became imminent). FDR's ham-handed attempt to influence Cardinal Mundelein's successor did not help him within the more conservative, isolationistic parts of the U.S. Catholic Church hierarchy. Tugwell, *supra* note 9, p. 513; Fogarty, *supra* note 6, pp. 25-26; Ickes Diaries, p. 110. FDR had very much wanted Monsignor Bernard J. Sheil to succeed his mentor; Sheil was not only personally sympathetic to FDR but he had also given a national radio broadcast 12 hours after Mundelein's death, urging

American Catholics to rally behind FDR on the neutrality law controversy (ultimately, Congress voted to repeal the arms embargo). FDR's related focus on moderating "the overwhelming isolationism of American Catholics" clearly influenced his sending Taylor to Rome. Tugwell, *supra* note 9, pp. 505-06. On November 3, 1939, Harry Hooker (an FDR business partner and close confidant of the president) wrote to Taylor, "congratulating [him] on the vital work which you did [on the embargo repeal], and which the World does not know about." (Taylor Papers, Cornell University). What Taylor's "vital work" in fact was remains unknown.

23. Fogarty, *supra* note 6, p. 24.

24. Fogarty, *supra* note 6, pp. 24-25; Fogarty, *supra* note 21, p. 262.

25. J. Farley, *Jim Farley's Story: The Roosevelt Years* (McGraw Hill 1948), pp. 217-18. Farley, after the appointment, sent Taylor a telegram, saying that the president had told him about it the day before and it "pleased me immensely." (Taylor Papers, Cornell University).

26. Fogarty, *supra* note 6, p. 25; Fogarty, *supra* note 21, p. 263; T. Morgan, *The Listening Post: Eighteen Years on Vatican Hill* (G.P. Putnam's Sons 1944), p. 188. J. Conway, "Myron C. Taylor's Mission to the Vatican 1940-1950," Church History (1975), p. 87; L. Pfeffer, *Church, State, and Freedom* (Beacon Press 1953), pp. 260-61. In his letters to all three men, FDR said he wanted to "encourage a closer association between those in every part of the world—those in religion and those in government—who have a common purpose." Only in his letter to Pius XII did the president add that he wanted to send "to you my personal representative in order that our parallel endeavors for peace and the alleviation of suffering may be assisted." FDR's letter to Pope Pius XII is reprinted in its entirety in The Holy See and the War in Europe, pp. 325-27.

27. "Taylor Welcomes Duties at Vatican," *New York Times* 1 (December 25, 1939). Interestingly, Taylor cited in this article the remarks the then Secretary of State had made to him at his home in 1936 as follows: "in effect that in the days soon to come all the forces of religion would need to align themselves together against a revival of paganism if civilization were to be saved." Interestingly, after World War II, Taylor remembered the quotation a little differently, replacing "paganism" with "communism." *See supra* p. 120 *and* note 13. *Time* magazine (January 1940) ran a lead article on the appointment, describing at great length "[t]he big man in the rumpled suit [FDR] scratch[ing] his pen steadily across the large white sheets [as he wrote to the Pope]."

28. *Id.* (quoting, for example, Rabbis Samuel H. Goldman and Herbert S. Goldstein).

29. O. Halecki, *Eugenio Pacelli: Pope of Peace* (Creative Age Press 1951), p. 160. The Pope, who viewed the United States as holding the balance of power in the world and was eager to enlist FDR's aid in attempting to stave off a full-fledged

European war, issued a prompt and detailed response to the president's letter on January 7, 1940, praising FDR's "courageous document" and "memorable message," and stating that the Vatican had "been deeply moved by the whole thought contained" therein. He went on to praise the "well-known qualifications" of Taylor and added that he was pleased the president's representative was being "sent to Us as the faithful interpreter of your mind regarding the procuring of peace and the abbreviation of sufferings consequent upon the war." This document is at the FDR Presidential Library and can be accessed at http://www.fdrlibrary. marist.edu/psf/box51 (the President framed the original of this letter.). On January 27, 1940, U.S. Ambassador to France, William Bullitt, sent Taylor a telegram, reporting that he had seen the Pope "a few days ago" and Pius XII had "expressed the greatest possible delight in your appointment.... He spoke of his visit to your home and of the charms of Anabel as well as your own." (Taylor Papers, Cornell University). For an excellent insight into the Pope's diplomatic training and his expectations for the Taylor mission, see J. Conway, "Pope Pius XII and the Myron Taylor Mission," *FDR, the Vatican, and the Roman Catholic Church in America, 1933-1945* (Palgrave Macmillan 2003) (eds. D. Woolner & R. Kurial).

30. W. Lippman, "Mr. Myron Taylor's Mission," *New York Herald Tribune* 14 (December 28, 1939).

31. E. Roosevelt, p. 209. Initially, the White House hoped for the best, announcing on December 27, 1939, that, out of 400 telegrams, only four were critical of Taylor's appointment. *See* "Drs. Buttrick and Adler Call on President: Two Peace Leaders See 'All in Agreement,'" *New York Times* 1 (December 28, 1939).

32. *See* "Baptists Protest Link to Vatican," *New York Times* 6 (December 29, 1939). For an excellent overview of the U.S. domestic political firestorm, *see* M. Carter, "Diplomacy's Detractors: American Protestant Reaction to FDR's 'Personal Representative' at the Vatican," *FDR, the Vatican, and the Roman Catholic Church in America, 1933-1945* (Palgrave Macmillan 2003) (eds. D. Woolner & R. Kurial).

33. *See* C. Goen, "Baptists and Church-State Issues in the Twentieth Century," *Civil Religion, Church and State*, pp. 118-19 (K.G. Saur 1992) (ed. M. Marty). Lutheran Church leaders also attended the White House meeting.

34. *See* F.D.R.: *His Personal Letters* (Duell, Sloan and Pearce 1947) (ed. E. Roosevelt), pp. 988-89.

The president was particularly sensitive about Taylor's diplomatic status—i.e., sending his "ambassador extraordinary" to the Vatican without the advice and consent of the Senate. On December 27, 1939, his spokesman told the White House press corps: "the President has the right to send a personal representative to any place, at any time, or on any occasion. There is no reason why [the

Taylor appointment] should lead to any assumption that it is a diplomatic move." And in a March 14, 1940, letter to Dr. Buttrick, FDR wrote that "Mr. Taylor is in Rome as my personal representative. This appointment does not constitute the inauguration of formal diplomatic relations with the Vatican. The President may determine the rank for social purposes of any special representative he may send; in this case the rank corresponding to ambassador was obviously appropriate." Graham, *supra* note 5, pp. 327-28.

35. On February 4, 1940, Harold Ickes observed in his diary that a key FDR ally was "considerably exercised over the appointment by the President of Myron Taylor...." Ickes, always looking at the political equation, "[o]f course ... agree[d] with this feeling, especially in view of the fact that, so far as I can see, the President got nothing in return for the appointment [*i.e.*, FDR had not been able to influence Cardinal Mundelein's successor—*see supra* note 20].... I have a feeling that one good rabble rouser could stir up considerable feeling in the Protestant sections of the country against the President for this appointment." Ickes, *supra* note 22, pp. 110-11. For a later critique of the Taylor appointment, see "Vatican Envoy Opposed," *New York Times* 12 (May 26, 1940); *see also* Carter, *supra* note 32, pp. 185-88 (detailing the pre–Pearl Harbor efforts of the *Christian Century* magazine); Graham, *supra* note 5, p. 334 (January 26, 1940, statement of the Executive Committee of the Federal Council of the Church of Christ in America: opposing "a permanent diplomatic relationship").

CHAPTER X

The First Taylor Mission

Before Myron Taylor could take on his mission to the Holy See, he had to first recover his health and strength. And so he and Anabel repaired to their winter villa in Palm Beach, Florida. While in Florida, the details of Taylor's first trip were taking shape in Washington.

Perhaps because of the touchy, domestic issues that arose in the wake of President Roosevelt's announcement, the White House and the State Department exchanged numerous drafts of the President's official appointment letter to Taylor. Ultimately, with all the bureaucratic nitpicking, FDR's signed letter was never dated (it was, however, sent before Taylor departed for Rome).[1]

By February, Taylor (and Anabel) were ready to travel to Rome. In meetings with FDR, Taylor was told that his principal mandate was to work with the Vatican in an attempt to persuade Mussolini not to join the war on Hitler's side. FDR's instructions were not purely altruistic, however. He also gave Taylor a written directive to ask the Vatican to muzzle Father Coughlin's rabid anti-Semitic and isolationistic screed, as well as to tell Vatican officials that "there is a great deal of anti-Jewish feeling in the dioceses of Brooklyn, Baltimore and Detroit and that this feeling is said to be encouraged by the church. The point to make is that of anti-Catholic feeling and that makes a general mess."[2]

On February 16, 1940, Mr. and Mrs. Taylor set forth by the Italian liner *Rex* from New York to Naples. Accompanying them was Undersecretary of State Sumner Welles. Over the opposition of Welles' fierce rival, Secretary of State Cordell Hull,[3] FDR had dispatched his "old boy-hood friend" Welles to visit with all of the warring European principals to get the facts firsthand and to see if some type of detente was possible.[4] FDR was thus trying anything and everything to forestall a larger worldwide conflagration (engulfing the United States).

On February 27, 1940, the president's "Ambassador Extraordinary" was received by Pope Pius XII in the Hall of the Little Throne.[5] In lieu of presenting diplomatic credentials, Taylor handed the Pope a letter handwritten by the president. FDR had undoubtedly calculated that such a personal touch would have a desired effect on its recipient. And it did. As existing photographs have memorialized, the Pope was visibly moved by FDR's handwritten letter (and Taylor reported back to FDR that it had had that effect).[6] The president's letter, dated February 14, 1940, reads in its entirety:

Your Holiness—

In my letter of December 23, 1939, I had the honour to suggest that it would give me great satisfaction to send to You my own representative in order that our parallel endeavors for peace and the alleviation of suffering might be assisted. Your Holiness was good enough to reply that the choice of Mr. Myron C. Taylor as my representative was acceptable and that You would receive him.

I am entrusting this special mission to Mr. Taylor who is a very old friend of mine, and in whom I repose the utmost confidence. His humanitarian efforts on behalf of those whom political disruption has rendered homeless are well known to Your Holiness. I shall be happy to feel that he may be the channel of communications for any views You and I may wish to exchange in the interest of concord among the peoples of the world.

I am asking Mr. Taylor to convey my cordial greetings to You, my old and good friend, and my sincere hope
that the common ideas of religion and humanity itself
can have united expression for the re-establishment of
a more permanent peace on the foundations of freedom
and an assurance of life and integrity of all nations under
God.

Cordially your friend,
Franklin D. Roosevelt

After the formal ceremony, the Pope and Taylor then had
a private audience for three-quarters of an hour. The discussion
focused on the prospects of peace, the war fervor among the German people and army (apart from Hitler), and the prospects of
Italy's joining the war (the Pope reported the Count Ciano—Il
Duce's son-in-law and Italy's Foreign Minister—was opposed to
the war; the Pope also reported that he had had no direct contacts
with Mussolini). After the session, Taylor, who was "impressed
by the Pope's diplomatic subtlety and shrewd prudence," excitedly
cabled FDR that Pius XII had offered "very close collaboration
with the President, through me, and daily access to the Pope, day
or night, whenever desired."[7]

At the same time of his first meeting, Taylor was establishing his base of operations in Rome. He took a large suite at the
Hotel Excelsior. An additional suite was booked for his aide, Harold Tittmann—an experienced American diplomat transferred
from Switzerland by the State Department. Taylor, Anabel, and
Mr. and Mrs. Tittmann began a whirlwind set of calls upon the
foreign ambassadors accredited to the Vatican. The Vatican diplomatic corps responded affirmatively to Taylor, finding him "large
in stature and generous of heart."[8]

The Pope was as good as his word, granting Taylor an unprecedented six more private audiences between February 27 and
May 23. These meetings—one of which, on March 18, included

President Roosevelt's handwritten letter to Pope Pius XII, acknowledging
the Pope's acceptance of Taylor as the president's representative

special mission to Mr. Taylor who is a
a very old friend of mine, and in
whom I repose the utmost confidence.
His humanitarian efforts in behalf
of those whom political disruption
has rendered homeless are well
known to Your Holiness. I shall
be happy to feel that he may
be the channel of communication
for any views You and I may
wish to exchange in the interest
of concord among the peoples
of the world.
                    I am asking Mr. Taylor

President Roosevelt's handwritten letter *(continued)*

to convey my cordial greetings
to You, my old and good
friend, and my sincere hope
that the common ideals of
religion and of humanity itself
can have united expression for the
reestablishment of a more permanent
peace on the foundations of freedom
and an assurances of life and
integrity of all nations under God.

Cordially your friend

Franklin D Roosevelt

President Roosevelt's handwritten letter *(continued)*

Welles—were mostly directed at how to persuade Mussolini to choose peace.[9] The Vatican believed that the president held the whip hand on influencing Mussolini, while FDR was of the view that the Pope's moral authority (and political influence in Italy) might be decisive.[10]

In the midst of these diplomatic efforts,[11] the Germans were not inactive. Worried about negative propaganda, the Taylor and Welles missions, Mussolini's leanings, and any potential geopolitical tiltings as to which of the belligerents was on God's side, the Nazis dispatched Joachim von Ribbentrop (the German foreign minister) to Rome. On March 11, 1940, von Ribbentrop met with the Pope at 11 a.m. After discussing the current status of Catholicism in Germany (and the political orientation of the clergy), the German foreign minister quickly came to the point. As noted by Monsignor Domenico Tardini (the Vatican's Secretary for Extraordinary Affairs), von Ribbentrop was adamant in "telling the Pope that Germany is very strong, that half the world is open to them, that they can get all the petrol they need from Romania[,] and that they will win this war without any doubt [sometime during] 1940. He gave this assurance without any trace of uncertainty. He repeated this more than once, raising his voice and gesticulating." By 12:10 p.m., the interview was over. Von Ribbentrop, who had entered with a "troubled and nervous face," departed the Pope "with a satisfied air."[12]

Taylor, meanwhile, kept up his efforts to help the president and Pius XII positively influence Il Duce for peace (at the same time Germany was pressuring Mussolini).[13] But there were other matters on Taylor's agenda as well. On March 8, for example, Taylor had a lengthy meeting with Cardinal Luigi Maglione, the Vatican Secretary of State.

At the March 8 meeting, Taylor started off by saying that they should postpone any specific discussion regarding peace efforts until Welles had returned from Berlin, Paris, and London. He then turned to the subject that was uppermost in his

Taylor with Monsignor Joseph Hurley in the corridor of the pontifical palace,
en route to visit with Cardinal Maglione, February 26, 1940

mind: the president's domestic political agenda. In explicit detail,
Taylor recounted FDR's written concerns that "anti-Jewish feeling" was being fomented by the Church in Brooklyn, Baltimore,
and Detroit, and that in the president's view might "re-awaken"
anti-Catholic prejudice in the United States.[14] Maglione had two
responses to FDR's "concerns": the first was to cite the "great work
of the late Pius XI in favor of the Jews," when his was "the only
important voice raised in Europe in their favour"; his second was
to invite Taylor to draft up a "note," which would then be referred
to the apostolic delegate in Washington (the Vatican, it seemed,
did not want to be drawn directly into this matter).

Undeterred, Taylor then moved on to Father Coughlin's "violent broadcasts and the misgivings caused by the excitable 'radio
priest.'" Because this subject had been teed up by FDR with then
Cardinal Pacelli (and the Church generally) four years earlier, as
well as that the Vatican had been asked to weigh in on Coughlin's

Taylor presenting his credentials, as well as President Roosevelt's
handwritten letter, to Pope Pius XII on February 27, 1940

activities since then on more than one occasion,[15] Maglione could
not swat this specific issue aside so blithely. Instead, he asked Taylor to draft up another "note," and promised that he would "study
the question."[16]

Taylor, not content with only domestic politics, next pressed
on to the internal politics of the Church itself. Still attempting
to find a prestigious position for Cardinal Mundelein's protégé,
Bernard Sheil, FDR had asked Taylor to see if he could pull levers
for Sheil's appointment as the new Bishop in Washington.[17] Using
an old rhetorical device (paralipsis), Taylor told Maglione that
"[a]lthough the President does not wish to make any recommendation," FDR wanted the Vatican to know that Sheil "would be
persona grata in Washington circles."[18] Maglione brushed aside the
attempted intervention by the non-Catholic American president,
saying that he did "not know anything about this nomination."[19]

Pope Pius XII reads FDR's letter delivered by Taylor on February 27, 1940

Making no headway on FDR's agenda, Taylor then turned to his own—based on years of having done business in a certain way. He invited Maglione to dine with him after Easter; Taylor also told the Secretary of State that he also wanted to sponsor events for "all the Ambassadors to the Holy See" and "all the Ministers to the Holy See." As to the former, Maglione assented, but with some caveats, the principal one being "that it would take place in a private room." As to the latter (and perhaps to temper Taylor's well-known, vast financial resources), Maglione felt compelled to note "the austerity imposed by the state of war."[20]

In the meantime, the Taylor approach to winning over Mussolini—"parallel action" by both the Pope and FDR—led to a frenzy of letter writing by both men, but with little effect. To the Pope's handwritten letter of April 24, Il Duce's April 30 response was outwardly respectful, but clear as to its author's leanings.

Mussolini blasted the "absurd 'Franco-British' demand that German troops, already on the march, should return to their starting points" before a peace conference proposed by him could be arranged. Mussolini concluded:

> I understand, Most Holy Father, Your wish that Italy be preserved from war. This has been possible till the present, but I cannot guarantee that it will be so to the end.
> We must take into consideration the will and intention of third parties.
> …
> I can assure You of one thing, Most Holy Father, and that is if Italy should go to war tomorrow, it would be indicated in the clearest manner to all, that honor, interest and posterity have demanded it.[21]

Roosevelt had been cool to Taylor's importunings to write more letters to Il Duce, thinking that two was enough. But with not only the Pope and Taylor urging him on, the British, French, and others doing so as well, FDR sent another message to Mussolini, which was delivered to him personally by Ambassador Phillips on May 1. That message tried to butter up Mussolini as having kept 200 million people at peace, but then warned that an expansion of the war could have serious repercussions, most of which would be difficult to foresee (but would likely include a rethinking by the three Americas—the United States as well as Latin and South America—of "their" position).[22] According to Ambassador Phillips, Mussolini carefully read FDR's message and stated that "he understood each of its points." Mussolini's formal reply to the president was that he did not understand why the three Americas would have to reconsider anything because of differences among European countries; as to a broadening of the war, peace could not be achieved until the issue of Italian liberty had been settled.[23]

On May 2, Taylor and Maglione met again. Taylor reported on FDR's efforts and Mussolini's initial reaction. According to Maglione, Taylor opined that Mussolini seemed to have left "the door open." The two men then discussed how to push the door farther open; Maglione suggested relaxing the blockade of Italy, as well as on having the Allies decide "[w]hat sacrifices could they accept to satisfy Italy." Taylor agreed with Maglione's suggestions and promised to pass those on to Lord Halifax (British Foreign Secretary) with his imprimatur.[24]

At the same time these men searched for a glimmer of hope, the Vatican was receiving authoritative news that the German Army was about to launch an attack on the Western Front, striking also at Holland and Belgium and possibly Switzerland.[25] Yet, because the Pope and his aides still believed that Roosevelt could somehow keep Italy out of this widening morass, they pressed Taylor to have FDR keep on with his letter-writing campaign. And the president complied, with additional letters dated May 14, May 27, and May 31. Mussolini by this point had made it clear he did not want to receive Ambassador Phillips any longer (not a good sign!); the letters were accordingly delivered to Count Ciano, the Italian Foreign Minister.[26]

Taylor was increasingly discouraged as these developments played out; so much so that he sent a telegram to the president on May 17, asking that he be ordered to return to Washington for consultation.[27] On May 19, Cordell Hull responded on behalf of FDR in a confidential message:

> Would approve the suggestions contained in your telegram if in June matters were more stabilized but I believe that under existing conditions it is unwise to plan more than twenty-four hours ahead on anything.[28]

Nine days before Hull's message, on May 10, Germany had launched its blitzkrieg against France, Belgium, Holland, and Luxembourg. Years later, Taylor spoke about the conflicting intelligence that was parlayed about in Vatican diplomatic circles just before the German offensive. He related, for example, discussions he had had with the French Ambassador to Italy. In March of 1940, Taylor had said to the Ambassador: "There is a lot of talk going around amongst some people on the strength of the Maginot line and the ability of the French army to withstand an attack. Why don't you go up to Paris and explore the situation, and come back and tell us about it?" According to Taylor, the Ambassador did just that, making a complete review of the situation, and reporting back to Taylor in April: "There is not the slightest doubt of the French army stopping the German advance. The Maginot Line will hold." At the same time the French Ambassador was speaking with much optimism, Taylor was also meeting with the Hungarian Prime Minister at the home of the Hungarian Ambassador to the Holy See.

According to Taylor, the Prime Minister was a "great geologist," who told him

> that the French Maginot Line would be breached—told me the very point where it would be invaded. He said the foundation at that point was not secure because it was undermined with quicksand. And that is the very place through which the Germans invaded Belgium and Luxembourg. Naturally I wired that to the President.[29]

Within weeks Germans stood on the edge of controlling all of the invaded nations, and an emboldened Mussolini decided that the time had come to throw his lot with Hitler. On June 10 (just a week before Marshal Pétain of France petitioned Germany for peace), Il Duce announced that Italy was entering the war as an Axis power.[30]

This caused the Vatican (in the words of Harold Tittmann) to be "gripped by anxiety almost amounting to despair." The Holy See thought that Mussolini's Blackshirts would invade the Vatican; they also worried that the Allies would now undertake to bomb the city of Rome. And while they took steps to get assurances on both fronts, those efforts left the Vatican leaders less than sanguine.[31]

With all of Europe on the precipice, Taylor became sick on June 15, thanks to an ill-prepared lobster at a dinner party.[32] On June 24, Anabel Taylor advised the President that her husband's illness was quite serious and that he would be operated on the next day by a New York–based doctor Mrs. Taylor had flown to Rome. Happily, the operation was a success, and as Taylor lay recuperating in his suite at the Hotel Excelsior he received a letter from FDR expressing "delight[] that you have come through this operation so well."[33]

As he recovered, Taylor made plans for his return to America, which was set for August 23. At his last meeting with the Pope on August 20, Taylor "found the Pope in a depressed state of mind." The belligerent nations were in no mood for compromise, and the Pope was "especially concerned over the future of Great Britain, which seemed very black indeed." Taylor tried to cheer the pope up "with visions of the vast potential of American military and economic aid"; to those visions and potential aid the pope replied that they might be "too little and too late."[34]

In his last meeting with Tittmann, Taylor told him that, because of his uncertain health, he could not set a firm date for his next visit to Rome. Tittmann was thus instructed by the State Department to return to Geneva, and the Taylor mission at the Vatican became inactive.[35]

Taylor returned to the United States with a letter from the pope to the president, dated August 22, 1940. The letter recounted the joint efforts at peace that had been undertaken, the fact that the Vatican was "redoubling" its efforts in that regard, and that the Vatican felt a "distinct sense of comfort in the thought that We shall not be without the powerful support of the President of the United States." The Pope also expressed thanks for FDR's sending Taylor to the Holy See:

> In light of experience, We now have further
> and ampler proof of the wisdom which inspired your

Excellency to dispatch your Representative to Us, as We also have cause to rejoice at the felicity of choice which led you to entrust this important post to the Honorable Myron C. Taylor.[36]

Notes

1. By a handwritten notation on the copy published in *Foreign Relations of the United States* (1939), Vol. II, pp. 873-74, it would appear that the letter was sent to Taylor on February 4, 1940. Determined to leave the nature and duration of Taylor's assignment vague, FDR closed his letter with the following:

> I may from time to time request you to serve as the channel of communication for any views I may wish to exchange with the Pope. You will, of course, communicate to this Government any matters which may come to your attention in the performance of your mission which you may feel will serve the best interest of the United States.

2. See *FDR: His Personal Letters* (Duell, Sloan and Pearce 1947) (ed. E. Roosevelt), p. 999.

3. Besides Hull's professional jealousy, William Bullitt (U.S. Ambassador to France) was also seeing red. The British also vehemently opposed the Welles mission, but at least their opposition was mainly grounded on geopolitical concerns. See B. Welles, *Sumner Welles: FDR's Global Strategist* (St. Martin's Press 1998), pp. 244-46.

4. In fact, Welles, at the age of ten, had been an attendant at FDR's wedding. FDR's "white lie" notwithstanding, Welles and the President did share a similar patrician background (Groton and Harvard) and outlook on world affairs. A couple of FDR's introductory letters on behalf of Welles can be found at *FDR: His Personal Letters*, p. 1001. Welles met with cordial receptions throughout Europe (with the exception of von Ribbentrop). In the end, however, he found no common points among the belligerents. See Welles, *supra* note 3, pp. 242-57.

5. Technically, because of Taylor's unique status he was not entitled to be received in the Hall of the Throne, where accredited representatives are welcomed. Coincidentally, their first meeting was on the Pope's birthday.

6. As the British Ambassador to the Holy See reported: "His Holiness has on two occasions blissfully informed me that the President signs letters to him 'your good old friend.' There is no doubt that the Pope is a victim of the President's notorious charm and political adroitness." A. Rhodes, *The Vatican in the Age of the Dictators (1922-1945)* (Holt, Rinehart & Winston 1973), p. 242.

7. J. Conway, "Pope Pius XII and the Myron Taylor Mission," *FDR, the Vatican, and the Roman Catholic Church in America, 1933-1945* (Palgrave Macmillan 2003) (eds. D. Woolner & R. Kurial), p. 145. In his more formal telegram to FDR, Taylor wrote: "Presentation ceremonials concluded with highest spiritual dignity and human understanding. His Holiness conveys through me his blessing and warmest regards to you personally. His eminence Cardinal Secretary of State joins in greetings and best wishes." (Taylor Papers, Cornell University). On March 21, the Pope formally met with Mr. and Mrs. Taylor in an elaborate ceremony. On this occasion, the Pope presented Mrs. Taylor with a large silver medal. *See* T. Morgan, *The Listening Post* (G.P. Putnam 1944), pp. 193-94.

8. O. Chadwick, *Britain and the Vatican During the Second World War* (Cambridge University Press 1986), p. 102; D. Alvarez, "The United States, the Vatican, and World War II," *Research Studies* 239, 242 (1972). In the words of British historian Chadwick: "Myron Taylor was a rhadamanthine kind of man; not pompous, but he seemed to survey humanity as from a pedestal. One Italian observer, who went to see him when he was ill in bed, had the impression that despite his prone position he was still sitting on a throne; and yet that beneath the august presence was a kindly person who was perfectly willing to listen." Chadwick, p. 101.

There has been a good deal of debate (then and later by historians) as to whether Taylor's lack of technical diplomatic status negatively affected his mission to the Vatican. *See, e.g.,* R. Graham, *Vatican Diplomacy* (Princeton University Press 1959), pp. 328-29. Professor Chadwick, I think correctly, terms it an advantage, because Taylor "could do what he liked ... [without] the wearisome [ambassadorial] protocol, ... [and] was exempt from the attentions of visiting Americans." Chadwick, *supra* note 8, p. 102.

Harold Tittmann, who wrote to his mother that he had "not the least idea what I am expected to do," did not have any direct dealings with the Pope or his advisors during Taylor's first mission to the Holy See. In his memoirs, however, he told of an interesting pre-Easter ceremony he attended with Taylor at Santa Maria Maggiore:

> The only light, coming from the small number of wax tapers distributed around the high altar, filtered dimly on the padded ceiling above, which had been covered centuries ago with gold from the New World. The lovely melodious "Miserere," the gradual extinction of the candles one by one and afterwards, the praying in complete darkness and silence when not even a bell was heard, and finally the resounding noise echoing down the ancient aisles produced by the beating on benches with iron bars to recall the disturbance of the

forces of nature at the approach of Christ's death, were all intensely dramatic. As we were leaving the basilica, Ambassador Taylor turned to me and grimly reflected that the noise caused by the beating on the wood could also represent the ferment then pervading Europe, the ominous developments of 1939 and 1940.

H. Tittmann, *Inside the Vatican of Pius XII* (Doubleday 2004), pp. 8-9.

9. Welles had previously met with Il Duce and Count Ciano on February 26. Handing Mussolini another handwritten letter by FDR emphasizing peace and friendship ("I shall hope to meet you one day, soon!"), Welles met an "icy" reception. Mussolini blustered that a "negotiated" peace was still possible, but not if the war spread. See Welles, *supra* note 3, p. 247; G. Ciano, *Diary: 1937-1943* (Enigma 2002), pp. 323-24. Welles had subsequent meetings with Mussolini and Ciano between March 16 and 19; nothing beyond diplomatic posturing, however, came of those talks. See Welles, *supra* note 3, p. 256; Ciano, pp. 331-33.

At the March 18 meeting with the Pope (and Taylor, who had insisted on being present "for the prestige of his own mission"), Welles gave a précis of his discussions with the various leaders of the belligerent nations (with an understanding that a more detailed briefing would come in the subsequent meeting with the Secretary of State). The Pope emphasized that a peace conference would not yield success at that point, and gave to Taylor a letter, dated March 16, which he asked to have Welles hand deliver to FDR. The letter, written in nineteenth-century diplomatic verbiage, thanked the president for sending the "Representative of Your Excellency," stated that the formal ceremony greeting Taylor "was enhanced by the autograph letter he bore from you and placed in Our hands," and expressed hope that the efforts of the Vatican and the U.S. government could bring about peace. (The Pope's letter is set forth in full in *The Holy See and the War in Europe*, pp. 369-71.) The Vatican later sought to have the Pope's letter simultaneously made public in both Washington and Rome. Ultimately, for reasons that remain unclear, the State Department nixed this idea. See April 6, 1940, memorandum from C. Hull to F. Roosevelt; April 1, 1940, memorandum from F. Roosevelt to C. Hull and S. Welles; March 30, 1940, memorandum from S. Welles to F. Roosevelt. (All of these memoranda are at the FDR Library in Box 51.)

At the March 18 meeting with Secretary of State Maglione (and Taylor), Welles reported on the results of his fact-finding mission. While the Allies (France and Britain) wanted a sound peace (by which they meant they wanted a modus vivendi whereby war would not break out every 20 years), the Germans were "certain of an overwhelming victory within a year." Welles asked Maglione about the chances for mediating a peace. The Vatican's Secretary of State replied that "[a]ny effort in this direction would, in the present circumstances, be doomed to failure and would compromise any future move which could be reserved at a more opportune moment." Welles agreed with Maglione, and told him he had already reported the same to FDR in a phone call (which the Italian government had tapped). As for the somewhat brighter possibility of keeping Italy out of the war, Welles told Maglione "very courteously, but with obvious sincerity," that the U.S. government had "great confidence in the influence of the most high and august moral power which the Pope can have in the present circumstances." This came in response to Maglione "remind[ing] Welles that the United States can do a lot and that all here have great confidence in President Roosevelt's good offices." Maglione's memorandum of this meeting is set forth in full in *The Holy See and the War in Europe: March 1939–August 1940* (Clonmore and Reynolds 1968) (eds. P. Blet, A. Martini, & B. Schneider), pp. 375-76. With respect to the taping of Welles' telephone, *see* Ciano, *supra* note 9, pp. 331-32.

10. Maglione, for example, told Taylor that FDR was the most powerful statesman in the West. The British apparently agreed with the Vatican. On April 18, 1940, the British Foreign Secretary, Lord Halifax, sent a detailed message to Taylor (via the British Minister to the Holy See, D'Arcy Osborne) in which he implored Taylor "for anything he could advise the President to do with a view to restraining Mussolini...." Tittmann, *supra* note 8, p. 11.

11. Joseph P. Kennedy, perhaps in an attempt to rehabilitate his diplomatic reputation, also made a trip to Italy during this period. He met with Taylor on March 5, but reported to his wife that he "didn't try to see the Pope, because my time was limited, I had no clothes, and I didn't really think it was politic because Taylor had just arrived." *Hostage to Fortune* (Viking 2001) (ed. A. Smith), p. 407. Kennedy later inserted himself into Welles' mission—to no constructive end. *See* Welles, *supra* note 3, pp. 250-54.

12. Monsignor Domenico Tardini's detailed memorandum, which the Pope dictated to him upon von Ribbentrop's departure, is set forth in full in *The Holy See and the War in Europe*, pp. 355-58. Several years later Taylor recounted a report on the von Ribbentrop visit he had received from a senior Vatican official (Monsignor Giovanni Battista Montini) on the night of March 11:

> We thought we should tell you of this interview of the Pope and Ribbentrop. Ribbentrop came in a very aggressive mood. He did not, however, give the Nazi salute; that was omitted. But instead of sitting down quietly and talking with the Pope and stating his case as you would expect a person to do, he stormed about the room. "This war will be over by September," he said. "It would not last that long except for the British meddling in it, which they have no right to do.

We can over-run France in a week. We can take Britain. Nothing can stop us. We are going to start the war on a certain day, (the approximate day was given.) We would have started it two weeks earlier but found our medical units were not quite ready or equipped. So we have postponed it two weeks. But by the first of September the war will be over and Europe will be in our hands." That was pretty bold.

The Pope then asked if Hitler's government was not treating the people of Poland very cruelly, treating the Jews especially cruelly. Ribbentrop said, "No. So far as the Jews are concerned, they should be exterminated. So far as the people of Poland are concerned, they have been our enemy, and we are treating them very well. We are feeding them and taking care of them." The Pope said, "Will you allow me to send two of my representatives into Poland to examine into the situation?" Ribbentrop answered, "I will talk with Hitler about that—but my answer would be no."

It was on that kind of note that this hour and a half of interview took place. The Pope could make no impression upon him at all. Ribbentrop left, and out in the corridor he nearly fainted, they had to give him coffee to brace him up.

Transcript of Meeting of Protestant Clergymen with Myron C. Taylor and Union Club (New York City, October 25, 1947) pp. 18-19 (Taylor Papers, Cornell University).

The German foreign minister also took time during his trip to Rome to pressure Il Duce to "accelerate" Italy's intervention in the war. According to Count Ciano, this pressure was sometimes counterproductive. On March 13, for example, he quotes Mussolini as "explod[ing]": "These Germans are unbearable; they don't give one time to breathe nor to think things over." Ciano, *supra* note 9, p. 330.

13. On April 18, for example, Taylor met with Secretary of State Cardinal Luigi Maglione, and asked him if the Pope would join FDR in a "parallel action" for peace—basically tag-teaming Mussolini. On April 19, Taylor sent a telegram to FDR with the following advice:

> I am definitely convinced that a communication from you to Mussolini would be timely and helpful and can be so worded as to contain no possibility of harmful results either to our own country, considering our neutral position, or to yourself. In any event, it seems to me that this is the only remaining effort you can make at this moment to try to circumscribe the war.

The next day, Maglione told Taylor that the Pope agreed to pursue the "parallel action" approach suggested by Taylor, but would do it in a manner to preserve the Vatican's publicly declared neutral status. *See* Tittmann, *supra* note 8, pp. 12-13. According to Anthony Rhodes, Taylor also suggested to Pius XII at some point that Mussolini might be bought off by a large bribe and/or the "internationalization" of Gibraltar. Rhodes, *supra* note 6, p. 243. Rhodes' book, which is without footnotes, does not document these suggestions. In neither the Vatican records nor the Taylor papers (both of which we have examined) could we find support for either "suggestion." In an April 24, 1940, discussion with Monsignor Joseph P. Hurley, Taylor did report that the French Ambassador told him that France was prepared to negotiate with Italy about numerous matters, including Gibraltar, and that the Allies were "prepared to make important concessions" to keep Italy out of the war. *See The Holy See and the War in Europe: March 1939– August 1940*, p. 396. In that same meeting, Taylor "mentioned the possibility" of the United States entering into the global conflict "if Japan ... thought fit to disturb the Pacific status quo." *Id.* pp. 396-97.

14. According to one historian, "[t]he fact that Roosevelt was trying to persuade a surefooted American Catholic Church that the persecution of a historically despised minority religion would rekindle a bout of Know-Nothingism, underscores the lengths that FDR was willing to go to quash Coughlinism." C. Gallagher, "A Peculiar Brand of Patriotism: The Holy See, FDR, and the Cast of Reverend Charles E. Coughlin." *FDR, the Vatican, and the Roman Catholic Church in America, 1933-1945* (Palgrave Macmillan 2003) (eds. D. Woolner & R. Kuriel), p. 273.

15. *See id.* pp. 269-72; G. Fogarty, "Roosevelt and the American Catholic Hierarchy," *FDR the Vatican and the Roman Catholic Church in America, 1933-1945* (Palgrave Macmillan 2003) (eds. D. Woolner and R. Kuriel), pp. 15-26.

16. The fact that the Church never addressed Coughlin's anti-Semitism has been ascribed by one historian as due (in the main) to the anti-Semitism of Monsignor Joseph P. Hurley—the individual put in charge of reviewing the Coughlin matter. *See* Gallagher, *supra* note 14, pp. 273-75.

17. In a separate memorandum to Taylor, dated February 11, 1940, FDR had expressed his disappointment that Sheil had not been appointed to replace Mundelein, and that Archbishop Samuel Stritch (who had been given the job) was "somewhat of a Fascist." Because Washington, DC, had just been made an archdiocese, FDR told Taylor that it would be "important" to have the first Bishop "be a reputable and liberal-minded Bishop. Bishop Bernard J. Sheil, who was understudy to Cardinal Mundelein would be an agreeable choice." Fogarty, *supra* note 15, p. 25. For at least one reason why FDR viewed Sheil as "an agreeable choice," *see* Chapter IX, pp. 131-32, note 22. FDR moved separately against

Stritch, utilizing his Postmaster General and Cardinal Spellman to bring him into line. Ultimately, Stritch rebuked any Coughlin-like sympathies and declared his support for the president's policies; Roosevelt thereafter proclaimed his delight to Spellman that the Chicago Diocese would be "pushing forward with the splendid social policies of the late Cardinal." G. Fogarty, *The Vatican and the American Hierarchy From 1870 to 1965* (Anton Hiersemann 1982), p. 266.

18. FDR had undoubtedly chosen that phrase in light of the importance the Vatican placed on it when it came to Taylor's appointment. *See* Chapter IX, pp. 130-31, note 21.

19. One historian has written about FDR's astonishing attempt to influence the Church as follows:

> Roosevelt may have compromised in regard to establishing diplomatic relations, but the Holy See was not going to allow the compromiser to intrude into the internal affairs of the Church. His urging the appointment of Sheil may have been one reason why Washington was left under the jurisdiction of Archbishop Michael J. Curley of Baltimore until his death in 1947—and why Sheil spent the rest of his days as an auxiliary of Chicago.

Fogarty, *supra* note 15, p. 25.

With respect to this specific meeting and Taylor pressing such matters generally, another historian has observed that while the Pope had believed FDR's decision to send Taylor to be a "noble and generous act," he soon learned that "Roosevelt's envoy had both more and less than such noble matters in mind." R. Tugwell, *The Democratic Roosevelt* (Doubleday 1957), p. 505.

As late as December 1940, the Roosevelt administration was continuing to lobby the Church in America for help with Coughlin, as well as for the appointment of Sheil as Bishop of Washington. *See* J. Blum, *The Secret Diary of Harold L. Ickes: The Lowering Clouds (1939-41)* (Simon & Schuster 1959), p. 382.

20. The memorandum of the March 8 meeting, which was prepared by Monsignor Joseph P. Hurley, is set forth in full in *The Holy See and the War in Europe: March 1939–August 1940*, pp. 352-54. A Taylor–Maglione dinner was set for March 27, 1940. Ultimately (and not consistent with the Secretary of State's gentle nudgings), it turned into a gala lunch in honor of Maglione at the Hotel Excelsior with a large cast of ambassadors and Church officials.

21. The full texts of the Pope's and Mussolini's letters are set forth in full in *The Holy See and the War in Europe: March 1939–August 1940*, pp. 395, 402-03.

22. Taylor had cast his net broadly in Rome, also seeking the views of Church officials not affiliated with the Vatican. Vincent McCormick, the Rector of the Gregorian University (and an American), had previously told Taylor that

the most "efficacious means" to keep Italy out of the war was for the "President [to] make it clear to the world that America will not look with indifference on a victory of Germany and Russia. If all the Americas joined in such a declaration, so much the better." Taylor forwarded McCormick's message to FDR, who apparently used it in the message delivered to Mussolini by Ambassador Phillips. Fogarty, *supra* note 17, p. 265. That Roosevelt felt so cavalier about speaking for "all the Americas" is interesting in and of itself.

23. Ambassador Tittmann has noted that Mussolini's last statement "might [have] mean[t] anything." Tittmann, *supra* note 10, p. 14. Presumably, it referenced Mussolini's view that Italy was imprisoned in the Mediterranean, and needed "windows on the Atlantic on the one hand and the Red Sea and the Indian Ocean on the other." See P. Blet, *Pius XII and the Second World War* (Paulist Press 1999), pp. 40-42.

24. Maglione's notes of Taylor's May 2 meeting are set forth in full in *The Holy See and the War in Europe: March 1939–August 1940*, pp. 404-05. The language *"the door open"* was emphasized by Maglione in his own notes. Taylor also told Maglione that he "could not talk about a *special point* included in President Roosevelt's message and in the conversation between Phillips and Mussolini." Maglione correctly intuited that FDR had made clear that "America will not remain indifferent in case of a defeat of the Allies."

25. Maglione's coded message to the Brussels' Nuncio, and the reply thereto, are set forth in full in *The Holy See and the War in Europe: March 1939– August 1940*, p. 406. See Blet, *supra* note 23, pp. 41-42.

26. Tittmann, *supra* note 8, pp. 14-15; Morgan, *supra* note 7, p. 195. FDR "made it clear to the Duce that he was ready to be instrumental in putting Italy's claims to the Allies. The U.S. President assured Mussolini that the outstanding questions would be given immediate attention, with the American Government acting on any solution agreed to between the parties for the ultimate purpose of bringing hostilities to an end." Quoted from Monsignor Tardini's memorandum, dated June 4, 1940 (*The Holy See and the War in Europe: March 1939–August 1940*, pp. 450-51). To the May 27 letters, Count Ciano told Phillips: "Italy will soon enter the war on the side of Germany." To the May 31 letter, Ciano told the U.S. Ambassador: "The date of Italian entry into the war has already been fixed." Morgan, *supra* note 7, p. 195.

27. Tittmann, *supra* note 8, p. 14.

28. Hull's telegram to Taylor is in both the Taylor Papers at Cornell and at the FDR Library.

29. Transcript of Meeting of Protestant Clergymen with Myron C. Taylor at Union Club (New York City, October 20, 1947) pp. 20-22 (Taylor Papers, Cornell University). Taylor also recounted having dinner in 1939 with the Prime

Minister of France, the French Foreign Minister, and the French Minister of Air; the Air Minister told Taylor that France had "no dependable planes."

30. From the Vatican's perspective, this period is well documented in Blet's *Pius XII and the Second World War*, pp. 42-47. *See also* London Apostolic Delegate Godfrey's June 10, 1920, memorandum to Cardinal Maglione, which is set forth in full in *The Holy See and the War in Europe: March 1939–August 1940*, pp. 451-53. According to Anthony Rhodes, Taylor suggested to the Pope that he threaten to excommunicate Mussolini if he did in fact declare war. Rhodes, *supra* note 6, p. 242. We have found no evidence to support Mr. Rhodes on this claim. There is, however, direct evidence that the U.S. Ambassador to France, William Bullitt, suggested that very thing to Paris Nuncio Valeri in mid-May 1940. In a May 15 memorandum to Cardinal Maglione, the Nuncio reported Bullitt's explicit recommendation of excommunication. The Nuncio, in response, first "reminded Mr. Bullitt of all the work done by the Holy Father to keep Italy out of the war and that it was largely due to his endeavors that Italy has kept peace until now." The Nuncio then added:

> the Holy Father should not be asked an impossible thing, something which, apart from any other consideration, so-called modern progress has ridiculed for more than a century, and which would have a more than dubious effect.

Nuncio Valeri's memorandum is set forth in full in *The Holy See and the War in Europe: March 1939–August 1940*, pp. 426-28. The Nuncio also noted that American Senator Jacques Bardoux had also just raised "on behalf of various colleagues of the Foreign Affairs Senate Commission, if the moment of excommunicating Hitler had also arrived." The Nuncio's response was that "apart from any other consideration, probably he had not even been baptized."

31. Tittmann, *supra* note 8, p. 17; Blet, *supra* note 23, p. 47. For example, while England said it would not attack the Vatican, it refused to guarantee the safety of Rome. There were rumors that the Pope would be forced to flee from Italy. C. Hull, May 22, 1940, memorandum to M.C. Taylor (Taylor Papers, Cornell University). The Vatican was also worried about its financial resources. Harold Ickes wrote in his diary on May 19, 1940, that "the gold of the Vatican has been sent to us for safekeeping. We now have buried underground at Fort Knox some nineteen billions of gold." Blum, *supra* note 19, p. 189. Ickes appears to have engaged in some hyperbole. On May 17, 1940, Taylor had sent FDR a "strictly confidential" telegram, conveying a Vatican request to allow "a sizeable amount of gold bars on deposit in a bank in a belligerent country" be transferred to a bank in New York. On May 22, the U.S. Treasury Department agreed to the request, and $7,665,000 of gold was shortly thereafter delivered out of England to the Chase

Manhattan Bank. For an overview of the United States' investment in protecting the Vatican's assets during World War II, *see* M. Phayer, *Pius XII, The Holocaust and the Cold War* (Indiana University Press 2008), pp. 103-07.

32. On that same day, the Vatican had asked Taylor to inform the U.S. government that Belgium was "in great danger of famine." Nothing of substance, however, was forthcoming in reply from the United States. Also went unmet was the Church's request that the U.S. government formally assist the efforts of the private "Commission for Polish Relief" (the USSR had sent 20,000 Poles to Siberia on April 15); FDR and the State Department told Taylor to tell the Vatican that the U.S. government could not fund or control the relief activities of private organizations. *See* M.C. Taylor April 26, 1940, letter to FDR (Taylor Papers, Cornell University); FDR May 24, 1940, memorandum to C. Hull (FDR Library, Box 51); C. Hull June 18, 1940, memorandum to FDR (FDR Library, Box 51); FDR June 18, 1940, letter to M.C. Taylor (FDR Library, Box 51).

33. FDR July 29, 1940, letter to M.C. Taylor (Taylor Papers, Cornell University). During Taylor's convalescence, the Pope dispatched Cardinal Maglione to visit him to convey the Pope's wishes for an early recovery. Morgan, *supra* note 7, p. 197. Roosevelt subsequently sent two telegrams to Taylor (August 5 and August 16) expressing further "delight" about his improved physical condition, while also cautioning Taylor that his health was FDR's "principal concern" (FDR Library, Box 51).

34. Tittmann, *supra* note 8, pp. 21-23.

35. As reported in *Time* on September 2, 1940, "Few thought ailing Envoy Taylor would ever return. But the Holy See's diplomacy, canniest in the world, had already taken a step to neutralize the effects of his departure. The day before the Taylor farewell the Pope appointed Monsignor Joseph Patrick Hurley, only U.S. member of his Secretariat of State, as Bishop of St. Augustine, Fla." Hurley's "unprecedented" appointment (it came only six days after the death of his predecessor) was widely perceived as a means by which Hurley could "continue his close cooperation with Mr. Taylor."

36. The Pope's letter is set forth in full in *The Holy See and the War in Europe: March 1939–August 1940*, p. 478. President Roosevelt's October 1, 1940, reply can be found in *FDR: His Personal Letters*, pp. 1068-69.

CHAPTER XI

The Second Taylor Mission

The November 1940 election saw FDR reelected to an unprecedented third term. And as 1940 turned to 1941, Taylor was at his Palm Beach home (Vita Serena), recovering from a second operation. He continued to keep abreast of developments at the Vatican,[1] but given his health, it was unclear what public role (if any) he would play going forward. There were rumors of him being replaced as FDR's emissary to the pope, as well as rumors of him being Joseph P. Kennedy's replacement at the Court of St. James.[2] But these were only rumors, as FDR told Taylor on March 4 not to "hurry the recuperation period," and that FDR had written the pope to expect "your return a little later on."[3]

Shortly thereafter, on March 11, the president signed the controversial Lend-Lease legislation. That law (premised upon FDR's campaign pledge to be the "great arsenal of democracy") allowed the president to "sell, transfer title to, exchange, lease, lend, or otherwise dispose of, to any such government [whose defense the president deemed vital to the defense of the United States] any defense article." Although seemingly open-ended, the law was understood (by Congress and the American public) to apply to providing assistance to Great Britain, then isolated and under the German attack known as the "Blitz." At the same time the nation was acting to help England, relations with Italy were quickly deteriorating: on June 14, the United States froze all Italian assets in the country; and by July 10, both countries ceased to have consular representations.[4] To bridge this latter gap, Harold

Tittmann was transferred by the State Department over to the Vatican to resume his prior duties as Taylor's assistant.[5]

With Tittmann on the ground in Rome, Taylor, much recovered, began to become more active. In particular, the State Department (prompted by Tittmann's warnings) advised Taylor to consult with the Apostolic Delegate in Washington (Archbishop Cicognani) about the "doubting Thomases" in the American Catholic hierarchy. Even the Vatican was concerned about certain church officials who had spoken out against U.S. policies and/or appeared to be in favor of a German victory. Taylor got some push back from Cicognani as to how broad based this concern was, but Cicognani did admit to certain Cardinals and Archbishops about having spoken in public against the United States entering the war.[6] (As we will shortly see, this issue would not go away, and would need to be addressed in a more comprehensive way.)

In May of 1941, Taylor decided to donate his Florentine home (Villa Schifanoia) to the pope, with the proviso that it be used for education in art and music under the direction of nuns (the gift was not made public until September 21, 1941, when Taylor was in Rome). And at the end of that same month, Taylor gave the address to the graduating class at the Cornell Law School. But such happy tasks were quickly overshadowed by Hitler's decision to invade Russia, which began on June 22, 1941.[7] That momentous act would predestine/determine geopolitical issues for the rest of the twentieth century, and would also give Taylor an important role in its outcome.

On July 6, Bishop Hurley (of St. Augustine, Florida) gave a radio address from Washington, DC, advocating that military support be given to the Soviet Union. This led to a political firestorm, with many U.S. Church officials publicly attacking and disagreeing with Hurley, which in turn caused Cicognani to write to Cardinal Maglione, the Pope's Secretary of State, bemoaning the public airing of dissent within the Church.[8] This dispute only served to highlight not only the isolationist views of many U.S. Catholics (lay and official) but also the Vatican's 1937 Encyclical Divini Redemptoris (Of the Divine Redeemer)—issued by Pope Pius XI (but authored by his Secretary of State, who would succeed him as Pope Pius XII). That Encyclical was an unabashed condemnation of the Soviet Union as dogmatically atheistic, and it forbade all Catholics from having anything to do with supporting that nation-state: "See to it, Venerable Brethren, that the Faithful do not allow themselves to be deceived! Communism is intrinsically wrong, and no one who would save Christian Civilization may collaborate with it in any undertaking whatsoever."

With that backdrop, however, the news of the German Army's swift and ever-growing conquest of Russian territory was grim and inescapable. FDR and his top advisors feared that if the Soviet Union were to be overrun and conquered, then stopping the Nazi regime when (not if) the United States ultimately became a belligerent might well prove impossible. But what to do about the 1937 Encyclical and the strong isolationist sentiments among many American Catholics (intertwined with the America First Committee)? If the United States attempted to help the Soviets militarily, the political backlash might prove too great.[9] In the words of FDR speechwriter (and later FDR biographer) Robert Sherwood, "[a]s a measure for coping with serious Catholic opposition to and for the Soviet Union, Roosevelt decided to send Myron C. Taylor, his special Ambassador to Pope Pius XII, on another mission to Rome."[10]

Before Taylor's trip (and behind the scenes), Archbishop Mooney from Detroit (who had publicly stood up to Father Coughlin) and Monsignor Ready (General Secretary to the National Catholic Welfare Conference)—in consultation with Taylor and Sumner Welles—had devised a strategy to thread the thorny needle of the 1937 Encyclical: that any aid provided by the United States would not constitute cooperation with communism, but would instead be directed at alleviating the suffering of the Russian people, people for whom the Church had always had special affection.[11] On September 1, FDR sent Taylor a detailed memorandum, directing him "to stress" several subjects when meeting with the pope and his advisors. Much of the document relates to postwar planning as the means of achieving the principles of the Atlantic Charter that FDR and Winston Churchill had enunciated after their meeting off of Newfoundland in August of 1941. Unfortunately, FDR also added: "It is worth noting that or [sic] best information is that the Russian churches are today open for worship and are being attended by a very large percentage of its population."[12] That sentence (as we will see) presaged a potent, potential roadblock for the success of Taylor's second mission to the Vatican. Nonetheless, on September 4—the same day the Germans attacked the USS *Greer*—Taylor left the United States, accompanied by his wife and carrying with him a personal letter from FDR to the Pope.

Arriving in Rome on September 8, Taylor's first meeting was with Cardinal Maglione on the morning of September 9; it lasted for two hours. At six o'clock, Taylor met with the pope; that lasted for one hour. Unlike the first Taylor Mission, in which President Roosevelt's handwritten, personal letter had so clearly pleased Pius XII, this one had the opposite effect. FDR's "personal" letter of September 3—designed to assuage the Vatican's grave concern about the freedom of religion in the Soviet Union—began with the following: "Insofar as I am informed, the churches in Russia are open. I believe there is a real possibility that Russians may as a result of the present conflict recognize freedom of religion in Russia, although, of course, without recognition of any official intervention on the part of any church in education or political matters within Russia." He went on, attempting to delineate between the Nazis and the Russians: "I believe . . . that the Russian dictatorship is less dangerous to the safety of other nations than is the German form of dictatorship. The only weapon which the Russian dictatorship uses outside its own borders is Communist propaganda...." And he concluded: "I believe that the survival of Russia is less dangerous to religion, to the church and such, and to humanity in general than would be the survival of the German form of dictatorship. Furthermore, it is my belief that the leaders of all the churches in the United States should recognize these facts clearly and should not close their eyes to these basic questions and by their present attitude on this question directly assist Germany in its present objectives."[13]

The Pope and his advisors were, to say the least, not impressed or convinced by the president's letter. Indeed, Monsignor Tardini (the Secretary for Extraordinary Affairs, the second-ranking position in the Secretariat of State) prepared at least seven memoranda containing the Pope's and his own incredulous reactions to FDR's representations. As Tittman would later write: "They were amazingly frank and sometimes humorous."[14] Tardini, for example, wrote that FDR either had no idea what he was talking about or was simply "apologizing for communism," given that religious persecution in the Soviet Union "has not diminished." He also wrote that what FDR really was seeking "from American Catholics and the authority of the Holy See—he wants to obtain a large advantage in American internal politics." He further wrote that the president's view that only Soviet propaganda had been used outside its borders was demonstrably false: "This is proved by the invasions of Poland, Estonia, Finland, Latvia, Lithuania, and Bessaradia." He also seemed quite surprised that the U.S. government had not thought through the likely consequences of a Soviet defeat of the Nazis—that is, communism's total domination of "continental Europe."[15]

After his first meeting with the Pope, Taylor met with U.S. Ambassador Phillips and his staff at the American Embassy in Rome, and shared the contents of FDR's letter with them. As Tittmann later wrote, they were "astonish[ed]"; in particular, Elbridge Durbrow, an expert on the Soviets, told Taylor there was "little hope that the Soviet government would change its attitude, regardless of what President Roosevelt had written in his letter to the Pope. He added that he could not understand how such a letter could ever have been written in the first place in view of all the contrary information that was on file at the State Department."[16]

Notwithstanding FDR's unhelpful kickoff to his mission, Taylor's various meetings with the pope and his advisors ultimately proved successful. Rather than attempt to do the impossible—that is, try to prove Roosevelt correct in his pronouncements—Taylor started off by stressing the United States' industrial capacity and its ability to produce military material: "an extraordinary power beyond everyone's imagination." As such, Hitler could not win the war, and the United States—if Germany attempted to prevent its supply of aid to Britain—would retaliate swiftly (and American public opinion would support such action).[17]

Of course, as the former CEO of the world's largest and most important industrial company, Taylor's views were entitled to great weight and brought some measure of comfort to a Vatican that was surrounded by totalitarianism and was generally pessimistic about Hitler's (to date) unbroken run of success. And just to emphasize the point, Taylor added that "if the defenders of civilization were in desperate need to save the world from Hitlerism, America would use every means to prevent its accomplishment."

Then Taylor moved on to the principles of the Atlantic Charter and FDR's hope that the pope could publicly weigh in and support the eight points concerning peace, individual freedoms, and world order set forth in that historic document. Because these principles were consistent with prior public pronouncements by the pope, Vatican officials saw no difficulty in doing so, so long as it did not seem to tie the pope directly to the specific war aims of "one camp." As Taylor reported to FDR: "The Pope readily agreed to make such a pronouncement at an opportune moment. He was of the opinion that it would be more harmful than helpful, his role of independence concerned, to make such a statement immediately without a sufficient occasion to inspire it. He agreed,

On his way to a papal audience, Taylor passes the pontifical Swiss Guard,
who have taken an oath of loyalty to the Pope

however, to do so at a reasonably early date. He exhibited no reluctance in so doing."

Having gotten through the easier parts of his agenda, Taylor then brought up the main event—how to deal with the Divini
Redemptoris, and would the Vatican help the president vis-à-vis
Lend-Lease aid to Russia. This issue was discussed over two days in
multiple sessions with both Cardinal Maglione and the pope. On
the second day, Taylor was informed that the concept of delink-
ing the Russian people from the Soviet state was one the Vatican
could support, but this message could not be seen as being issued
from or dictated by the Pope or the Vatican. Instead, guidance
would be sent to the Apostolic Delegate in Washington to have
the message delivered in America by a high-ranking member(s)
of the Church.

As part of the foregoing discussions, Taylor was asked that the president endeavor to get some statement from the Soviets on the issue of religious freedom. Taylor, citing to possibly helpful sections of the Russian Constitution, assured the Pope that FDR was doing exactly that.[18]

One more topic—not on Taylor's agenda—was discussed at length: the Pope asked Taylor to have the American government use its influence to dissuade the British from bombing Rome— something on which the British military had been making public threats. Given the "very great historical and artistic importance" of the Vatican and its buildings, if any "were to be hit, the Holy See could not remain silent."[19] Taylor understood the pope's concerns and agreed to raise the matter with Churchill on his return trip to America, as well as with the president in Washington.

On September 23, his second set of Vatican meetings completed, Taylor (and Mrs. Taylor) left Rome and headed first to Lisbon. FDR had asked Taylor to take the temperature of António de Oliveira Salazar, the "benevolent dictator" of Portugal. Obviously, Portugal (and Spain) (both neutrals) were of strategic and geographic importance, and FDR wanted to know where Salazar stood at present. Unfortunately, Taylor's report back was not encouraging. Concerned about an imminent German invasion, Salazar did not want the United States to enter the war; although he thought that Britain and America together "might destroy Hitler personally," Nazism "was the new social, political and economic evolution in Europe." Salazar further opined that the best solution would be to "Britain's agreeing to the incorporation of the Ukraine into Germany as part of her vital 'living space,' and that, without the Ukraine, Russia could not continue much of a military threat."[20]

Taylor then went on to England, where he separately met with both Churchill and Anthony Eden (the Foreign Secretary) about the Church's concern about England bombing Rome. Taylor made no progress with either man, however; indeed, the Foreign

Office went so far as to contrast the Pope's concern for Rome with his silence on the Nazi's bombing of London, as well as their other war atrocities.[21]

Even before Taylor reached the United States, FDR was getting reports on how successful Taylor's mission to the Vatican had been. Ambassador Phillips, while Taylor was still in Rome, had cabled the president: "Myron has a way with him which plays exceedingly well in all Vatican circles."[22] On October 7, Tittmann wrote Sumner Welles: "I thought you might like to know that I have heard from several chiefs of Mission accredited to the Holy See, as well as from personalities within the Vatican itself, that Myron Taylor's visit to Rome has had a definitely heartening effect on the Pope. In view of the doubt regarding the international situation with which the Holy Father is known to be beset, it seems to me that this should be an important accomplishment and, in itself, well worth the trouble Mr. Taylor took to make the voyage."[23] And two days later, FDR sent Taylor a copy of the pope's September 20 letter to the president (which Taylor had carried back to Washington). The pope had praised Taylor as "a devoted and conscientious bearer of tidings from your Excellency and who remains a welcome link between you and Us." In his cover note, FDR added: "You well deserve all that he says about you."[24]

All that remained now was for the Church to fulfill its pledge to play ball on Lend-Lease aid to Russia. With Taylor back in Washington, ensconced in his suite at the Mayflower Hotel, and taking on a few extra (domestic) duties for the president,[25] Cicognani was conferring with Mooney and Ready (and Taylor) on how best to effectuate the Vatican's hidden-hand strategy to back FDR's plan to aid Russia. Ultimately, they came up with the idea of having an outspoken isolationist Church leader—Archbishop McNicholas of Cincinnati—deliver the message. With time of the essence—not only were German troops closing in on Moscow but a second Lend-Lease appropriations bill was pending in Congress and over 90% of available Lend-Lease funds had already been allocated[26]—McNicholas was summoned to Washington and given his marching orders by Cicognani.[27]

In a pastoral letter published on October 30 (which received national coverage), McNicholas wrote: "If we keep in mind the clear distinction that Pope Pius made between the system of atheistic communism, which he condemned, and the Russian people, whom he loved, we shall be able to rid ourselves of much perplexity regarding the Russian situation.... We must not forget the suffering and persecuted people of Russia, deprived of freedom and put in bondage, have still some rights."[28] Fittingly, on that same day, FDR cabled Joseph Stalin that he had approved up to $1 billion of war materials be provided to the Soviet Union in expedited fashion.[29] But FDR waited awhile for the McNicholas letter to sink in and take effect. As Sherwood wrote: "It is an indication of Roosevelt's concern for public opinion that he did not formally include the Soviet Union among the recipients of Lend Lease until November 7."[30]

In the words of the leading historian on the decision to aid Russia in 1941, because of "Myron Taylor's special mission to the Vatican" which had secured the Church's overt approval of such aid, "[s]o perished the great dread of the President that the encyclical of Pius XI would provide a sanction for equating aid to Russia with aid to communism and thereby permit his opponents to insist with telling force that his program was in conflict with the doctrines of the church."[31] In reflecting upon Taylor's contribution to this historic result (which was "given no great amount of publicity"), Sherwood wrote: "Taylor was one who really deserved the somewhat archaic title of 'Ambassador Extraordinary.'"[32]

Within a matter of weeks, everything changed in America with the Japanese attack at Pearl Harbor, and with Germany's subsequent declaration of war on December 11 (followed by Italy on the same day).[33] On December 17, with Ambassador Phillips and his embassy staff expelled from Italy, both Taylor and Welles separately wrote FDR on the need to keep Tittmann in Rome (he would shortly move into quarters in Vatican City).[34]

And before the year was up, Taylor had taken on yet another task. At the request of Secretary of State Cordell Hull, he joined an elite group of officials in the government (and "several prominent persons from outside the government with special qualifications") on the Advisory Committee on Postwar Foreign Policy—a concept that was endorsed by FDR as follows: "I heartily approve."[35]

Notes

1. *See, e.g.,* S. Welles February 3, 1941, memorandum to M.C. Taylor reporting on Tittmann's status and lamenting the need for the kind of "confidential information" from the Vatican that we were getting "during the time you were in Italy" (Taylor Papers, Cornell University); FDR February 11, 1941, memorandum to M.C. Taylor (regarding his preferred choice for the new Apostolic Delegate in Washington) (Taylor Papers, FDR Library) (two days later Bishops Cicognani and Hurley met with Taylor at his home in Florida, presumably to discuss that matter); Taylor February 15, 1941, letter to Missy LeHand (enclosing a January 9 letter from Count Vladimir d'Ormesson, former French Ambassador to the Vatican) (Taylor Papers, FDR Library); H. Tittmann, *Inside the Vatican of Pius XII,* p. 23 (Doubleday 2004).

2. *Id.* pp. 29, 33; WCF December 22, 1940, telegram to M.C. Taylor (Taylor Papers, Cornell University).

3. FDR March 4, 1941, letter to M.C. Taylor (Taylor Papers, FDR Library); G. Fogarty, *The Vatican and the American Hierarchy From 1870 to 1965,* pp. 270-71 (Anton Hiersemann 1982).

4. Tittmann, *supra* note 1, p. 31

5. That became official on April 21, 1941. Tittmann, *supra* note 1, p. 34. Tittmann thereafter had a number of meetings with the Pope and other Vatican officials to discuss Washington's posture vis-à-vis the war and the Vatican's concerns about a possible/likely German victory. Tittmann, *supra* note 1, pp. 34-55. At one unique, private audience with the Pope on June 19, the Pope urged Tittmann to wire Taylor immediately in New York City to contact Archbishop Spellman and ensure that a secret bank account(s) held in a New York bank(s)—known only to the Pope—be identified to the Treasury Department so that they would not be frozen. Tittmann, *supra* note 1, p. 45. For Taylor's interactions generally with the Vatican regarding its assets in U.S. banks, *see* M. Phayer, *Pius XII: The Holocaust and the Cold War,* pp. 96-112 (Indiana University Press 2008).

6. G. Fogarty, "Roosevelt and the American Catholic Hierarchy," *FDR, the Vatican, and the Roman Catholic Church in America, 1933–1945*, pp. 26-27 (ed. D. Woolner & R. Kurial) (Palgrave 2003). Tittmann, *supra* note 1, pp. 46-48.

7. The historiography of Operation Barbarossa is immense. *See, e.g.,* R. Evans, *The Third Reich at War* (Penguin Press 2009); S. Kotkin, *Stalin: Waiting for Hitler, 1929–1941* (Penguin Books 2019).

8. Fogarty, *supra* note 6, pp. 27–28; J. Conway, "Myron C. Taylor's Mission to the Vatican 1940–1950," *Church History* (Vol. 40), pp. 89-90 (March 1975); Fogarty, *supra* note 3 p. 272.

9. As Robert Sherwood, FDR's speechwriter, close confidant, and later biographer, later wrote: "There were some impatient people who thought that the President exaggerated the strength of Catholic sentiment, but it was his way to tread with extreme wariness whenever religious sentiments were involved; he knew a lot more than his advisors did about those sensitivities." R. Sherwood, *Roosevelt and Hopkins: An Intimate History*, p. 384 (Harper & Brothers 1948). Roosevelt (and Sherwood) were clearly correct, given vituperative opposition to helping Russia that had already been voiced by some Church officials. For example, the Bishop of Buffalo had publicly stated that Catholics would be justified in not serving in the U.S. military if it were allied with the Soviet Union. So sensitive was the president to this issue is shown by how FDR handled it in two separate press conferences. On August 16, asked if he contemplated extending Lend-Lease to Russia, FDR bluntly answered "No." As late as September 30, he was asked if he intended to have Russia covered by Lend-Lease, FDR replied: "I don't know. That is the thing that nobody knows at this present time." R. Dawson, *The Decision to Aid Russia, 1941*, p. 269 (North Carolina Press 1959).

10. *Id.*; M. Taylor (ed.), *Wartime Correspondence Between President Roosevelt and Pope Pius XII*, pp. 54–58 (Macmillan 1947).

11. Monsignor Ready August 23, 1941, letter to S. Welles (Taylor Papers, Cornell University); S. Welles August 25, 1941, memorandum to M.C. Taylor (Taylor Papers, Cornell University); S. Welles August 25, 1941, memorandum to FDR (Taylor Papers, Cornell University); M.C. Taylor August 30, 1941, telephone message/memorandum to FDR (Taylor Papers, FDR Library); Fogarty, *supra* note 6, p. 28; Fogarty, *supra* note 3, p. 273; Dawson, *supra* note 9, p. 234.

12. FDR September 1, 1941, memorandum to M.C. Taylor (Taylor Papers, FDR Library).

13. O. Halecki, *Eugenio Pacelli: Pope of Peace*, pp. 166-67 (Creative Age Press 1952); Dawson, *supra* note 9, pp. 235-36.

14. Tittmann, *supra* note 1, pp. 59-62.

15. *Id.*

16. *Id.* p. 62. What constituted the basis of FDR's thinking or evidence for his letter remains a mystery. We do know that (undoubtedly at the request of Taylor in his August 30 telephone message/memorandum—*see supra* note 11) FDR did ask Russian Ambassador Harriman to seek some help on this front when he would be negotiating terms of aid to Russia with Stalin on September 28-30 in Moscow. Sherwood, *supra* note 9, pp. 387-93. In a memorandum Harriman later wrote, he reported that "[t]hroughout the week" on "every occasion" he had explained "the American political situation and public opinion regarding Russia, particularly in relation to the religious subject, and urged both statements and action be taken to indicate to America that the Soviets were willing to allow freedom of worship not only in letter but in fact. Everyone [including Stalin] at least nodded 'Yes.'" Harriman went on to express his belief that at best the Soviets would give "lip service" to the issue, with "religious worship … tolerated only under closest G.P.U. scrutiny." *Id.* pp. 391-92. Taylor got discouraging reports from Russia on the issue of religious freedom—see the October 5, 1941, letter from Leopold Braun, the Chaplain to American Catholics in Moscow (Taylor Papers, FDR Library); ("completely bewildered and literally stupefied" by FDR's letter; "Every single Catholic member or clergy in the USSR has been arrested, imprisoned or exiled!!!"); and a subsequent historical analysis from George Kennan from the U.S. Embassy in Moscow. Tittmann, *supra* note 1, p. 68.

17. Besides the Tardini memoranda, the best accounts of Taylor's sessions are in his September 21, 1941, memorandum to FDR and Secretary of State Hull (Taylor Papers at the FDR Library) and in P. Blet, *Pius XII and the Second World War*, pp. 122-25 (Paulist Press 1999). *See also* Tittmann, *supra* note 1, pp. 59-66; Conway, *supra* note 8, pp. 90-91; Fogarty, *supra* note 3, p. 273.

18. *See supra* note 16.

19. Memorandum re: Bombing Rome Given Myron Taylor September 17, 1941, by His Holiness Pope Pius XII (Taylor Papers, FDR Library).

20. Sherwood, *supra* note 9, p. 400.

21. Conway, *supra* note 8, p. 91. As noted in Chapter I, Taylor returned to the issue of the Allies not bombing Rome on several occasions during the war at the Pope's urging. Churchill, influenced by England's domestic politics, would not agree with Taylor's importunings. And FDR told Taylor that he felt obliged to defer to the English prime minister on this matter. Yet Taylor's repeated efforts (and constant pressure from the Vatican) did have the ultimate effect of sparing the Vatican from any significant harm. Cornell Government Professor Matthew Anthony Evangelista recently published an article concluding that Taylor's "bombing" diplomacy was a "failure." *Myron Taylor and the Bombing of Rome: The Limits of Law and Diplomacy* (June 8, 2020). But as Professor Evangelista does acknowledge, Taylor really was not in a decision-making position on that issue;

all he could do was advise the policy makers of his views (and those of the Vatican). Furthermore, what had once been an unthinkable breach of international law and norms—the aerial bombing of civilian targets and major metropolitan areas—became widely accepted as a matter of course during World War II. *See, e.g.,* R. Overy, *The Bombers and the Bombed* (Penguin 2014); M. Hastings, *Armageddon: The Battle for Germany, 1944–1945* (Knopf 2004); M. Hastings, *Retribution: The Battle for Japan: 1944–1945* (Knopf 2008); *The Papers of George Catlett Marshall* (Vol. 2), pp. 676-81 (Johns Hopkins University Press 1986) (ed. L. Bland, S. Ritenour & C. Wonderlin) (General Marshall's November 15, 1941, restricted press conference where he revealed that, if war came with Japan, the United States would "set the [Japanese] paper cities on fire. There won't be any hesitation about bombing civilians—it will be all out war.").

22. W. Philips September 9, 1941, cable to FDR (President's Secretary File, FDR Library); Conway, *supra* note 8, p. 91.

23. H. Tittmann October 7, 1941, memorandum to S. Welles (Taylor Papers, FDR Library). On October 22, 1941, FDR forwarded this document to Taylor. *See also* S. Welles February 20, 1941, memorandum to M.C. Taylor (Taylor Papers, Cornell University).

24. FDR October 9, 1941, memorandum to M.C. Taylor (Taylor Papers, FDR Library). Not surprisingly, the Pope's letter makes no mention of the USSR lend-lease issue; instead, it alludes (in a very general fashion) to the Atlantic Charter principles. Tittmann, *supra* note 1, p. 63.

25. For example, Taylor advised FDR on labor issues in the steel industry (M.C. Taylor October 18, 1941, memorandum to FDR; Taylor Papers, Cornell University), as well as meeting with John L. Lewis at the Mayflower regarding the pending coal strike (M.C. Taylor October 29, 1941, memorandum; Taylor Papers, Cornell University). Notwithstanding Taylor's prior workings with Lewis and Lewis' high opinion of Taylor (*see* Chapter VII), that did not stop Lewis from launching a public broadside against J.P. Morgan and Taylor with respect to the pending strike. That led to Morgan's partner Thomas Lamont (also a long-standing Director of U.S. Steel) sending FDR a detailed memorandum on November 3, 1941, entitled "The Lewis Diatribe Against J.P.M. and M.C.T." After recounting Taylor's role in saving U.S. Steel and his courageous deal in finding labor peace with Lewis, Lamont concluded: "I have known M.C.T. thirty-five years. I know from him, though he does not wear his heart on his sleeve, that his ambitions have long been to retire from industry and to spend the last part of his life in the sort of public service which he has recently been rendering. I know how quick you were, with your acute perceptions, to take advantage of his support almost from the day of your first inauguration, and how since then he has continued to help in many constructive fields. You have undoubtedly found that he has his own views

and expresses them in a quiet and helpful and cooperative way. I do not assume to say that he is always in agreement with all others, but if he is not, he makes it known, not in a belligerent fashion, but in a clear and helpful way. He does not hesitate to change his views, but always maintains an open mind. That is why he can get on in negotiation with men even like Lewis.... I am telling you nothing new when I say that ... M.C.T. has never been, and never will be, any man's man!" (Lamont Papers, Baker Library, Harvard Business School). On November 10, FDR replied to Lamont, first questioning why Lewis did it "after all the sound and successful negotiations between Myron and Lewis." Lewis' "attitude ... must have made Myron's blood boil, even though he is slow to anger and exceedingly just.... I have come reluctantly to the conclusion that Lewis' is a psychopathic condition." (Taylor Papers, Cornell University).

26. Dawson, *supra* note 9, p. 237

27. Fogarty, *supra* note 6, p. 29; Fogarty, *supra* note 3, pp. 273-75; Conway, *supra* note 8, p. 90; Blet, *supra* note 17, p. 126; Tittmann, *supra* note 1, pp. 63-64. Taylor was also working in October with Church officials to neutralize any potential trouble from Father Coughlin on aid to Russia. Fogerty, *supra* note 3, p. 274.

28. Dawson, *supra* note 9, pp. 267-68. The pastoral letter was on page 6 of the October 31, 1941, *New York Times* and put in the Congressional Record by Senator Mead of New York. *Id.* An editorial in the *Michigan Catholic* on that same day took the same tack, as did the annual meeting of Catholic Bishops in Washington on November 12-13. *Id.* And ultimately the Pope made reference to his concern for the Russian people in his 1941 Christmas message.

29. Sherwood, *supra* note 9, p. 396. With the Nazis only 30 miles from Moscow, FDR famously wrote on a Harry Hopkins November 25, 1941, memorandum about logistical issues concerning delivery: "OK but say to them from me: Hurry, Hurry, Hurry! FDR." *Id.* at 398-99.

30. *Id.* pp. 297-98. Ultimately, $11 billion of war materials were "leased" to the Soviet Union with "no serious issue" raised. *Id.* p. 398.

31. Dawson, *supra* note 9, p. 268.

32. Sherwood, *supra* note 9, p. 398.

33. B. Simms & C. Laderman, *Hitler's American Gamble* (Basic 2021).

34. Fogarty, *supra* note 3, p. 280; Tittmann, *supra* note 1, p. 681.

35. C. Hull, *The Memoirs of Cordell Hull*, pp. 1632-33 (Macmillan 1948).

CHAPTER XII

1942 and the Third Taylor Mission

The Postwar Advisory Committee had its first meeting on February 12, 1942.[1] As envisioned, its purpose was not to prepare definitive plans. Instead, because President Roosevelt anticipated difficult compromises with America's Allies (both England and the Soviet Union) regarding the postwar world, he gave Sumner Welles different marching orders: "What I expect you to do is to prepare ... the necessary number of baskets and the necessary number of solutions for each problem. When the time comes, all I have to do is reach into a basket and fish out solutions that are sound and from which I can make my own choice."[2] The work of the Committee (whose existence was kept a secret) was performed mainly by subcommittees. Myron Taylor would come to chair the subcommittee on postwar foreign economic policy (which became known as the Taylor Committee); he also participated on the subcommittee addressing territorial problems (chaired by Isaiah Bowman, President of Johns Hopkins University) and on a special subcommittee anticipating the need for an international organization (initially chaired by Welles).

Taylor's economic policy committee (in the words of Cordell Hull) ultimately "formulated far-reaching plans for postwar economic policies and for the creation of international agencies in the field of economics and social problems."[3] As far as Welles' subcommittee, within short order it had on the drafting board an international political organization called the "United Nations Authority."[4] Taylor's work on the various subcommittees continued during the war years when he was unable to get back to Rome; in keeping with the chronological narrative of this Taylor biography, highlights of Taylor's contributions in these areas will be identified as they occurred.[5]

Just as the Advisory Committee was getting off the ground, there was an exchange between Taylor and FDR that reflects the personal bond between the two men. On February 14, Taylor sent (via Grace Tully, FDR's private secretary) a newspaper clipping from New York about an American "Cliveden Set" in Washington (and other cities) plotting a peace "short of military victory."[6] FDR responded to Taylor on February 17: "Who in the name of all that is mysterious are the members of the American "Cliveden Set" in Washington or elsewhere? It beats me! Let me know the next time you are in Washington. F.D.R."[7] The subject was still on the president's mind later that same day when, at a press conference, he characterized an argument against aid to Russia as being "on a par with other arguments that are set up by the Cliveden set of Washington."[8] At the same time Taylor was giving FDR grist for use in the domestic political mill, he was also sending on to the president a detailed British document setting forth that government's view of its postwar relationship challenges/rivalries (geopolitical, economic, etc.) with the United States.[9]

During the winter, spring, and early summer months, Taylor's principal activities related to the start-up work of the subcommittees to which he had been assigned (including yet another one on securities problems, chaired by Norman Davis of the American Red Cross).[10] Interestingly, during this period his involvement in Church/Vatican affairs seems to have been at a low ebb.[11] Taylor's seeming noninvolvement all changed, however, when it became known that certain German diplomats had been contacting Church officials to see if the Vatican would "sound out various powers" about possible peace protocols.[12] Although Harold Tittmann told Cardinal Maglione on August 8 that "the U.S. government cannot for a moment conceive of peace with the AXIS until

Hitlerism is completely annihilated,"[13] FDR was very concerned with this development (at this point in the war, no American Army had taken any offensive action).[14] As such, FDR wrote to Welles on August 13: "I agree it would be very useful for Myron Taylor to go back to the Vatican for two or three weeks. But how can we get him there? F.D.R."[15]

On August 22, Tittmann received a telegram from the State Department advising him of FDR's decision and asking that he arrange for Taylor to be allowed to come to Rome. Tittmann immediately contacted Monsignor Montini for his assistance; he, in turn, formally requested Taylor's safe passage to the Italian Ambassador to the Holy See. Initially, the Italian government's response was negative; but ultimately Mussolini's son-in-law, Italian Foreign Minister Count Ciano, approved Taylor's trip, citing to the terms of the 1927 Lateran Treaty, which gave accredited diplomats access to the Vatican.[16]

With Taylor's safe passage assured, Taylor's trip to Rome was made public on September 2.[17] The next day FDR wrote to the pope, expressing that he was "very happy that Mr. Myron C. Taylor is going back to the Vatican to see You.... He will tell You of all that has gone on in America since he last saw you [sic], and he will tell You how important I believe it to be that we maintain close contacts and close relationships."[18] A key part of what Taylor intended to tell the Pope was set forth in a memorandum prepared not by Taylor or the State Department but instead by Archbishop Mooney, Bishop Hurley, and Monsignor Ready (all of whom had played a key role in the Lend-Lease aid to Russia episode). This memorandum, which Welles shared with the president on September 4,[19] stated that now that the United States is "fighting against the very things which the Popes [sic] condemned, our conviction of complete victory is one with our confidence in the unwavering tenacity with which the Holy See will continue its magnificent moral leading." The country was united in waging this "just war," and all Americans have been "profoundly impressed by the searing condemnation of Nazi religious persecution" issued both by the pope and his predecessor, Pius XI. "Among the architects of this unity are the foremost Catholic leaders in our country.... Their public sentiments ... can be summed up ...: Prosecute the war to a victorious conclusion." Then, after stressing again (twice) that "anything less than complete victory would endanger the principles we fought for and our very existence as a nation," the memorandum expressly references (twice) the Nazi peace feelers—seeking a "treacherous peace"—and warning the Holy See that it must resist "peace without victory" overtures profferred by the Nazis "through devious channels," no matter "how strong a pressure the Axis powers may bring to bear upon the Vatican."[20] On the same day that FDR received that document, the Secretary of State received a cable from the American Legation in Bern, reporting on the efforts of the Vatican to help Jews in France and Italy. According to the cable, the Church had been more successful in Italy than in France. The information was to be treated in a "most confidential manner" at Maglione's request: "The Vatican fears that their channels for the alleviation of suffering might be closed to them if their various demarches became generally known and talked about."[21]

Four days later, the Secretary of State asked Taylor to sound out the "British Government's attitude towards the Vatican" concerning "the recent rumors that the Vatican will be used by the Axis in the near future to support peace proposals. Do the British believe that the Pope would lend himself to the maneuver of this character? Since you go to London after Rome, you may, of course give the British the benefit of your opinions in the light of your recent visit to the Holy See."[22]

And then the next day, just before Taylor's departure from Washington, the president's Advisory Committee on Political Refugees met with Taylor.[23] At that meeting Taylor was informed of the historic telegram sent from Switzerland by Gerhart Riegner to Rabbi Stephen Wise in New York City (received on August 28), in which the Nazi plan to kill between three and four million Jews by poison gas was disclosed.[24] Reigner's telegram was the first writing to the outside world of the Nazi's plans for the Holocaust.

On September 12, Taylor left New York City (without Mrs. Taylor) on his third mission to the Pope. On September 13, he arrived in Lisbon, where he was met by his appointed escort from the Vatican, Monsignor Vagnozzi.[25] From Lisbon, the pair first flew to Barcelona, Spain, where they were met by the American Consul; and from Spain they flew to Rome, where they arrived on September 17 to "some commotion"—"Italian and German planes were posted all around the field due to the war situation" and goose-stepping German soldiers were much in evidence.[26] As per Count Ciano's directive, the pair was greeted by Vatican officials and whisked through customs.[27] When the Italian authorities marked Taylor's passport with a seal of the date of his arrival, Taylor remarked that his "passport was acquiring a unique value … because it would probably be the only passport in the world at war showing that a diplomat had landed in enemy territory and subsequently returned safely to his own country."[28] Thereafter, Taylor and the Church officials were swiftly driven in an official Vatican limousine, with police escort, directly to the Vatican.

The morning after Taylor's arrival, Montini came to welcome him, but also to probe for the topics Taylor planned to raise on his visit. Taylor, however, begged off, claiming exhaustion from his trip (and wanting to restudy the various memoranda he had brought to present to the pope and his top advisors).[29] Obviously, he recovered in short order, because Tittmann would later write: "Even though 68 years old, Myron Taylor was an indefatigable worker. He would rise at 5 a.m. and work until 8 a.m., when he would eat a hearty breakfast. From then on, he would meet a steady stream of visitors, with spurts of dictation in between. The pace he set left us exhausted, but he continued fresh as a daisy."[30]

Taylor met (alone) with the pope on September 19, September 22, and September 26. The first meeting lasted two hours,

Myron C. Taylor, Harold H. Tittmann Jr., and various church officials
in the corridor of the Apostolic Palace

which was the longest audience ever accorded to a diplomat by Pius XII.[31] It undoubtedly took so long because Taylor both read and commented on the entire memorandum prepared by Mooney, Hurley, and Ready.[32] Besides the warning(s) against the German peace-feelers, Taylor wanted to emphasize to the pope that the sheer, overwhelming industrial might of the United States would undoubtedly crush the Axis powers:

> The world has never seen such an avalanche of war weapons, manned by skilled mechanics and stout-hearted freemen, as we shall loose in 1943 and 1944 against the Axis. In some few sectors, we have already taken the offensive, months ahead of our original plans. That offensive will rise in irresistible crescendo, more and more rapidly, more and more powerfully, until totalitarianism,

with its menace to religion and freedom, is finally and utterly crushed.[33]

And, of course, as the former CEO of the world's largest industrial company, Taylor had great credibility on that subject.

At their second meeting, on September 22, the pope handed Taylor a written response to the Taylor memorandum.[34] In that document the pope replied that he had "never thought in terms of peace by compromise at any cost ... On certain principles of right and justice there can be no compromise." He also wrote that "[w]e will never approve and we will still less favor a peace that gives free reign to those who would undermine ... the foundation of Christianity and persecute religion and the Church."[35] The Pope further assured Taylor that the United States "need have no fear that any pressure from outside the Vatican will make it change its course." These papal expressions may well have encouraged FDR to blurt out the demand of unconditional surrender at the Casablanca Conference in January of 1943.[36]

At that same audience Taylor gave the pope a memorandum on cooperative efforts between the United States, Great Britain, and the Soviet Union being a means to induce religious tolerance in the latter. As with his prior visit, this met with little enthusiasm. Tardini later wrote that "this memorandum demonstrates the error and illusion of the Americans, who believe it possible that the Communist Government, once victorious, would enter as a gentle little lamb in the European family of nations. The truth is quite different. If Stalin wins the war, he will be the lion which will devour all of Europe. I told Taylor that neither Hitler nor Stalin will be able to remain quiet and calm in a family of European nations. I am amazed that such obvious matters are not recognized by such high level political leaders."[37]

After his September 22 audience with the pope, Taylor then met with Tardini. Tardini's memorandum of that meeting emphasized Taylor's message that "the US feels strong, is sure of victory and is not afraid of a long war," while also detailing how little the

United States understood the "European situation" and that this "could cause [postwar] Europe enormous problems."[38] Taylor also called on "the necessity of a word from the Pope against such huge atrocities by the Germans … I said in reply that the Pope has already spoken several times to condemn crimes by whomsoever they are committed. I added that some people want the Pope to condemn by name Hitler and Germany, which is an impossibility. Taylor said to me: 'I didn't ask this. I have not asked that he condemn Hitler by name.' I said again: 'The Pope has already spoken.' Taylor said: 'He can repeat it.' And I could not but agree."[39]

Three days later Taylor met with Maglione for an hour and one half.[40] Taylor began the meeting by giving a comprehensive overview of the postwar planning work already underway by the U.S. government (including the establishment of a world organization); Maglione "expressed his pleasure" that such important work was being undertaken. Taylor then returned to the subject he had raised with Tardini: "that the Holy Father should again speak out against the inhuman treatment of refugees and hostages—and especially of the Jews—in occupied territories."[41] Maglione replied that "the Holy See has been working incessantly for the relief of the unfortunate peoples of the occupied countries and very particularly for refugees and for the Jews…. [R]epresentatives of the Catholic Church in various countries … have been quite outspoken in their condemnation of this inhuman treatment…. His Holiness has on many occasions condemned this treatment of peoples … and has declared that the blessing or the malediction of Almighty God would descend upon rulers according to the manner in which they treat the peoples under their rule. This … was quite a strong statement—as strong, in fact, as it is possible to make without descending to particulars, a course of action which would immediately draw his Holiness into the field of political disputes, require documentary proof, etc." Taylor nonetheless persisted and urged the pope to speak out again. In response, Maglione assured Taylor that "the Pope will certainly avail himself of the first opportunity to restate His position in very clear terms."[42]

With respect to Maglione's need for "documentary proof," the next day Taylor forwarded to Maglione a memorandum sent to him by the State Department which it had received from the Geneva Office of the Jewish Agency for Palestine, dated August 30, 1942.[43] The document cited "two reliable eye-witnesses (Aryans)" who attested to, among other things: (1) the liquidation of the Warsaw Ghetto, with all Jews without any distinction being shot and their bodies used for making fats and fertilizer; (2) whole-scale mass executions in various European locations (e.g., "There is not one Jew left in the entire district east of Poland, including occupied Russia."); (3) Jews being deported from Germany, Belgium, Holland, France, and Slovakia and "sent to be butchered"; and (4) a "large part of the Jewish population deported to Lithuania and Lubin has already been executed." Based on this document Taylor asked Maglione if the Vatican could confirm these reports and, if so, "whether the Holy Father has any suggestions as to any practical matter in which the forces of civilized public opinion could be utilized in order to prevent a continuation of these barbarities." As Tittmann would later write, Taylor's memorandum was the first written documentation of the "extermination" of the Jews in Poland to come to the Vatican, "rather than persecution, which we all knew about."[44]

On September 26 Taylor had his last audience with the pope. A good part of the meeting had to do with responding to various requests made by FDR and Taylor, as well as handing Taylor a private letter to the president (thanking him for Taylor's visit).[45] He also handed Taylor a memorandum regarding the Pope's opposition to bombing civilian populations: "[I]f aerial bombardments must continue to form part of this harrowing war, let them with all possible care be directed only against objects of military value and spare the homes of non-combatants and the treasured shrines of art and religion [this last reference was obviously meant to be the Vatican]."[46] With respect to Poland, the Pope objected to the Polish government-in-exile's eagerness for him to denounce the Nazis. He was in a "delicate" position, having already resisted Nazi demand for public approval of the German invasion of Russia, as well as its demand for public condemnation of Allied bombing of Cologne. The pope explained that he had sent numerous confidential communications to a variety of Polish officials (in Poland and London), all with sympathy for the plight of the Polish people. Furthermore, the pope emphasized, he had consistently protested Nazi misdeeds to German authorities through diplomatic channels.[47]

On September 27, Taylor had his final meeting with a Vatican official. At this session, he presented to Tardini his initial reaction(s) to the Pope's memorandum of the prior day.[48] He noted at the outset that the Church had been silent when the Germans and Japanese had bombed civilian populations (attaching photographs of Church property in England damaged by bombs), but now raised objections at the point when the Allies "are strong enough to bomb military objectives in Germany." Notwithstanding that such a glaring inconsistency might cause "many conflicting reactions," Taylor vowed: "(1) to discourage, in London and Washington, indiscriminate bombing and to urge that targets be confined to munitions plants and communication centers; [and] (2) to have the public warned to move away from danger zones."[49]

As Taylor flew out of Rome on September 28 there was much speculation about his visit, especially among the Axis powers.[50] *Der Bund*, a publication based in Bern, Switzerland, called the Taylor mission "extraordinary," "paradoxical and strange," with a "dense cloud of rumors" hovering around the "political atmosphere of the Vatican."[51] Was he seeking terms of a negotiated peace, or was he seeking to have the pope side with the Allies; or perhaps Taylor was seeking the pope's help in the U.S. elections in November?

While Taylor was still in Rome, Count Ciano had received a German proposal "that we give Myron Taylor as 'solemn booing."[52] Mussolini's reaction was a bit stronger. Calling Taylor a "buffoon," Il Duce directed Ciano to tell the Vatican: "Concordat or no Concordat, if Myron Taylor tries to return to Italy he will end up in handcuffs."[53]

Taylor's first stop was Spain. But before he got there, very bad weather almost caused the plane to make an emergency landing at the military airport of Alghero in Sardinia (manned by Italian and German troops). The pilot, concerned for Taylor's safety, disregarded the airport's directive to "land immediately," flying instead for "half an hour at an altitude of about 300 feet, [with] the plane shaking dangerously over the black sea."[54]

The highlight of Taylor's stopover in Spain was an unscheduled meeting with General Franco on September 30, which was called at Franco's request. Attended only by Franco, Spain's Foreign Minister, U.S. Ambassador to Spain Carlton Hayes, and a translator, the meeting went for an hour and a half. As Hayes recounted in his memoirs,[55] the dialogue was "almost exclusively between General Franco and Mr. Taylor." Franco delivered a lecture in defense of Hitler and against "barbarous and oriental, communistic Russia." In Hayes' words, "Mr. Taylor's rebuttal was masterful." Besides dissecting the logic of Franco's exposition on the causes of war, Taylor went on to give an "emphatic account of America's power and determination to win the war." Hayes would write in his memoirs that Franco's enthusiasm about joining the war "afterwards softened … attributable in no small degree … of meeting and hearing Myron Taylor." And in his letter to the president of the same day on the visit of "the great Myron Taylor," Hayes wrote: "The Taylor visit, aside from being a great personal boon to me, has come at the right psychological moment for the American cause in Spain."[56] It was, of course, more than just the "right psychological moment" because the American "Torch" landings in North Africa would commence on November 8th; and a nonneutral Spain could have had a significant impact on the success of those landings.[57]

From Spain Taylor traveled on to Lisbon where he met Dr. Salazar for the second time on October 2. According to his memorandum of his conversation with the Portuguese leader,[58] Taylor began by briefing Salazar on the U.S. government's postwar planning activities. He then moved on to a favorite topic: that Germany would suffer a "complete defeat" under the weight of America's industrial/military might. Taylor also told Salazar of his low opinion of Franco's grasp of geopolitical issues—an observation that amused Salazar, who indicated "that he shared my estimate of the General's mental processes." Taylor next turned to America's determination "to crush Japan." Citing the number of men who would be in uniform within the next year (ten million), he also cited how America's steel production—at present— dwarfed "the whole of the Axis and Axis controlled countries." The two men then compared notes on the people in Germany and Italy and their enthusiasm (or lack thereof) for the war. It seems clear from their meeting that, with America now in the war (and bolstered by Taylor's words), Salazar's pessimism from the prior year about Nazism being the future wave of Europe had changed dramatically.[59]

From Lisbon Taylor flew on to London where (as promised) he pressed Winston Churchill on not targeting Rome for aerial bombing at an October 5 dinner party hosted at 10 Downing Street by Churchill, with his family, and U.S. Ambassador John Winant in attendance. As recounted in Chapter I, Churchill did not accede to Taylor's requests.[60] Per his directive from Cordell Hull, Taylor also shared with the Churchill dinner party the "complete victory" memorandum he had presented to the Pope and the pope's response thereto. On behalf of her husband, Clementine Churchill wrote to Taylor on October 8, thanking him "for the great privilege enjoyed by myself and my daughters in being allowed to have knowledge of the wonderful and historic document which you presented to His Holiness, the Pope. I feel your visit to the Vatican may have far reaching results."[61]

On October 12, Taylor touched down back in America. Shortly thereafter, he heard from Welles that Tittmann had received an 'informal unsigned statement" from Maglione on October 10, responding to Taylor's September 26 memorandum detailing the extermination of Jews in Poland and elsewhere.[62] The unsigned document set forth that "[r]eports pertaining to the severe measures taken against non-Aryans have also arrived at the Holy See from other sources, but thus far it has been impossible to verify their accuracy."[63] It went on to represent that "[e]very opportunity is being undertaken by the Holy See, however, to mitigate the suffering of these unfortunate people." Welles also reported to Taylor that Tittmann "regrets" the Vatican "was not more helpful," but he had "received the impression [from Maglione] that the Vatican had no practical suggestions to make … [and] that there is little hope of restraining Nazi barbarities except through sheer physical force coming from without."[64]

Undeterred, Taylor went to work with his old friends at the National Catholic Welfare Conference (Monsignor Ready, et al.) in drafting a pastoral directed to American Catholics. Issued on November 14, the document addressed a host of issues raised by an entire world at war. Most relevant, it set forth that the United States was "associated with other powers in a deadly conflict against [other nations that were] intent in waging war to bring about a slave world."[65] Because that represented a basic "conflict of Principles," it made "compromise impossible."[66] The pastoral also expressed the "deepest sympathy to our brother bishops in all countries … where religion is persecuted, liberty abolished, and the rights of God and of man are violated." Not stopping there, it espoused a "deep sense of revulsion against the cruel indignation heaped upon the Jews in conquered countries and upon defenseless peoples not of our faith." And it further protested "against disporatic tyrants who have lost all sense of humanity by condemning thousands of innocent persons to death in subjugated countries as acts of reprisal; by placing other thousands of innocent victims in concentration camps, and by permitting unnumbered persons to die of starvation."

The issue of bombing had also come up again, as Archbishop Cicognani contacted Taylor in a panic on October 28 over an "urgent communication" from the Vatican regarding Anthony Eden's just issued, public declaration that the British "have as much right to bomb Rome as the Italians have to bomb London. We shall not hesitate to do so to the best of our ability and as heavily as possible if the course of the war should render such bombing helpful and convenient."[67] Taylor promptly met with the Apostolic Delegate on the matter and then wrote two letters on November 2 to FDR seeking an immediate audience (at which FDR suggested an "independent course of action, subject to consultation with the military").[68] Thereafter, from his Florida home Taylor called the president to follow up on FDR's "independent course of action" idea.[69] In that call Taylor asked for instructions on what to tell the Pope on the U.S. government's position regarding bombing.[70] After giving the matter "much thought," however, FDR wrote to Taylor that adopting an "independent course of action different from that of our principal associate in the war" was not advisable.[71]

In the meantime, the national press in America headlined the rapidly spreading news of the Nazi atrocities against the Jews of Europe.[72] And this in turn (among other things) led to a December 17 Joint Declaration by the Allied Powers (led by the United States and Great Britain) against the Nazi's persecution of the Jews. Noting "Hilter's oft-repeated intention to exterminate the Jewish people in Europe," the Declaration condemned the deportation of Jews from the occupied countries to Eastern Europe and specifically called out what the Germans were doing in Poland— "the principal Nazi slaughter-house." The Allies then reaffirmed "their solemn resolution to ensure that those responsible for these crimes shall not escape retribution."[73]

On the same day of the Joint Declaration, Taylor sent another memorandum to the president, relaying a message he had received from the Apostolic Delegate on negotiations the Vatican had had with the Italian government to remove Axis military hardware from Rome, and asking if this approach might provide the means for sparing the city.[74] The following day, FDR wrote to Hull:

I really think that England and the United States could agree not to bomb Rome on condition that the city itself, outside of the Vatican, be not used in any shape, manner, or form either by the Germans or the Italians for war purposes. I understand that today most of the Italian Departments have left Rome with their civil and military personnel, but that Germans, who are of course all military, are using Rome as central headquarters. I should think that we ought consider it is up to the Vatican itself to propose that Rome be demilitarized. If that is accomplished, there is no reason for us to bomb it.[75]

Hull then followed up with British Ambassador Halifax on this idea of Rome becoming an "open city" (i.e., one completely demilitarized).[76] With Taylor urging the president and Hull on with their efforts with the British, Hull recorded in his memoirs that Halifax sent him a memorandum on January 12, 1943, "stating that his government had decided, somewhat reluctantly, to abandon its idea, partly as a result of our attitude."[77] Thus, while the issue of bombing Rome was not finally settled and would in fact continue until Rome was conquered by the Allies in June of 1944, Taylor's persistence had at least moved the needle a bit.[78]

On December 23, Welles sent FDR a letter, informing the president that his December 1 letter to the Pope regarding Taylor's trip had not gotten through to the Vatican.[79] As such, Taylor had suggested that FDR's reply be cabled to Tittmann (via Bern) and included in a Christmas message to the Pope (to be delivered by Tittmann). FDR agreed, and his Christmas message to the Pope (drafted by Welles) stated that the Pope's letter "brought to me by my personal representative, has given me the greatest pleasure as did a memorandum by Your Holiness in response to his explanation of the position and objectives of this Government and people and of their accomplishments and preparations for defensive war.... It has given me the greatest satisfaction and I am greatly heartened again to receive from Your Holiness such positive assurances which will enable us to continue our efforts along parallel lines."

As the calendar year's end approached, it was also time for the Pope's annual Christmas message. Prompted by the pledges made to Taylor in September, as well as the British Ambassador to the Holy See giving the Pope the London version of the Allies' December 17 statement on Nazi atrocities against the Jews,[80] the Pope used the end of his message to state that countries had no right to "herd people around as though they were a lifeless thing," and he acknowledged the "anguished cries" of the victims of "arbitrary attacks." He concluded by invoking his hope that the war would come to an end so as to benefit all the war's victims, a "wish humanity owes to the hundreds of thousands of people who, without any fault of their own and sometimes because of their nationality or race alone, have been doomed to death or progressive extermination."[81] The immediate reaction to the Pope's message in the West was positive (a *New York Times* editorial, for example, called the Pope a "lonely voice crying out of the silence of a continent"),[82] while the Italians and Germans were furious and contemplated action against the Vatican.[83] Western diplomats assigned to the Vatican noted their approval, while at the same time expressing their wish that the Pope had gone farther and had been more specific.[84]

That was the immediate reaction to the Pope's message. The historical literature about it since, however, has labeled the 1942 Christmas message as a "lightning rod" in the debate about Pope Pius XII and the Holocaust.[85]

Notes

1. C. Hull, *The Memoirs of Cordell Hull*, p. 1634 (Macmillan 1947). Besides Hull and Welles, the government members included Dean Acheson, Adolph Berle, Herbert Feis, and Leo Pasvolsky. Nongovernment members, besides Taylor, included Isaiah Bowman (president of Johns Hopkins University), Norman Davis (chairman of the American Red Cross), Hamilton Fish (head of the Council

on Foreign Relations and editor of *Foreign Affairs*), Anne O'Hare McCormick (foreign affairs columnist for the *New York Times*), and Benjamin Cohen (general counsel of the National Power Pricing Committee). To avoid the postwar problems that plagued Woodrow Wilson, special care was to balance the Committee's membership (which would grow over time) to ensure bipartisanship. *Id.* p. 1635.

2. S. Welles, *Seven Decisions That Shaped History*, p. 182 (Harper & Brothers 1950). Given the well-known rivalry between Hull and Welles, it is unsurprising that each man's memoirs take a greater share of the credit for the idea, formation, and work of this committee.

3. Hull, *supra* note 1, p. 1636.

4. *Id.* p. 1637.

5. In Welles' and Hull's memoirs, both men singled out Taylor's important contributions. *See* Welles, *supra* note 2, p. 21 ("Myron Taylor, whose broad grasp of international affairs, and whose experience and knowledge of economic problems, made his co-operation invaluable."); Hull, *supra* note 1, p. 715 (Taylor "became one of the moving spirits in our work of initiating and developing the outlines of a proposed world peace organization.").

6. M.C. Taylor February 14, 1942, letters to G. Tully and FDR (Taylor Papers, FDR Library).

7. FDR February 17, 1942, memorandum to M.C. Taylor (Taylor Papers, FDR Library).

8. *FDR: His Personal Letters*, p. 1286 (Duell, Sloan and Pearce 1947) (ed. E. Roosevelt). FDR's outburst only fed the story as the press then wanted to know who was in the "set." FDR's public airing of the Cliveden Set also brought a protest from a member of the English Cliveden Set (Nancy Astor) to FDR's wife. That in turn led the president to seek the counsel of Sumner Welles on how to deal with the Waldorf Astors: "I am a bit troubled because I do not want to be rude. The facts are that irrespective of any concerted move, the 'Cliveden Set' in 1937, 1938, and 1939 was comprised of people who belonged to the Chamberlain school in England. They were not subversive but they were proved wrong by hindsight.... The term 'Cliveden Set' became a symbol of not just appeasement but of a failure to evaluate the world situation as it really was. When I spoke to the press I was, of course, speaking generically ... without any reference to Nancy or Waldorf personally. We have had and still have people in Washington who contribute very much the same theory. They have been proved wrong but have continued on in their wrongheadedness whereas Nancy and Waldorf had not. For example, I would call the McCormack-Patterson-Hearst-Roy Howard [conservative-isolationist publishers] the 'Cliveden Set' in this country. I cannot call them unpatriotic, but I can certainly classify them as thoroughly mistaken, but mistaken in the present when they have been proved wrong as to the past. FDR." Welles, in

turn, suggested that Mrs. Roosevelt reply to the Astors using the president's own words. *Id.* 1321-22.

FDR also called the aforementioned publications "The Dawes House Set"—after the country estate outside Washington owned by Cissy Patterson, Editor of the *Washington Times-Herald*. Patterson publicly countered by attacking the "Yellow Potomac Set," who, according to Patterson, was "more concerned with keeping their jobs than with winning the war." R. Martin, *Cissy: The Extraordinary Life of Eleanor Medill Patterson,* p. 437 (Simon & Schuster 1979).

9. M.C. Taylor February 25, 1942, memorandum to G. Tully (with attachment) (Taylor Papers, FDR Library). *See also* S. Welles August 19, 1942, memorandum to FDR attaching Leopold Amery's (British Secretary of State for India) July 30, 1942, letter to Taylor (Taylor Papers, FDR Library).

10. Besides the memoirs of Hull and Welles, a 1949 publication by the State Department ("Postwar Foreign Policy Preparation: 1939-1945") details Taylor's significant involvement in the various subcommittees.

11. For example, Taylor appears to have played no role in the U.S. government's initial reactions/objections to Japan's asking to have (and being granted) an official representative to the Holy See in early 1942. This episode is well dealt with in H. Tittmann, *Inside the Vatican of Pius XII,* pp. 102-10 (Doubleday 2004) and P. Blet, *Pius XII and the Second World War,* pp. 127-31 (Paulist Press 1999).

12. Blet, *supra* note 11, pp. 132-33.

13. Blet, *supra* note 11, p. 133; Tittmann, *supra* note 11, p. 126.

14. FDR August 3, 1942, memorandum to R. Close (Minister of the Union of South Africa) citing a presidential memorandum of the same date setting forth the U.S.'s defensive war aims for 1942. E. Roosevelt, *supra* note 8, pp. 1337-39.

15. FDR August 13, 1942, memorandum to Welles (Taylor Papers, FDR Library).

16. Tittmann, *supra* note 11, pp. 126-27; H. Tittmann September 4, 1942, telegram to C. Hull (Taylor Papers, Cornell University). Tittmann later wrote that he heard second hand that Mussolini had made the final decision. Tittman, *supra* note 11, p. 127. With Taylor's trip now approved, Tittmann then made arrangements to give up his bedroom in the Vatican for Taylor's use during his visit. Tittman, *supra* note 11, p. 127-28.

17. M.C. Taylor September 2, 1941, memorandum to FDR (Taylor Papers, FDR Library).

18. E. Roosevelt, *supra* note 8, p. 1345.

19. S. Welles August 14, 1942, memorandum (with attachment) to FDR (Taylor Papers, FDR Library).

20. *Id. See also* G. Fogarty, *The Vatican and the American Hierarchy From 1870 to 1965,* pp. 284-85 (Anton Hiersemann 1982) (Fogarty I); G. Fogarty,

"Roosevelt at the American Catholic Hierarchy," *FDR, the Vatican, and the Roman Catholic Church in American: 1933-1945*, p. 31 (ed. D. Woolner & R. Kurial) (Palgrave 2003) (Fogarty II).

21. American Legation September 4, 1942, cable to C. Hull (Taylor Papers, Cornell University). *See also* Tittmann September 4, 1942, telegram to Hull (Taylor Papers, Cornell University).

22. C. Hull September 8, 1942, memorandum to M.C. Taylor (Taylor Papers, FDR Library).

23. The Committee had been constituted in May of 1938 and had worked with Taylor regarding the Evian Conference and his subsequent work on the Intergovernmental Committee on Political Refugees. *Refugees and Rescue: The Diaries and Papers of James G. McDonald*, pp. 130, 136, 138-39, 146, 152, 154-55, 169-80, 188, 190-91, 241-42, 276-77 (ed. R. Breitman, B. Stewart & S. Hochberg) (Indiana University Press 2009).

24. *Id.* p. 298. *See also* G. Riegnar, *Never Despair: Sixty Years in the Service of the Jewish People and the Cause of Human Rights*, pp. 35-54 (Chicago 2006); W. Laqueur & R. Bretnar, *Breaking the Silence: The German Who Exposed the Final Solution*, pp. 152-56 (Hanover 1994); B. Welles, *Sumner Welles: FDR's Global Strategist*, pp. 230-31 (St. Martin's Press 1997).

25. On June 10, 1949, Monsignor Vagnozzi, by then the Apostolic Delegate to the Philippines, sent to Taylor (at his request) a rough copy report of "our historical trip of 1942" (Taylor Papers, Cornell University). This report (except for a few errors as to dates) is the most detailed record extant of Taylor's trips in and out of Rome in 1942. By the terms of Count Ciano's approval of Taylor's visit, at all times while in Rome (and not in the Vatican) the president's representative had to be accompanied by a Vatican official.

26. *Id. See also* Transcript of Meeting of Protestant Clergymen with Myron Taylor at Union Club (New York City, October 20, 1947) at pp. 25-26 (Taylor Papers, Cornell University).

27. Tittman had asked if he could go to the Rome airport to greet Taylor, but was refused (per Count Ciano's directive). Tittmann, *supra* note 11, p. 128.

28. Vagnozzi, *supra* note 25, p. 2.

29. Tittmann, *supra* note 11, pp. 128-29.

30. *Id.* p. 130.

31. *Id.* p. 129.

32. Taylor's September 19, 1942, "statement" to the Pope is in the Taylor Papers at the FDR Library, as are his summary of all of his three audiences with the Pope. *See also* R. Rychlate, *Hitler, the War, and the Pope*, pp. 203-05 (Sunday Visitor 2010). It appears that no Vatican official ever suspected the original

authors of the "Taylor" memorandum. Fogarty I, *supra* note 20, p. 285; Fogarty II, *supra* note 20, p. 31.

33. Blet, *supra* note 11, p. 133; J. Conway, "Myron C. Taylor's Mission to the Vatican 1940-1950," *Church History*, p. 92 (Vol. 44) (March 1975).

34. It appears to have been drafted by an American in Rome (Vincent McCormick) at the request of Pius XII's confidant Robert Leiber, Fogarty I, *supra* note 20, p. 285; Fogarty II, *supra* note 20, p. 31.

35. Blet, *supra* note 11, p. 134; Fogarty I, *supra* note 20, pp. 285-86; Fogarty II, *supra* note 20, p. 31.

36. Fogarty I, *supra* note 20, pp. 286, 291; Fogarty II, *supra* note 20, p. 31; Tittmann, *supra* note 11, p. 125.

37. Tittmann, *supra* note 11, pp. 131-32; Blet, *supra* note 11, p. 134.

38. Tittmann, *supra* note 11, pp. 132-33.

39. O. Chadwick, *Britain and the Vatican During the Second World War*, p. 213 (Cambridge Press 1986); Blet, *supra* note 11, p. 134.

40. Two versions of this meeting exist—Taylor's memorandum and a memorandum prepared by Father Carroll (an American Priest at the Vatican), who sat in on the meeting. Both documents are in the Taylor Papers at Cornell and at the FDR Library.

41. This quotation (as well as the others from this conversation) come from Carroll's memorandum, *supra* note 40. *See also* Chadwick, *supra* note 39, pp. 213-14.

42. Another part of this meeting was directed to Taylor's expressing the U.S. government's continued displeasure with the Vatican's granting Japan's request to have an ambassador appointed to the Holy See (*see supra* note 11). According to Carroll's memorandum, Taylor closed this portion of the meeting noting America's "sad experience" with Japan and warning that "the Vatican should be cautious in [its] dealings with the Japanese representatives, lest the latter get the Vatican into serious trouble." Maglione "enjoyed this very much and assured Mr. Taylor that the Holy See would be on its guard always and intimated that it would not be taken in as easily as 'some of our friends.'" Taylor's memorandum recorded that Maglione "smilingly responded that they were under no illusions."

43. This document can be accessed online at the Jewish Virtual Library. *See also* Tittmann, *supra* note 11, p. 120; Chadwick, *supra* note 39, p. 214; B. Welles, *supra* note 24, p. 231; Blet, *supra* note 11, p. 159; M. Phayer, *Pius XII: The Holocaust and the Cold War*, p. 46 (Indiana University Press 2008); R. Erbelding, *Rescue Board: The Untold Story of America's Efforts to Save the Jews of Europe*, p. 22 (Doubleday 2018).

44. Tittmann, *supra* note 11, p. 120.

45. Blet, *supra* note 11, p. 135.

46. The Pope's September 26, 1942, memorandum is in the Taylor Papers at the FDR Library.

47. Tittmann, *supra* note 11, pp. 115-17. Later that same day Taylor met with Tardini to say goodbye. Taylor again tried to put a good face on the U.S.'s Russian ally, stating that it would be necessary for the U.S.S.R. to become part of the family of nations. To that Tardini replied: "Stalin would not be suitable as a member of any family." *Id.* p. 132.

48. Taylor's September 27, 1942, memorandum is in the Taylor Papers at the FDR Library.

49. Blet, *supra* note 11, pp. 135-36; Tittmann, *supra* note 11, p. 133; Fogerty I, p. 285.

50. Tittmann, *supra* note 11, p. 130; Vagnozzi memorandum (*see supra* note 25). Incredibly, on the same day that Taylor left Rome Welles sent him a memorandum listing the overseas expense per diem at $8 per day (Taylor Papers, Cornell University). It is unclear whether Welles was attempting some humor.

51. The *Der Bund* (October 2, 1942) translation is in the Taylor Papers at Cornell.

52. G. Ciano, *Diary: 1937-1943*, p. 548 (Enigma 2002). Ciano's reaction to this proposal was: "How foolish! I can't say whether it is more ridiculous or disgusting. It would appear that the inventor of this idea was that cripple Goebbels. It doesn't even deserve an answer."

53. *Id.* p. 556. Notwithstanding, Taylor said he was "not afraid of risks. I have lived a long life, and I have got more than I could possibly desire. I am very happy to dedicate my remaining days to the cause of world peace, and no danger or risk would prevent me from doing what I can for such a cause." Vagnozzi memorandum, *supra* note 25.

54. Vagnozzi memorandum, *supra* note 25. While Vagnozzi was "whispering prayers," he noted that Taylor "looked very cool and unconcerned." After one particularly bad bump I could not refrain from telling him: "I feel very nervous"; he answered dryly, without the slightest trace of emotion: "Everybody does." *See also* Transcript of Meeting of Protestant Clergymen with Myron Taylor, pp. 26-27 (Taylor reported that "[a]ll aboard the plane thought the Germans were going to kidnap me.").

55. *Wartime Mission in Spain: 1942-1945*, pp. 70-73 (MacMillan 1945); *see also* Hayes October 6, 1942, report on Taylor's visit to Spain (Taylor Papers, FDR Library).

56. *Id.* p. 72.

57. Transcript of Meeting of Protestant Clergymen with Myron Taylor, p. 24. While in Spain Taylor reported to the president (1) that he had "absolutely"

convinced the Pope and Vatican authorities that "we would prosecute the war until Hitler and Nazism were destroyed," and (2) we would give the Italian people "adequate assistance" in the future to abandon Hitler ("this impressed the Pope and the Vatican authorities greatly."). M.C. Taylor September 29, 1942, letter to FDR (Taylor Papers, FDR Library).

58. The undated memorandum is in the Taylor Papers at the FDR Library.

59. Taylor would later state (although it is not in his memorandum) that he broached the subject of an Allied air base in the Azores. Transcript of Meeting of Protestant Clergymen with Myron Taylor, p. 25. In August 1943 Salazar agreed to lease bases in the Azores to the British; and on December 1, 1943, U.S. and British air forces were allowed access to Lajes Field. These facilities proved critical to winning the Battle of the Atlantic with German u-boats.

60. Tittmann, *supra* note 11, p. 133. *See also* M. Evangelista, "Myron Taylor and the Bombing of Rome: The Limits of Law and Diplomacy," *Diplomacy & Statecraft*, p. 285 (June 8, 2020).

61. W. Churchill October 8, 1942, letter to M.C. Taylor (Taylor Papers, FDR Library). She added: "I shall never forget last Monday evening." Taylor would later state that it was Winston Churchill on December 5 who called the Pope's memorandum "a great historical document." Transcript of Meeting of Protestant Clergymen with Myron Taylor, p. 39.

In her diary, Mary Churchill (the Prime Minister's youngest daughter) recorded the evening as follows: "Home in the evening.... The Winants, Diana (who's going to have another baby—hooray) & Mr. Myron Taylor (USA envoy to Vatican). It was v[ery] interesting. Messages from Mr. Taylor to Pope & vice versa read. Most beautiful language & very encouraging." *Mary Churchill's War: The Wartime Diaries of Churchill's Youngest Daughter*, p. 168 (ed. E. Soames) (Pegasus Books 2022).

62. S. Welles October 21, 1942, memorandum to M.C. Taylor (Taylor Papers, Cornell University and FDR Library); *see also* Tittmann, *supra* note 11, p. 120; Blet, *supra* note 11, pp. 159-60.

63. The other sources appear to have been Casimir Papée, the Polish Ambassador to the Vatican, and various Jewish organizations. Blet, *supra* note 11, p. 159.

64. On Taylor's September 26, 1942, memorandum Maglione had annotated: "I do not believe we have any information confirming this very serious news. Isn't this correct?" Blet, *supra* note 11, p. 159.

65. Fogarty I, *supra* note 20, pp. 286-87; Fogarty II, *supra* note 20, pp. 31-32.

66. In the aftermath of Taylor's reports to the president, clearly someone in the administration leaked to the press. *See, e.g.*, "Pope Wants Allies to Win,"

New York Post (October 31, 1942); "Pope Is Said to Believe Peace Hinges on Total Defeat of Axis," *Washington Evening Star* (October 31, 1942).

67. A. Cicognani October 28, 1942, letter to M.C. Taylor (Taylor Papers, FDR Library). *See also* Conway, *supra* note 33, p. 93. For the British government's exasperation regarding the Vatican's pleas vis-à-vis bombing, *see* Chadwick, *supra* note 39, p. 216.

68. Both Taylor November 2, 1942, letters to FDR are in the Taylor Papers at the FDR Library.

69. In the interim, Secretary of State Hull had opposed a course of action "independent" of the British. Hull, *supra* note 1, p. 1560.

70. November 30, 1942, memorandum for the President (Taylor Papers at the FDR Library).

71. FDR December 4, 1942, letter to M.C. Taylor (Taylor Papers, FDR Library). Hull had drafted FDR's response to Taylor. C. Hull December 3, 1942, letter to FDR (Taylor Papers, FDR Library). At Taylor's request, Ambassador Winant sent to Welles a memorandum regarding the October 5 dinner party at 10 Downing Street. J. Winant December 8, 1942, memorandum to S. Welles (Taylor Papers, FDR Library).

72. On November 25, the *New York Herald Tribune*'s front-page headline read: "Wise Says Hitler Has Ordered 4,000,000 Jews Slain in 1942." On that same day, the *Chicago Daily Tribune* (on page 4) reported: "2 Million Jews Slain by Nazis, Dr. Wise Avers." B. Welles, *supra* note 24, p. 231; Erbelding, *supra* note 43, p. 293 n.23.

73. The U.S. version of the Allies' Joint Declaration can be accessed online at the Jewish Virtual Library. Soviet officials added a sentence in the statement issued from London indicating the victims "reckoned in many hundreds of thousands." C. Hull December 11, 1942, cable to London (National Archives and Records Administration); Chadwick, *supra* note 39, p. 217. The *New York Times* ran a front-page headline on December 18, 1942: "11 Allies Condemn Nazi War on Jews."

74. Hull, *supra* note 1, p. 1560; Evangelista, *supra* note 60, pp. 289, 302 n.65.

75. Hull, *supra* note 1, pp. 1560-61, Conway, *supra* note 33, p. 93 n.30.

76. FDR December 30, 1942, letter to F. La Guardia ("in regard to making Rome an Open City, I hope for good news soon."); E. Roosevelt, *supra* note 8, p. 1383. *See also* Fogarty I, *supra* note 20, p. 288.

77. Hull, *supra* note 1, p. 1562.

78. Conway, *supra* note 33, p. 93. Interestingly, despite Professor Evangelista's blanket conclusion regarding Taylor's "failed" diplomacy on this issue (*see* Chapter XI, pp. 171-72, note 21), he makes no reference to FDR's December 18 memorandum to Hull or Halifax's change of position in January 1943.

79. S. Welles December 23, 1942, letter to FDR (with attached telegram, transmitted on December 26, 1942) (Taylor Papers, FDR Library). FDR's December 1, 1942, letter can be found at E. Roosevelt, *supra* note 8, pp. 1373-74.

80. Chadwick, *supra* note 39, p. 217; Blet, *supra* note 11, pp. 160-61. See *supra* note 73.

81. Chadwick, *supra* note 39, p. 218; Blet, *supra* note 11, p. 161; Phayer, *supra* note 43, p. 53; Tittmann, *supra* note 11, p. 123; A. Rhodes, *The Vatican in the Age of Dictators (1922-1945)*, p. 272 (Holt, Rinehart & Winston 1973).

82. December 25, 1942, p. 16 ("The Pope's Verdict").

83. Mussolini: "The Vicar of God ought never to open his mouth." Chadwick, *supra* note 39, p. 218. The Germans fumed that the Pope "virtually accuses the German people of injustice toward the Jews, and he makes himself the spokesman of the Jews, who are war criminals." Blet, *supra* note 11, p. 161; Chadwick, *supra* note 39, pp. 218-19. Ribbentrop, believing the Pope was abandoning neutrality, ordered the German Ambassador in Rome, Von Bergen, to threaten retaliation. The Pope, to Von Bergen's face, told him "he did not care what happened to himself; but that a struggle between Church and State could have only one outcome, the defeat of the State." Von Bergen also reported back to Ribbentrop: "Pacelli is no more sensible to threats than we are." Chadwick, *supra* note 39, p. 218; Rhodes, *supra* note 81, pp. 273-74. Ribbentrop should not have been surprised by the Pope's response, having received a tongue lashing in March of 1940 for Nazi atrocities against Christians and Jews in a private audience with the Pope. On March 14, 1940, the *New York Times* headlined this meeting "Jews' Rights Defended" ("The Pontiff, in burning words he spoke to Herr Ribbentrop about religious persecutions, also came to the defense of the Jews in Germany and Poland."). See M. Gilbert, "Hitler's Pope," *The American Spectator* (August 18, 2006). Later, in 1943 with the fall of Mussolini, Hitler contemplated kidnapping the Pope. D. Kurzman, *A Special Mission: Hitler's Secret Plot to Seize the Vatican and Kidnap Pope Pius XII* (DaCapo Press 2007).

84. Chadwick, *supra* note 39, p. 219; Blet, *supra* note 11, p. 161. Tittmann met with the Pope on December 30, 1942. As Tittmann reported back to the State Department, the Pope believed his words were clear enough "to satisfy all those who had been insisting in the past that he utter some word of condemnation of the Nazi atrocities." When Tittmann demurred, the Pope "seemed surprised when I told him I thought there were some who did not share his belief." The Pope's reply was that "he thought it was plain to everyone that he was referring to the Poles, Jews and hostages when he declared that hundreds of thousands of persons had been killed or tortured through no fault of their own because of their race or nationality." He further told Tittmann: "when talking of atrocities he could not name the Nazis without at the same time mentioning the Bolsheviks

and this he thought might not be wholly pleasing to the Allies." Tittmann signed off his report with: "Taken as a whole [the Pope] thought his message should be welcomed by the American people and I agreed with him." Tittmann, *supra* note 11, pp. 123-24. In a 1961 speech, Tittmann amplified upon his December 30 audience with the Pope, while basically reiterating the substance of his 1942 report back to Washington. *Id.* pp. 124-25.

85. C. Rittner & J. Roth, *Pope Pius XII and the Holocaust*, p. 4 (Leicester University Press 2002). This "lightning rod" posits two polar opposite camps regarding the Pope's role vis-à-vis the Holocaust. In one camp, Pius XII was Hitler's Pope. *See, e.g.,* J. Cornwell, *Hitler's Pope: The Secret History of Pius XII* (Penguin 1999); M. Phayer, *The Catholic Church and the Holocaust* (Indiana University Press 2000); S. Zucotti, *Under His Very Windows: The Vatican and Holocaust in Italy* (Yale University Press 2001), D. Goldhagen, *A Moral Reckoning: The Role of the Catholic Church in the Holocaust and Its Unfulfilled Duty of Repair* (Knopf 2002). In the other camp, the Pope has been defamed and instead, by his moral leadership and conduct, he should be canonized. D. Dalin, *The Myth of Hitler's Pope: How Pope Pius XII Rescued Jews from the Nazis* (Regnery 2005); R. Rychlak, *Hitler, the War, and the Pope* (Our Sunday Visitor 2010); G. Thomas, *The Pope's Jews: The Vatican's Secret Plan to Save Jews From the Nazis* (St. Martin's Press 2012); M. Reibling, *Church of Spies: The Pope's Secret War Against Hitler* (Basic Books 2015). It is not the goal of this biography of Taylor to try to resolve this "lightning rod" debate. However, perhaps the nuanced views of Tittmann, who was in the Vatican from when it was surrounded for thousands of miles in every direction by totalitarian regimes from 1941 (and when America had made no significant military contribution to defeating the Axis powers) until Rome was liberated in June of 1944, should be given weight in evaluating what the Pope could/should have said and done in 1942 and thereafter. Tittmann, *supra* note 11, pp. 94-96, 118-20. Furthermore, it is encouraging—for those who want to try to understand the "messy middle" of complex historical events—that one of the anti-Pius XII authors—Michael Phayer—subsequently published a more nuanced book setting forth his revised views of the Pope's role vis-à-vis the Holocaust. M. Phayer, *Pius XII: The Holocaust and the Cold War* (Indiana University Press 2008) (*e.g.,* pp. 53-64: regarding the 1942 Christmas Message, the Pope "did not keep silent. The … address assuaged negative opinion about Pius XII in the western hemisphere and directly led the bold Dutch Church to challenge the Nazi Holocaust.") For the most recent historiography on this matter, *see* D. Kertzer, *The Pope at War: The Secret History of Pope Pius XII, Mussolini, and Hitler* (Random House 2022). In any event, this biography will only detail what Taylor did vis-à-vis the Vatican in this area, as well as the other areas in which he made important contributions.

CHAPTER XIII

1943: Work in Washington and Deposing Mussolini

Between January 14 and 24 of 1943, FDR and his military advisors met with Winston Churchill and his military advisors in Casablanca. The ostensible purpose of the conference was to plot the next steps in the war (e.g., invading Sicily, opening up a second front in Western Europe). At a press conference on the last day, FDR announced that "peace can come to the world only by the total elimination of German and Japanese war power.... The elimination of German, Japanese, and Italian war power means the unconditional surrender of Germany, Italy, and Japan."[1] Some observers thought this inflexible policy was a mistake[2]; and one of those included the pope, who labeled the demand as "idiotissima!"—the pope and his advisors believed it would not only destroy Italy and Germany but also ensure Russian domination of Europe after the war.[3] As will be documented, the disconnect between the Pope's September 22, 1942, memorandum to Myron Taylor and FDR (as a result) being emboldened to issue his "unconditional surrender" demand at Casablanca would create significant diplomatic work for Taylor until the end of World War II.

By the end of that same month, Cordell Hull's relationship with Sumner Welles had reached a breaking point (ultimately, it would lead to Welles' forced resignation).[4] One immediate effect of that breakdown was that Hull assumed leadership of the Subcommittee on Political Problems that was fleshing out a postwar international body.[5] Thereafter, Taylor was one of a small group of men Hull took to the White House on a regular basis to work on the proposed structure and workings of that organization with the president.[6]

Taylor was also very busy in the winter, spring, and summer of 1943 with respect to economic postwar planning—the newly constituted Taylor Committee formally replaced two separate economic subcommittees in April of 1943.[7] Designed to facilitate intergovernmental cooperation between cabinet agencies, the Taylor Committee's broad mandate included agriculture, aviation, international monetary standards, creation of a world bank, trade agreements, inland transportation, power, labor standards and social security, telecommunications, and food distribution.[8]

While all of that work was important, Taylor did not lose sight of the deteriorating political situation in Italy and its implications for a possible cessation of hostilities between America and that country. In fact, Taylor was intent on "sow[ing] the seeds of getting rid of Mussolini's government."[9] On February 18, the Apostolic Delegate cabled the Vatican that Taylor had told him several times that the "American government will find it useful to have some reliable information on the form any new [Italian] government would take, on retaining the royalty, and on who might be the prime minister."[10] Initially, because of a concern that the Holy See would be seen as interfering in the country's internal political affairs, the Vatican put off responding to Taylor's inquiries.[11] But as the war in North Africa wound down and it seemed probable that the Anglo-Allies would soon turn their full (military) attention to Italy, the Vatican pivoted and decided to become involved.[12]

On May 12, Cardinal Luigi Maglione, on behalf of the pope, met with Count Ciano. Il Duce's son-in-law expressed his frustration at the box in which the Italian government found itself, but ultimately reported back to Maglione that Mussolini believed "under the present conditions there is no alternative, and Italy will continue to wage war."[13] As to the United States, the Vatican moved on two tracks. On May 19, the pope wrote to the president, recalling Taylor's representations to him in both 1941 and 1942 that "America has no hatred of the Italian people," and expressing a simple "hope and prayer" that they and their "treasured shrines of Religion and Art" would be spared from destruction.[14] On May 21, in a memorandum worked on by the Pope Pius XII, Cardinal Maglione, and Monsignor Tardini, the Vatican sent its response to Taylor's inquiries. It had four points: (1) the Holy See wants to remain above and outside of international power politics; (2) the Italian people continue to be attached to the monarchy; (3) it belongs to the King, and not outsiders, to chose his ministers; and (4) the Vatican had no names to suggest.[15]

As an interesting footnote to history, in the midst of this critical diplomacy Winston Churchill was visiting Washington and was scheduled to make his second address to a joint session of Congress on May 18, 1943. FDR requested seven tickets for the presidential box. Grace Tully, per the president's directive, handed out the coveted tickets to Mr. and Mrs. Taylor, the Duke and Duchess of Windsor, Lord Leathers (the British Minister of Transport), and John Rutherford (the step-son of the president's long-time mistress, Lucy Mercer Rutherford) and his wife.[16] Given Taylor's nineteenth-century Victorian sense of propriety,[17] one can only imagine what he would have thought about his friend (FDR) and his sense of propriety.[18]

On May 28, Taylor had a frank, one-on-one meeting with the Apostolic Delegate.[19] That caused Archbishop Cicognani to fire off a historic cable to the Vatican the next day. He reported that Taylor told him Italy faced one of its gravest hours in history, and that the Vatican had to tell "whoever has the means for acting" that it was urgent for the Italian people to separate themselves from Mussolini and the Germans and to form a new government. While the United States was prepared to negotiate with a new government (and not bomb Rome), if a new government was not formed massive destruction of Italy would follow.[20] Because Taylor's message had the tone of an ultimatum, and given the Vatican's difficult relationship with Mussolini (and the Holy See's ongoing fear of what would happen to Rome), the Pope and his advisers reacted cautiously.[21]

On June 4, the Vatican cabled Cicognani: "The Holy Father would like to know whether this conversation took place with the agreement of, or the consent of, the President or the Government or if only, as stated, upon his [Taylor's] own initiative. It will be very delicate now to speak specifically of the new government because it is a pending internal matter that depends *upon the will of the Sovereign.*"[22] That same day Taylor met with Cicognani and also gave him a document responding to the June 4 cable; Taylor affirmed that he had "spoke[n] only upon my initiative."[23]

When Taylor reported to FDR on the Pope's message and his response, the president said: "Myron[,] this is the first break in the war. It is wonderful."[24] What both men understood by the Vatican's response was that the Holy See was now prepared to contact King Emmanuel (the Italian Sovereign) to try to move Italy away from Mussolini and the Axis powers. At FDR's instruction Taylor went back to Cicognani and reported that he, Taylor, was prepared to go back to the Vatican at FDR's direction and serve as an intermediary between the Holy See and Washington regarding "every initiative undertaken by Italy to extricate itself from the war."[25]

Two days later the pope instructed Tardini to draft a message for the King of Italy. Before it could be delivered (and while the Vatican was still debating how best to approach Victor Emmanuel III), FDR in a press conference on June 11 directly addressed the Italian people. He told them that if they deposed Mussolini and the Germans were removed from Italy, then the Allies would ensure the Italian people could choose their own government and ultimately Italy could take its place in the family of nations.[26] This, as Taylor explained to Cicognani, was in fact an ultimatum (but one that did not include the term "unconditional surrender").[27]

On June 16, the president formally responded to the pope's May 19 letter. Drafted by Hull, it incorporated the substance of Admiral Leahy's memorandum of June 14 (which noted the British intention to bomb "military objectives such as the railroad yards and facilities in Rome ... [and that] our general staff had agreed with the British"). Noting that Americans valued "the religious shrines and the historical monuments of Italy," FDR pledged that "[a]ttacks against Italy are limited, to the extent humanly possible, to military objectives." Furthermore, "our aviators are thoroughly informed as to the location of the Vatican and have been specifically instructed to prevent bombs from falling within the Vatican City."[28]

The following day, papal representatives met with King Emmanuel. He was told that "the president's [June 11, 1943] message also corresponds to the intentions of the Allies, which the Holy See knows from an official source [i.e., Taylor]."[29] The King was also told that the Vatican had informed FDR that it does not intervene in Italy's internal political affairs, and left such matters to the monarchy, who "is well regarded and loved by the Italian people, and the government depends upon Your Majesty." At that point, the King smiled and said, "I am not like the pope."[30]

The Vatican's concerns about bombing only heightened as it was becoming evident that the Allies would soon take a military offensive somewhere in Italy.[31] That caused Taylor to send a brief note to FDR on June 28, "wondering if we were to say to the Vatican that if the Holy See would guarantee that all military installations, activities, and personnel were removed, and the use of the railroad facilities for all military purposes were abandoned, the City will not be bombed."[32] Taylor's "wondering" prompted FDR to write Hull on the same day, citing to Taylor's language in an effort to have Rome declared an "open city." Noting that this "would require the cooperative consent of the British," FDR added: "I agree with Myron that it is worthwhile discussing."[33]

But the bombing issue was still not resolved when, on July 10, the war was joined in Italy with the Allies' invasion of Sicily.[34]

Shortly thereafter, a number of Italian churches in Turin and Catania were destroyed by Allied bombers. And then on July 19 (after having dropped leaflets the day before warning of bombing the next day, mainly to be aimed at the railway marshalling yards), British planes bombed Rome, hitting a number of residential parts of the city, killing more than 1,500 people, and heavily damaging the Basilica of San Lorenzo Fuori le Mura. The Pope not only issued a statement condemning the bombing but he also visited the bombed basilica and prayed among the ruins (a gesture that received worldwide attention).[35] On July 24, Taylor reported to FDR and Hull of a meeting he had had with Cicognani regarding the bombing. He reported that the "Pope's statement ... was intentionally moderate and phrased so that it might not be used by the Nazis or Fascists to the disadvantage of the Allies.... [T]he Pope will continue his effort ... to persuade the Government to remove everything of a military character from Rome. He does not believe that the possibility of the Holy Father being a medium for removal of Italy from the war is at an end."[36] But the Pope's earlier intervention with the King, the Allies' rapid advances in Sicily, and the July 19 bombing of Rome made Cicognani's predictions a tad moot; on that same day in Rome, King Emmanuel "asked" for Mussolini's resignation (he was subsequently imprisoned) and requested Marshal Badoglio to form a new government.[37]

On July 26, Taylor met with Cicognani and later that day reported to FDR and Hull on the substance of this conversation. The Apostolic Delegate foresaw the "ultimate withdrawal of Italy from the war," but also predicted difficulties with the German Army on the mainland of Italy. Taylor noted that "[i]t seems obvious that the negotiation medium now can only be General Eisenhower and the King and/or Marshal Badoglio." And in the context of seeking to preserve the Italian fleet (the fourth largest in the world) for Allied use, Taylor observed that a "negotiated peace" with Italy (as opposed to "unconditional surrender") might yield a better result, in a shorter time, and save "the lives of thousands of men."[38]

Initially, Badoglio vowed to continue the war effort, but after extended negotiations between General Eisenhower and the new Italian government, Italy officially surrendered on September 8. That good news, however, was accompanied by the corresponding bad news that the German Army was entering Rome and would soon be in control of the city.[39] Just before each of those events, Taylor had been lobbying the Apostolic Delegate to have the pope use every effort to protect Italian Jews from being evacuated.[40]

With Rome now effectively cut off from the outside world (and the King and Badoglio having fled Rome), Taylor's attention for the remainder of 1943 was mainly redirected to postwar planning.[41] At Hull's request, he sent on to the Secretary of State two documents regarding how best to reorganize the subcommittees to ensure better harmony and work product, with authority and responsibility for policy determination more "clearly defined." Among other things, he also questioned whether he should remain as Chair of the Economic Subcommittee.[42] He did remain, however, chairing (among other things) a meeting with a British economic delegation concerning multilateral trade issues on September 20 in Washington.[43]

Taylor's last efforts during 1943 were directed to helping shape postwar planning vis-à-vis Russia. On October 6, he sent a detailed memorandum to Hull outlining the "political, security and economic problems" looming in shaping a peaceful world with Russia, a country that (1) wanted "her territorial ambitions ... satisfied," (2) wanted "her security ... assured," and (3) "wanted her economy ... not to adversely affected." Keys to addressing these daunting issues, in Taylor's view, were (1) Russia committing to "certain restraints" on its ambitions, (2) satisfactorily dealing with the disarming of Germany, (3) determining what role the Allies should play in allowing for Germany's economic recovery, (4) defining what role (if any) Russia would play in an international monetary system, (5) to what extent Russia would want "foreign capital assistance (loans)," (6) what trade and commodity arrangements could be reached with Russia, and (7) whether

Russia would participate in "regional economic arrangements …, especially in East or Central Europe." Taylor ended his prescient memorandum with an old, familiar theme: "It would seem helpful, in the interest of every high stake in the post-war world, even though intangible, for Russia to clarify whether her policy toward religion will be such as to eliminate the old antagonism and fear against her which arose from her official atheism."[44]

Notes

1. R. Atkinson, *An Army at Dawn*, pp. 293-94 (Henry Holt 2002). Roosevelt added: "It does *not* mean the destruction of the population of Germany, Italy, or Japan, but it does mean the destruction of the philosophies in those countries which are based on conquest and subjugation of other people." *Id.* Churchill was surprised that FDR made the "unconditional surrender" demand public in that press conference, and there is evidence that suggests he was not in favor of including Italy in the demand. *Id.* Following up with a radio address to the American public on February 12, FDR (seeming to invoke the December 17, 1942, joint declaration by the Allies) explained that "we mean no harm to the common people of the Axis nations. But we do mean to impose punishment and retribution on their guilty, barbaric leaders." *Id.*

2. For example, U.S. General Albert Wedemeyer, a key War Department planner, warned that "unconditional surrender would unquestionably compel the Germans to fight to the very last." Atkinson, *supra* note 1, p. 294.

3. P. Kent, "The War Aims of the Papacy, 1938-45," *FDR, the Vatican, and the Roman Catholic Church in America, 1933-1945*, p. 166 (ed. D. Woolner & R. Kurial) (Palgrave 2003); J. Conway, "The Vatican and U.S. Wartime Diplomacy." *FDR, the Vatican, and the Roman Catholic Church in America, 1933-1945*, pp. 147-48 (ed. D. Woolner & R. Kurial) (Palgrave 2003); G. Fogarty, *The Vatican and the American Hierarchy From 1870 to 1965*, p. 291 (Anton Hiersemann 1982); H. Tittmann, *Inside the Vatican of Pius XII*, pp. 146-47 (Doubleday 2004).

4. B. Welles, *Sumner Welles: FDR's Global Strategist*, pp. 341-54 (St. Martin's Press 1997).

5. C. Hull, *The Memoirs of Cordell Hull*, p. 1638 (Macmillan 1948).

6. *Id.* p. 1693. Hull's memoirs give a good feel for how this work developed over time. *Id.* pp. 1638-55.

7. Organization and Procedures of Committee on Post-War Foreign Economic Policy, April 2, 1943 (Taylor Papers, FDR Library); *Postwar Foreign Policy*

Preparations 1939-1945, pp. 9-11 (State Department 1949); C. Hull May 4, 1943, letter to M.C. Taylor (Taylor Papers, Cornell University).

8. *See, e.g.,* June 24, 1943, Memorandum re Procedure in Discussions Concerning Monetary Stabilization (Taylor Papers, FDR Library). With respect to the issue of postwar food distribution in a world with so many displaced people, FDR—after consulting with Hull, Welles, Taylor, Bowman, and Pasvolsky—held a press conference on February 23, 1943, to reveal the postwar plans underway to deal with the problem. *Id.* p. 12.

9. Transcript of Meeting of Protestant Clergymen with Myron Taylor at Union Club (New York City, October 20, 1947) at p. 30 (Taylor Papers, Cornell University).

10. P. Blet, *Pius XII and the Second World War*, p. 203 (Paulist Press 1999). At this same time Archbishop Spellman had traveled from the United States to the Vatican and spent approximately two weeks there conferring with Church officials. *See* FDR February 7, 1943, memorandum to Hull, *FDR: His Personal Letters*, pp. 1399-1400 (ed. E. Roosevelt) (Duell, Sloan and Pearce 1947); Fogarty, *supra* note 3, pp. 291-93; G. Fogarty, "Roosevelt and the American Catholic Hierarchy," *FDR, the Vatican, and the Roman Catholic Church in America, 1933-1945*, pp. 32-33 (ed. D. Woolner & R. Kurial) (Palgrave 2003). The only thing he later reported in writing to the president about his conversations with the pope was that he (the pope) was deeply grateful for Taylor, for whom he had the "highest esteem and appreciation." Fogarty *supra* note 3, p. 293. About the deteriorating political and economic situation in Italy, Spellman was quite detailed in what he told FDR, with "anti-German feeling … very strong and deep," and the "only obstacles to peace that I see are Mussolini and the fact that if peace was obtained, then the Germans would retaliate by bombing Rome." *Id.* With respect to the treatment of Croatian Jews, Spellman had received assurances that the Vatican was "intervening" on their behalf. *Id.* n.46.

11. Blet, *supra* note 10, p. 203. At the same time, Taylor was in frequent contact with the Apostolic Delegate regarding efforts to help Jews in Europe. *E.g.,* M.C. Taylor March 1, 1943, letter to A. Cicognani (deportation of non-Italian Jews) (Taylor Papers, Cornell University); M.C. Taylor March 22, 1943, letter to S. Welles (the pope's follow-up regarding the March 1, 1943, letter) (Taylor Papers, Cornell University); A. Cicognani March 6, 1942, cable to L. Maglione (Taylor appeal regarding the deportation of Yugoslavian Jews) (Taylor Papers, Cornell University); M.C. Taylor March 26, 1943, cable to the State Department (regarding the treatment of Polish, Bulgarian, and Romanian Jews) (Taylor Papers, Cornell University) [This document is also on display in the Holocaust Museum in Washington, DC.]; A. Cicognani May 15, 1943, letter to H. Morgenthau (regarding the Pope's interest "in the persecuted Jews in Europe") (copying Taylor, who

thanked Cicognani in a May 18, 1943, letter for the "careful and sympathetic attention which your Excellency and the Holy See have given this difficult matter") (both documents are in the Taylor Papers at Cornell).

12. Blet, *supra* note 10, p. 203; J. Conway "Myron C. Taylor's Mission to the Vatican 1940-1950," *Church History*, p. 94 (Vol. 44, March 1975).

13. *Id.* pp. 203-04. See M.C. Taylor May 14, 1943, memorandum to FDR (suggesting he go to Madrid, Lisbon, or the Vatican "to be in closer touch with developments") (Taylor Papers, Cornell University); FDR May 21, 1943, memorandum to C. Hull (with handwritten "Tell M.T. not time just now") (Taylor Papers, FDR Library).

14. Tittmann, *supra* note 3, pp. 147-48; Conway, *supra* note 12, p. 93; Blet, *supra* note 10, p. 204. On May 14, 1943, Taylor wrote a memorandum to FDR detailing "American prestige in Italy of late" as a result of "machine gunning, from low altitude, civilians on roads and in the streets by American bombers." (Taylor Papers, Cornell University).

15. Conway, *supra* note 12, p. 94; Blet, *supra* note 10, pp. 204-05. Interestingly, the pope appears to have been ready to suggest some names, but Tardini objected. Blet, *supra* note 10, p. 205.

16. R. Willis, *FDR and Lucy: Lovers and Friends,* pp. 113-14 (Routledge 2004); *see also* J. Persico, *Franklin & Lucy,* p. 290 (Random House 2008).

17. *See* Chapter VII, pp. 89-92, note 64.

18. Also during this time period Taylor was advising FDR regarding a proposed trip to Rome by Joseph Davies, the former Ambassador to Russia. In his memoir and the film based thereon (*Mission to Moscow*), Taylor reported that Davies had baldly asserted that "religion in Russia was in fact free. This ... is not in accord with the facts." Accordingly, Taylor suggested that Davies "refrain" from making any public statement(s) on this subject, "making it less difficult for you to deal with this question in due course." M.C. Taylor May 6, 1943, memorandum to FDR (Taylor Papers, FDR Library).

19. *See* M.C. Taylor's May 28, 1943, memorandum (Taylor Papers, Cornell University).

20. Blet, *supra* note 10, p. 205; Conway, *supra* note 12, p. 94.

21. Blet, *supra* note 10, p. 205; Conway, *supra* note 12, pp. 94-95. The Pope told Tardini it was necessary to contact the King (secretly) and tell him of Taylor's message. *Id.*

22. The Vatican's June 4, 1943, cable is in the Taylor Papers at Cornell. At the same time, Taylor was asking the Vatican to intervene to protect Dr. William Filderman, President of the Union of Jewish Congregations of Roumania, who was under house arrest in Bucharest and was threatened with deportation to a concentration camp. *See* M.C. Taylor June 2, 1943, letter to A. Cicognani; A. Cicognani

June 3, 1943, letter to M.C. Taylor (Taylor Papers, Cornell University). *See also* R. Trisco, "The Department of State and the Apostolic Delegate in Washington During World War II," *FDR, the Vatican, and the Roman Catholic Church in America, 1932-1945*, pp. 239-40 (ed. D. Woolner & R. Kurial) (Palgrave 2003).

23. Both Taylor's June 4, 1943, memorandum of his June 4 conversation and his June 4, 1943, memorandum to Cicognani are in the Taylor Papers at Cornell.

24. Meeting with Protestant Clergymen, p. 32.

25. *Id.*; Blet, *supra* note 10, pp. 205-06. Interestingly, a June 4, 1943, State Department memorandum on Taylor's initiative referenced a second option regarding unconditional surrender, which was never acted upon. (Taylor Papers, Cornell University).

26. Blet, *supra* note 10, p. 206; Conway, *supra* note 12, p. 95.

27. *Id.* The next day Cicognani not only reported Taylor's comment to the Vatican, he also wrote to Taylor: "The Holy See must remain outside the competition of politics." Because the Italian people were "very attached to the monarchy," he must appoint the premier—"an imposed premier would not be acceptable to the Italian people." A. Cicognani June 12, 1943, memorandum to M.C. Taylor (Taylor Papers, Cornell University).

28. C. Hull June 15, 1943, letter to FDR (with attachments) (Taylor Papers, FDR Library); Conway, *supra* note 12, p. 95. On the Hull draft, FDR made handwritten notations and sent them to "Former Naval Person" (aka Churchill), explaining "His letter to me was not a request not to bomb Rome but he spoke of the historic places and also spoke of the Holy See which I suppose includes the churches outside the Vatican." Professor Evangelista, in his article concluding that Taylor's efforts vis-à-vis bombing constituted "failed diplomacy," puts forth the Leahy memorandum as front and center proof of that "failure." M. Evangelista, "Myron Taylor and the Bombing of Rome: The Limits of Law and Diplomacy," *Diplomacy & Statecraft*, pp. 290-91 (June 8, 2020) (*see* Chapter XI, pp. 171-72, note 21; Chapter XII, p. 197, note 78). It seems a bit of a stretch to call a formal pledge by the president *not* to bomb the Vatican as constituting categorical "failed" diplomacy. In any event, the Pope was not mollified by FDR's letter (mostly because of ongoing British insistence *not* to spare the Vatican). On June 25 Cicognani reported to Taylor that if Rome were to be bombed (for whatever reason), "the Holy Father will voice his open protest to the world." A. Cicognani June 25, 1943, memorandum to M.C. Taylor (Taylor Papers, Cornell University).

29. Blet, *supra* note 10, pp. 207.

30. *Id.* p. 207. On the same day of that audience with King Emmanuel, a small group of U.S. military and State Department officials—and Taylor—began meetings to give "urgent consideration to terms for Italy that had been drafted in

the War Department." *Postwar Foreign Policy Preparations 1939-1945*, pp. 131-32 (State Department 1949).

31. Evangelista, *supra* note 28, p. 291; Tittmann, *supra* note 3, p. 149.

32. M.C. Taylor June 28, 1943, memorandum to FDR (Taylor Papers, Cornell University); Evangelista, *supra* note 28, p. 291.

33. E. Roosevelt, *supra* note 10, pp. 1432-33; Tittmann, *supra* note 3, pp. 151-52. Curiously, the FDR June 28, 1943, memorandum does not appear in Professor Evangelista's article. Hull replied on June 29, citing the practical difficulties of the Vatican ensuring "the carrying out of the various commitments," especially given that the Germans and Mussolini "have not scruples particularly in this critical moment." C. Hull June 29, 1943, memorandum to FDR (Taylor Papers, FDR Library). On that same day, Taylor met with Cicognani asking for the Vatican's help vis-à-vis Jewish refugees in Italy. (M.C. Taylor June 29, 1943, memorandum to A. Cicognani; Taylor Papers, Cornell University). The Apostolic Delegate responded on July 3 that he was "confident that the Holy See would do everything possible to forestall further calamities for these unfortunate victims of the war." (Cicognani July 3, 1943, memorandum to Taylor; Taylor Papers, Cornell University.) *See also* Trisco, *supra* note 22, p. 240. Interestingly, at the same moment Taylor was trying to come up with ways to save the Vatican from aerial bombing, he was also interacting with the Holy See on the creation of a "Hebrew Home" in Palestine. On June 24, he sent to Hull, Welles, and Long a June 22 letter from Cicognani that reflected the Vatican's lack of enthusiasm for a "Hebrew Home" there. In that letter, three objections were noted: (1) it "would be a severe blow to the religious attachment of Catholics to this land," (2) the Jews did not have an absolute right to land "they left nineteen centuries before," and (3) with the geopolitical problems it would create with Arabs, "it would not be too difficult to find a more fitting territory than Palestine." (M.C. Taylor June 24, 1943, memorandum to C. Hull, et al. (with attachment); Taylor Papers, Cornell University).

34. J. Holland, *Sicily '43: The First Assault on Fortress Europe* (Atlantic Monthly 2020); R. Atkinson, *The Day of Battle: The War in Sicily and Italy, 1943-1944* (Abacus 2003). FDR on that same day sent a message to the Pope assuring him that "[t]hroughout the period of operations, the neutral state of the Vatican City, as well as the Papal domains throughout Italy, will be respected." Tittmann, *supra* note 3, pp. 157-58. This did little to assuage the concerns of the Vatican. *Id.*; Conway, *supra* note 12, p. 95. *See* A. Cicognani July 15, 1944, letter to M.C. Taylor (Taylor Papers, FDR Library). Just before the Sicily invasion, FDR was taken up with two Taylor-related issues. The first was informing Averell Harriman at the U.S. Embassy in London that he believed "the proposed trip of Myron" to the Vatican "will give rise to understandable rumors and might generally be misconstrued by the American public and our Allies." FDR July 7, 1943, cable to Harriman

(Taylor Papers, FDR Library). Hull had previously advised the president on this matter, concluding that "Mr. Taylor's happy relations with the Apostolic Delegate in Washington make him particularly useful here." C. Hull July 1, 1943, memorandum to FDR (Taylor Papers, FDR Library). The second was the president's July 7 request that Taylor continue his work on the Intergovernmental Committee on Refugees, given the "refugee problems created by the enemy powers." FDR July 7, 1943, letter to M.C. Taylor (Taylor Papers, FDR Library and Taylor Papers, Cornell University). Taylor responded in two letters (July 13 and July 14). Perhaps foreshadowing what would take place in 1944 with the creation of the War Refugee Board, Taylor bluntly told the president that he had "not been in harmony with much that had taken place" with the ICR, especially in the "recent past" (Taylor had previously declined to chair the U.S. delegation to the April 1943 Bermuda Conference on refugee issues, believing it would "likely fail" to produce results—he was, unfortunately, correct in that assessment); in the second letter, he took up FDR's suggestion of a designee to do the day-to-day ICR work and nominated Robert Pell, a State Department official who had worked with Taylor for several years. M.C. Taylor July 13, 1943, and July 14, 1943, letters to FDR (Taylor Papers, Cornell University). Not surprisingly, Pell was quite frustrated by Long's "unrelenting attack on the work" of the ICR. R. Breitman & A. Lichtman, *FDR and the Jews*, pp. 176, 221 (Belknap Press 2013). The president responded to Taylor's letters on July 29, thanking him for staying on the ICR and approving Pell. FDR July 29, 1943, letter to M.C. Taylor (Taylor Papers, Cornell University).

35. Conway, *supra* note 12, pp. 95-96; Blet, *supra* note 10, pp. 207-08; Tittmann, *supra* note 3, pp. 162-72; Evangelista, *supra* note 28, p. 294. Remarkably, the Basilica's mosaic floor tiles were recovered and set ultimately back in place. D. Larkin, "Echoes From the Roman Ghetto," *New York Times*, T1 (July 14, 2013).

36. M.C. Taylor July 24, 1943, memorandum to FDR and C. Hull (Taylor Papers, FDR Library).

37. Conway, *supra* note 12, p. 96; Blet, *supra* note 10, p. 209: Evangelista, *supra* note 28, pp. 296-97; Fogarty, *supra* note 10, p. 35; R. Katz, *The Battle for Rome*, p. 21 (Simon & Schuster 2003).

38. M.C. Taylor July 26, 1943, memorandum to FDR and C. Hull (Taylor Papers, FDR Library).

39. Conway, *supra* note 12, p. 86; Blet, *supra* note 10, pp. 211-14; Katz, *supra* note 37, pp. 29-30; Tittmann, *supra* note 3, pp. 174-89.

40. A. Cicognani August 28, 1943, letter to M.C. Taylor (Taylor Papers, Cornell University); *see also* Evangelista, *supra* note 28, p. 298. As with the Holocaust generally (*see* Chapter XII, p. 199, note 85), the Pope and the Church's role in protecting/saving the Jews of Rome and in nearby areas is a subject of heated debate. E.g., S. Zuccatti, *Under His Very Windows: The Vatican and Holocaust in Italy*

(Yale University Press 2001); M. Phayer, *Pius XII: The Holocaust and the Cold War*, pp. 85-89 (Indiana University Press 2008); Katz, *supra* note 37, pp. 61-85, 395-96; Blet, *supra* note 10, pp. 214-18; Tittmann, *supra* note 3, p. 190. As with the broader debate, it is not the goal of the Taylor biography to try to resolve this debate.

41. FDR August 18, 1943, letter to M.C. Taylor ("just as well" safe conduct could not be arranged to allow Taylor to return to the Vatican) (Taylor Papers, FDR Library). During the period between September 1943 and June 1944—while the Germans and the Allies were in fierce combat in and around Rome (and the papal villa at Castel Gandolfo was bombed on four occasions) relations between the Church (in America and in Rome) and the U.S. government were at a low ebb. Fogarty, *supra* note 10, pp. 36-37; Conway, *supra* note 12, pp. 96-98; Trisco, *supra* note 22, pp. 229-39.

42. M.C. Taylor August 14, 1943, memorandum to C. Hull (Taylor Papers, FDR Library). Just before Welles left the State Department (August 22, 1943), Vice President Wallace asked him if Taylor was doing good work on the Postwar Committee. Welles replied, "Yes, excellent work ... he had grown in stature enormously." (Wallace Oral History at Columbia University). Welles was succeeded as Undersecretary of State by Edward Stettinius, who had been Taylor's protégé at U.S. Steel (and who later succeeded him as CEO in April of 1938). *See* M.C. Taylor November 18, 1943, handwritten note to FDR (Taylor Papers, FDR Library).

43. C. Hull September 3, 1943, memorandum to M.C. Taylor (Taylor Papers, Cornell University); Informal Economic Discussion Meeting at Department of State, Room 474 (September 20, 1943) (Taylor Papers, FDR Library). Taylor chaired similar sessions with Canadian delegations in Washington on January 3-7, 1944, and in New York on February 12-13, 1944. *Postwar Foreign Policy Preparations 1939-1945*, p. 193 (State Department 1949).

44. M.C. Taylor October 6, 1943, memorandum to C. Hull (Taylor Papers, FDR Library). Just as the year was ending Archbishop Mooney was telling Taylor that the Church continued to be highly skeptical about Russia after the war: "Surely ... [FDR] is too wise to fail to see the shadows which the still unresolved enigma of Russia throws across the picture.... [T]o list the Soviet Union among the 'democratic nations' is to invite a reaction of cynicism and disillusionment that can well be fatal to our highest hopes for a good peace." Archbishop Mooney December 13, 1943, letter to M.C. Taylor (Taylor Papers, Cornell University).

CHAPTER XIV

1944: The United Nations and Back to Rome

A ngered and frustrated by the bureaucratic barriers the State Department (i.e., Breckinridge Long) had erected in 1943 to block the Treasury Department's efforts to save 70,000 Romanian Jews—who had hoped to escape on Romanian ships using Vatican insignia—Henry Morgenthau (FDR's Hyde Park neighbor and friend, as well as being the long-serving Secretary of the Treasury) convinced the president to issue Executive Order No. 9417 on January 22, 1944; that order established the War Refugee Board (WRB).[1] With cabinet representation (besides Morgenthau, it included Cordell Hull and Henry Stimson, the Secretary of War) it was hoped that the WRB would be able to take effective and concrete action to somehow save the "victims of enemy persecution" in Europe.[2]

But with "meager resources and authority" (and continued problems with the State Department), the WRB faced long odds.[3] It appears that another obstacle (at least initially) was in its way: Myron Taylor. Although Taylor had proposed the creation of a single international agency in 1942 to deal with the problems of displaced peoples,[4] and notwithstanding the fact that he was clearly disenchanted with the recent performance of the Intergovernmental Committee on Refugees (ICR),[5] Taylor tried to "influence" his former protégé Edward Stettinius, who was now the Undersecretary of State, into defining "the relationship and the future scope" of the WRB and the ICR.[6] Taylor escalated this to the president,[7] who in turn asked Morgenthau and Stettinius to resolve the matter with Taylor. Ultimately, Taylor reported to FDR that the "initial uncertainties" regarding the relationship between the ICR and the WRB had been resolved and "[t]he two groups now find themselves in perfect harmony." But in the May 25 letter containing that report, Taylor also tendered his resignation from the ICR, which FDR accepted on June 5 with "especial regret" and "great reluctance."[8]

At the same time Taylor was raising his bureaucratic concern(s) about the WRB, he was also hard at work on the Subcommittee on Territorial Problems under the leadership of Isaiah Bowman. That group was focused on a topic not unrelated to that of the WRB: what to do with the massive refugee population (approximately 20 million people) that was being created as a result of the war's devastation.

One priority for the Bowman group was to figure out what to do regarding the issue of Palestine. With the formation of a League of Arab States (encouraged by Britain) as background, on March 14, 1944, Taylor wrote a memorandum to Hull, expressing his concern over efforts "to encourage a consolidation of the Arab world." Such efforts, Taylor felt, are "filled with dangers of many sorts." Among Taylor's worries was the fact that "we in this country know all too little about [the Arab world]." He added, with amazing prescience: "Perhaps one thing the world has to fear in the future is the strong aggregation of people bound by ties of blood and religion, especially those who are almost fanatical, now separated into groups and tribes and states, may join themselves together to oppose ... the relative smaller numbers of the Anglo-Saxon world."[9]

Two weeks later Hull responded to Taylor's memorandum. Clearly influenced in his thinking by British Foreign Secretary Anthony Eden, Hull cited at length a 1941 speech by Eden: "It seems to me both natural and right that cultural and economic ties between the Arab countries, yes, and the political ties too, should be strengthened. His Majesty's government for their part will give full support to any scheme that commands general approval." Hull then went on to pooh-pooh Taylor's concerns, opining that "the difficulties existing to Arab unity are far from negligible, and the initial steps in that direction would in all probability be only cultural and economic lines."[10]

Unfortunately, as history has shown, both Hull and Eden were wrong.[11] The year 1945 saw the implementation of the Arab League Pact. Later that year the Arab League boycotted Jewish businesses in Palestine to oppose the formation of Israel. And in 1947, the British withdrew support for its Mandate of Palestine, stating that it was unable to find a solution acceptable to both the Jews and the Arabs. Later that same year, the United Nations opposed the partition of Palestine into two states—one Jewish, one Arab—with Israel declaring independence in 1948.[12] Most historians agree that the contemporary roots of the Arab–Israeli conflict, and probably Muslim extremism, stem from this post–World War II period.[13]

Also at this same time, Taylor informed Hull that he wanted to step away from representing the U.S. government in economic discussions with English delegations.[14] Hull just slotted Taylor into another critical task: ensuring bipartisan support for the rapidly coming-to-fruition plans for the United Nations.

All of the planning for an international organization, which began in 1942, had entered an accelerated phase by the end of 1943. Between December 9, 1943, and July 8, 1944, the original eight-man (later nine-man) group—which included Taylor—met 70 times to hammer out the details of the plan.[15] Hull (and FDR) were determined not to make the mistakes Woodrow Wilson had made in keeping out the political opposition vis-à-vis post-World War I planning and the League of Nations, so the Secretary of State made a conscious effort to bring in Senators of all stripes to discuss the work in progress.[16] Hull also wanted "three of the ablest men in America" (Charles Evans Hughes, retired Chief Justice of the Supreme Court—who had also been Secretary of State and the Republican candidate for president in 1916; John W. Davis, the Democratic candidate for president in 1924—and senior partner of Davis Polk & Wardwell; and Nathan L. Miller, the former Republican governor of New York and long-time general counsel of U.S. Steel) to study the draft of what would become the United Nations; and the man Hull asked on April 19 to act as intermediary with all three was Myron Taylor.[17] Those consultations all were productive to the end work product, but this Taylor biography will focus on only one—the interactions with Hughes.

Taylor was a particularly good choice to consult with Hughes because Hughes had been his favorite law professor when Taylor was at Cornell Law School (and later Taylor would donate the funds to build a residential dormitory at the Law School in Hughes' honor).[18] Hughes, although reluctant to get involved, said he would "do his duty as a citizen."[19] Hughes' first comments related to the size of the Security Council: "As long as the great powers control the decisions as to the use of force, there would not seem any harm in enlarging the number of smaller powers which would be in a position to be consulted and give their views."[20] After a May 5 conference at Hughes' home with all four men, Hughes sent Taylor a memorandum proposing seven specific changes to the proposed charter of the organization.[21] One additional issue needed further work—and it had come up in Hull's meetings with various senators: could the president order American military forces into combat at the request of the Security Council without congressional approval. On May 7, Hull discussed the issue with Hughes. And on May 8, Taylor followed up. Hughes first told Taylor he "could not undertake to give any opinion on constitutional questions." That said, Hughes told Taylor that any provision requiring prior congressional approval before the Security Council could act would emasculate both the charter and the organization. Hughes then offered a historical observation to his student of 50 years before: "Our Presidents have used our armed forces repeatedly without authorization by Congress when they thought the interests of the country required it."[22] Hull subsequently expressed his gratitude for Hughes' "extremely helpful comments," many of which were ultimately adopted in the United Nations Charter.[23]

At the request of FDR and Hull, Taylor was next asked to contact "several eminent Republicans" with ties to Governor Thomas Dewey (the party's presumed presidential nominee in 1944) and share with them the draft of the United Nations plan.[24] Taylor did so, but also reported back to Hull that "a direct approach" to Dewey had not yet been made—"dictated, on second thought, by the doubt whether a definitive statement might not be under some circumstance misused, and that he is only one of several in the field up to the moment.... I am following the matter closely but do not want to make a wrong move at this time which might injure the project."[25] Taylor never got to make another move on this front, however, because he was soon to return to Rome.

Of course, Taylor could not get back until the U.S. Army first had driven the enemy out of the city. By the beginning of June 1944, they were poised to do just that.[26] Just before they did move on Rome, the pope gave an address to the Saint College of Cardinals on June 2 (the feast of St. Eugene). Clearly concerned that Rome might be destroyed in a siege of the city, the pope spoke against a peace based on the spirit of vengeance, and "deprecated the confrontation of the German people with a choice between complete victory or complete destruction, since the dilemma would serve to prolong the war."[27] Already under ongoing pressure from both Great Britain and Russia on his undefined unconditional surrender policy,[28] FDR expressed his displeasure about the pope's June 2 address to Archbishop Spellman.[29] Thus, when Rome fell to Mark Clark's 5th Army on June 5, FDR's first instinct was to get Taylor back to the Vatican to convince the Pope to play ball on what had become a geopolitical hot potato.[30]

On June 7 (the day after D-day), FDR wrote to Stettinius (who was Acting Secretary of State in Hull's absence): "What do

Taylor with General Mark Clark at the U.S. 5th Army
headquarters north of Rome in July 1944

you think of Myron Taylor leaving as soon as possible to go to the
Vatican? I think he might be very useful there. I hope he is well
enough to do it."[31] One week later (having already alerted the Vatican), FDR formally wrote to Taylor expressing his "desire that you
proceed to Rome at the earliest possible moment. Your special tal-
ents are needed there at this important period of our representation in Rome and in Italy."[32] Four days later, the president wished
Taylor "Happy Voyage!" and informed him that he was arranging
for his "Missus" to be able to join him shortly.[33]

Taylor arrived in Rome on June 19. And while he found the city essentially intact, the nation and its population were in very poor shape and facing a shortage of critical food and medical supplies. Taylor had, in fact, been aware of these problems before he arrived (through the Apostolic Delegate), and in April had established American Relief for Italy Inc.—an organization that became a focus of much of his efforts after he returned to Rome.[34] Taylor's relief organization, in short order, would raise approximately $6 million in public funds and distribute over $37 million in relief supplies to the Italian people.

Two days after his arrival in Rome, Taylor met with the pope for an hour and a quarter; that was followed by another hour-long meeting with Cardinal Luigi Maglione. The Pope was relieved that Rome and its historic artifacts had survived; he also asked about the president's health.[35] Taylor, following the president's directive, started right in on the Pope's June 2 address, stressing "at length that the destruction of the German Army and its unconditional surrender remained the policy of our government." The Pope responded by delineating between the Nazi Party, the German Army, and the German people. The pope also expressed concerns (once again) about the religious situation in Russia, as well as the fate of Poland upon the conclusion of the war. Both men agreed to resume discussing these issues the following week.[36]

On June 23, Taylor reported to the president on his exchanges with the Pope and Maglione. FDR wrote back to his emissary: "That you shall have been able, especially in the course of your very first conversation with the Pope on this occasion, to correct false impressions and present with such force and clarity our fundamental policy that Germany shall be compelled to sue for unconditional surrender was particularly gratifying." The president ended his letter by asking Taylor to thank the Pope for the Holy See's "frequent action ... on its own initiative ... to render assistance to the victims of racial and religious persecution."[37]

Taylor next met with the Pope on June 29 and July 12. On both occasions he went over his list of presidential objectives:

Sacks of flour are unloaded from a truck in Rome after its liberation in
June 1944 thanks to the efforts of American Relief for Italy Inc.

"First: to convince the Pope and other Vatican authorities that
the German army must surrender unconditionally; second: that
cooperation with Russia in the interest of victory and permanent
world peace is essential; third: that an International Organization
must be created at as early a date as possible to implement the
settlement of world problems and to insure future peace." The Vatican's concern about Poland took up a fair amount of these meetings (given its large Catholic population), as well as the "broader
question" of Russia's attitude regarding religious freedom.[38] After
the July 12 papal audience, Taylor had a long meeting with Monsignor Domenico Tardini, who provided him a memorandum on
the Vatican's analysis of Russia's attitudes and postwar aims (a
memorandum Taylor sent on with his report to the president).[39]
FDR's response to Taylor was to veto the idea of trying to get a

statement from our "most sensitive" Russian allies—it would be "highly dangerous" to "attempt to force … any frontal assault." And "from your report, [the Vatican] is wary of statements and intent on concrete application."[40]

While Taylor kept on repeating the "unconditional surrender" mantra at every opportunity with Vatican officials, the July 20 attempt on Hitler's life prompted a Vatican telegram to the Catholic nuncio in Berlin to "do what diplomatic decorum seems to require in such a case."[41] That appears to have led to German peace feelers going out to Church officials in Berlin and Spain. On September 21, the Pope relayed these feelers to Taylor; not surprisingly, the feelers went nowhere.[42]

Taylor had been fairly generic in his first meetings with the pope about describing the international organization on which he (and others) had worked so long and hard. On September 1 (the fifth anniversary of the war), the pope made a radio address. In it, he cited to his 1939 Christmas message in which he had expressed hope that an international organization would be created that was "really capable of preserving the peace according to the principles of justice and fairness against any possible future threat."[43] The next day the Pope informed Harold Tittmann that he had deliberately inserted that into his address because of Taylor's frequent references to the planned United Nations. On September 4, Taylor formally thanked the Pope: "I am deeply pleased … that you accepted my suggestion with respect to the international organization for peace and incorporated it in your allocution. This gives me infinite satisfaction."[44]

This exchange appears to have whetted the Vatican's appetite to know more about the organization, as Taylor started to pepper Washington for permission to share further information with the Pope.[45] Initially, the State Department was reluctant to do so, but ultimately FDR approved sharing the draft document agreed to at the Dumbarton Oaks Conference.[46] On October 17, Taylor met with the Pope and told him that he would deliver to him a copy of that document (which he did that day);[47] at that same audience,

Myron C. Taylor in an informal discussion with Pope Pius XII

the Pope agreed to "make a special appeal for the salvation of the Jews of Hungary at [Taylor's] request."[48]

Most of Taylor's remaining work in 1944 in Rome was dedicated to getting food and supplies to the Italian people.[49] That work made Taylor so popular in Italy that the Grand Master of the Order of Malta planned to honor him.[50]

After the president's reelection on November 7, Taylor sent FDR two notes of congratulations, including with one a set of Vatican stamps (for FDR's collection).[51] Taylor then turned to a document he had obviously spent a fair amount of time preparing.

On November 10, Taylor wrote a 16-page letter to the president, which he began: "I would like to say a few words" about his experiences since FDR "telephoned Anabel and me suggesting this mission."[52] He then reviewed, on an annual basis, what he viewed was his track record as the president's "Personal Representative to Pope Pius XII."[53] Taylor then foresaw "a new cycle" that would involve "the long and difficult road of military occupation and control," with a host of attendant, difficult challenges "in the post war world." In a final section he entitled "The Future," Taylor concluded his letter to the president as follows:

> I do not believe that I should embark upon this new cycle of history at the Vatican. Therefore, Mr. President, mindful of your generosity, your unfailing support and constant friendliness, I offer my resignation to become effective upon the surrender of Germany. To suggest an earlier retirement would mean that I have deserted the colors. That I have never done and I have no desire to begin now.

But one last task had to be done before 1944 ended. On November 28, Taylor once more met with the pope, this time to discuss how unconditional surrender would actually work. It had three components: (1) the act of unconditional surrender would eviscerate the myth of the German Army's invincibility, (2) the actual surrender terms would be short and simple, and (3) the agreement would have to be signed by the highest German authority still existing.[54] Because Taylor left a document with the pope setting forth these same points, Tardini was charged with writing a response. He thereupon prepared two documents—one on the term "unconditional surrender," and the other on what it meant to relinquish power to a foreign conqueror. On December 10, the Pope looked at both and instructed Tardini to send Taylor only the second document. There would be no purpose sending the "unconditional surrender" document given that Taylor considered the concept "an incontestable dogma regarding which he had not requested any advice from the Vatican."[55]

Notes

1. J. Blum, *The Morgenthau Diaries: Years of War, 1941-1945*, pp. 214-23 (Houghton Mifflin 1967); R. Breitman & A. Lichtman, *FDR and the Jews*, pp. 231-37, 262-75 (Belknap Press 2013); C. Hull, *Memoirs of Cordell Hull*, pp. 1539-40

(Macmillan 1948). Important works on the WRB include R. Erbelding, *Rescue Board: The Untold Story of America's Efforts to Save the Jews of Europe* (Penguin 2018); R. Breitman & A. Kraut, *American Refugee Policy and European Jewry, 1933-1945* (Indiana University Press 1987).

2. By this point neither the Intergovernmental Committee on Refugees, nor FDR's Advisory Committee on Political Refugees had accomplished anything of significant relief for European refugees during the war. Blum, *supra* note 1, p. 209; *Refugees and Rescue: The Diaries and Papers of James G. McDonald 1935-1945*, pp. 313-10 (ed. R. Breitman, B. Stewart & S. Hochberg) (Indiana University Press 2009).

3. Breitman & Lichtman, *supra* note 1, p. 272. FDR ordered $1 million be set aside for administrative expenses. Blum, *supra* note 1, p. 202.

4. Breitman, Stewart & Hochberg, *supra* note 2, p. 327.

5. *See* Chapter XIII, pp. 212-13, note 34.

6. M.C. Taylor March 3, 1944, letter to FDR (Taylor Papers, Cornell University); Erbelding, *supra* note 1, pp. 81-82. Much of this bureaucratic taffy-pull played out in March and April of 1944. *Id.*

7. M.C. Taylor March 3, 1944, memorandum to FDR (Taylor Papers, Cornell University).

8. M.C. Taylor May 25, 1944, letter to FDR (Taylor Papers, Cornell University); C. Hull June 3, 1944, memorandum to FDR (with attachments) (Taylor Papers, FDR Library); FDR June 5, 1944, letter to M.C. Taylor (Taylor Papers, FDR Library). His deputy Pell also resigned from the ICR at that time.

Also in this period, Taylor kept up his concern regarding Allied bombing, as well as rendering Rome an "open city." *See, e.g.,* FDR January 31, 1944, letter to M.C. Taylor (with attachments) (Taylor Papers, FDR Library); M.C. Taylor March 13, 1944, letter to FDR (with attachment) (Taylor Papers, FDR Library); FDR March 21, 1944, letter to M.C. Taylor (Taylor Papers, FDR Library). The Vatican's extreme concern about the bombing in 1944 is well set forth in H. Tittmann, *Inside the Vatican of Pius XII*, pp. 199-204 (Doubleday 2004).

9. M.C. Taylor March 14, 1944, memorandum to C. Hull (Taylor Papers, Library of Congress). *See also* C. Stewart, "The Man Nobody Knows," *New York Archives*, p. 11 (Summer 2009).

10. C. Hull April 1, 1944, memorandum to M.C. Taylor (Taylor Papers, Cornell University). *See also* Stewart, *supra* note 9, p. 11.

11. *See* Chapter VIII, note 46. The U.S. government's (and, in particular, the State Department's) deference to the British on policy regarding the Arab world during World War II has been well documented. *See, e.g.,* Blum, *supra* note 1, pp. 209, 224; Breitman & Lichtman, *supra* note 1, pp. 92, 117-119, 224. Roosevelt's naivete concerning the Arab world is perhaps best exemplified by his

experience preparing for and meeting with King Saud aboard the USS *Quincy* on February 14, 1945, after the Yalta Conference. Stunned by the King's hatred of Jews, and vehement opposition to a Jewish settlement in Palestine, only upon reflection would the president belatedly acknowledge the failure of his meeting with the King, as well as the "fanaticism" that Taylor had warned of the year before. Breitman & Lichtman, *supra* note 1, pp. 299-305.

12. A. Radosh & R. Radosh, *Harry and Zion: Truman's Coup* (Harper 2009).

13. Stewart, *supra* note 9, pp. 11-12.

14. M.C. Taylor April 13, 1944, memorandum to C. Hull (Taylor Papers, Cornell University); C. Hull April 29, 1944, memorandum to M.C. Taylor (Taylor Papers, Cornell University). As such (and with his imminent return to Rome in June 1944), Taylor played no role in the July 1944 meetings that led to the Bretton Woods Agreements. *See* B. Steil, *The Battle of Bretton Woods* (Princeton 2013) (the protagonists of this book—John Maynard Keynes (the British delegate) and Harry Dexter White (the American delegate)—both served on the Taylor Committee). *The Price of Vision: The Diary of Henry Wallace, 1942-1946*, p. 262 (ed. J. Blum) (Houghton Mifflin 1973). It was, of course, inevitable that the Treasury Department would take the lead on the Bretton Woods meetings. Hull, *supra* note 1, p. 1154; Blum, *supra* note 1, pp. 233-35. That the Taylor Committee's two years of "formulating far-reaching plans for postwar economic policies and for the creation of internal agencies" was critical to the ultimate Bretton Woods Agreements is without doubt. Hull, *supra* note 1, p. 1636; *Postwar Foreign Policy Preparation*, pp. 191-93 (State Department 1949).

15. *Postwar Foreign Policy Preparation*, pp. 247-48.

16. The first such meeting with eight senators took place on April 25, 1944. *Id.* pp. 263-64.

17. Hull, *supra* note 1, p. 1654; *Postwar Foreign Policy Preparation*, pp. 263-64.

18. *See* Chapter III, p. 16. Taylor was also a good choice for Miller, since Miller had worked for him at U.S. Steel. John W. Davis, moreover, was a very old social friend of Taylor's.

19. M. Posey, *Charles Evans Hughes*, pp. 393-94 (Macmillan 1951).

20. *Id.* p. 794.

21. *Id.* p. 794-95.

22. *Id.* p. 795.

23. *Id.*

24. *Postwar Foreign Policy Preparation*, p. 286.

25. *Id.* According to Hull, because of Taylor's (and others') efforts, the 1944 Republican national convention adopted a plank favoring an international organization. Hull, *supra* note 1, p. 1670.

26. *See* R. Atkinson, *The Day of Battle* (Henry Holt 2007); R. Katz, *The Battle for Rome* (Simon & Schuster 2003).

27. P. Kent, "The War Aims of the Papacy, 1933-45," *FDR, the Vatican, and the Roman Catholic Church in America, 1933-1945*, pp. 166-67 (ed. D. Woolner & R. Kurial) (Palgrave 2003); P. Blet, *Pius XII and the Second World War*, pp. 257-58 (Paulist 1997). The Pope added: "Those who are animated by such a sentiment [i.e., unconditional surrender] move forward as if in a hypnotic dream through the chasms of unspeakable sacrifice and also force others to a destructive and bloody struggle." *Id.*

28. On January 17, 1944, April 1, 1944, and April 5, 1944, the president had sent separate memoranda to Hull about his unconditional surrender difficulties with Russia and England—all of these documents are in *FDR: His Personal Letters*, pp. 1485-87, 1504-05 (ed. E. Roosevelt) (Duell, Sloan and Pearce 1950); *see also* Blet, *supra* note 27, p. 258. As he had in Casablanca, FDR cited Hull to Grant and Lee at Appomattox; but that analogy is/was not historically accurate (to say the least). R. Atkinson, *The Army at Dawn*, pp. 294-95 (Henry Holt 2002).

29. Blet, *supra* note 27, p. 258.

30. J. Conway, "Myron Taylor's Mission to the Vatican 1940-1950," *Church History*, p. 98 (Vol. 44 March 1975). Interestingly, the day after the Pope's June 2 address, the German high command informed Field Marshal Albert Keserling, the Senior German commander in the Mediterranean: "Führer decision. There must not be a battle of Rome." R. Atkinson, *The Day of Battle*, p. 568 (Henry Holt 2007).

Professor Evangelista (who concluded that Taylor's efforts vis-à-vis bombing constituted "failed diplomacy"—"Myron Taylor and the Bombing of Rome: The Limits of Law and Diplomacy," *Diplomacy * Statecraft* (June 29, 2020)—*see* Chapter XIII, p. 211, note 28; Chapter XII, p. 197, note 78; Chapter XI, p. 171, note 21) stops his analysis/coverage short of 1944. Thus, his article fails to acknowledge what Hull wrote in his memoirs (*supra* note 1, p. 1563):

> The center of Rome was, in fact, not bombed, although Allied planes dropped bombs on the city's railroad yards. The Allied advance was carried out so as to encircle the city and force the Germans to retire without contesting the capital street by street, which would have wrought great destruction. When the Allies reached Rome they found the city comparatively untouched, with the exception of the fact that the Germans, on leaving, had crippled its water supply.

For a fascinating recording of the Germans' evacuation from Rome from inside the Vatican, *see* Tittmann, *supra* note 8, pp. 207-10.

31. FDR June 7, 1944, memorandum to E. Stettinius (Taylor Papers, FDR Library).

32. FDR June 13, 1944, letter to M.C. Taylor (Taylor Papers, Cornell University). FDR added: "The high esteem in which you are held by His Holiness and the authorities of the Holy See is matched only by the confidence which I repose in your ability to interpret the valiant actions of our armed forces and the high purpose of the people of the United States in the present titanic struggle." [an obvious reference to the unconditional surrender policy].

33. FDR June 17, 1944, letter to M.C. Taylor (Taylor Papers, Cornell University). On June 23, Anabel Taylor sent a handwritten note to FDR (care of Grace Tully) thanking him for arranging for her to join her husband in Rome. The following day, the president sent a memorandum to Stettinius asking him "to get a seat on a plane for Mrs. Myron Taylor about the tenth of July or shortly thereafter." These documents are in the Taylor Papers at the FDR Library.

34. FDR April 6, 1944, letter to M.C. Taylor (Taylor Papers, FDR Library); *see also* H. Stimson August 23, 1944, letter to M.C. Taylor (Taylor Papers, Cornell University); C. Hull October 11, 1944, letter to M.C. Taylor (Taylor Papers, Cornell University); C. Hughes November 28, 1944, letter to M.C. Taylor (Taylor Papers, Cornell University); T. Lamont December 14, 1944, letter to M.C. Taylor (Taylor Papers, Cornell University). For the Apostolic Delegate's role in addressing the food (and other) problems of Rome, *see* R. Trisco, "The Department of State and the Apostolic Delegation in Washington During World War II," *FDR, the Vatican, and the Roman Catholic Church in America, 1933-1945*, pp. 231-39 (ed. D. Woolner & R. Kurial) (Palgrave 2003).

35. Whether the Vatican had any inside source on FDR's precarious grasp on life is unknown. *See* R. Ferrell, *The Dying President: Franklin D. Roosevelt, 1944-1945* (University of Missouri Press 1978). There is no evidence that Taylor was ever aware (or made aware) of the president's health at this point, or up until his death in April 1945.

36. Blet, *supra* note 27, pp. 258-59.

37. Taylor's June 23 letter is part of C. Hull's July 8, 1944, memorandum to FDR in the Taylor Papers at the FDR Library. FDR's undated response to Taylor is in the Taylor Papers at Cornell and in the Taylor Papers at the FDR Library. *See also* Taylor June 28, 1944, and June 30, 1944, letters to FDR (Taylor Papers, FDR Library). After the June 21 papal audience, Maglione prepared a memorandum on Soviet policy that stated, among other things: "Its intention to occupy the Baltic countries, a part of Poland, and the Balkans does not agree with the Atlantic

Charter and could seriously compromise the cause of peace." Blet, *supra* note 27, p. 259.

Interestingly, it appears that FDR in 1944 at least twice contemplated "clarifying" what unconditional surrender would mean to the German people; on both occasions Churchill talked him out of such a "clarification." R. Dallek, *Franklin Roosevelt: A Political Life*, p. 592 (Penguin 2017); N. Hamilton, *War and Peace*, p. 270 (Houghton Mifflin 2019). For a strong critique of the unconditional surrender policy, *see* T. Fleming, *The New Dealers' War* (Basic Books 2001).

38.   Conway, *supra* note 30, p. 98. Taylor told the Pope about his discussions with Russian Ambassador Maisky in London just prior to his arrival in Rome regarding a possible statement that "would be agreeable" to Stalin. Kent, *supra* note 27, pp. 169-70. The Vatican, however, wanted actions, not statements.

39.   M.C. Taylor July 14, 1944, and July 17, 1944, letters to FDR (Taylor Papers, FDR Library). Blet, *supra* note 27, p. 259-60.

40.   FDR's September 20, 1944, letter to M.C. Taylor is in the Taylor Papers at Cornell. *See* J. Conway, "Pope Pius XII and the Myron Taylor Mission," *FDR, the Vatican, and the Roman Catholic Church in America, 1937-1945*, p. 98 (ed. D. Woolner & R. Kurial) (Palgrave 2003).

Thereafter, Taylor and Tardini continued to write (and often share) memoranda with dramatically different hopes and analyses of possible outcomes for postwar Europe vis-à-vis the Russians. Blet, *supra* note 27, pp. 260-61. *See also* Taylor August 4, 1944, letter to FDR (Taylor Papers, FDR Library); M.C. Taylor August 9, 1944, letter to C. Hull (Taylor Papers, FDR Library); M.C. Taylor August 11, 1944, memorandum of meeting with the Pope (Taylor Papers, FDR Library); M.C. Taylor August 14, 1944, letter to FDR (Taylor Papers, FDR Library).

In recounting his various activities, Taylor also reported on the multitude of people who were arriving in Rome for audiences with the Pope (*e.g.*, Churchill, Stimson, Forrestal, Patterson, McCormack, etc.). After meeting the Pope, Churchill told Taylor that he was "a very forthright and powerful personality." D. Kertzer, *The Pope at War*, p. 435 (Random House 2022). FDR responded: "I take it that many American firemen are keeping you more than busy. I begin to realize the old saying 'that all roads lead to Rome,'" FDR August 22, 1944, letter to Taylor (Taylor Papers, FDR Library).

41.   Blet, *supra* note 27, pp. 261-62.

42.   Blet, *supra* note 27, pp. 262-63. The peace feelers were either (1) that the Anglo-Allies drop unconditional surrender and reach a peace with Germany, which would enable Germany to continue against Russia, or (2) that Germany would reach an accord with Russia.

43.   Blet, *supra* note 27, p. 278.

44. M.C. Taylor September 4, 1944, letter to Pius XII (Taylor Papers, FDR Library).

45. *See, e.g.,* M.C. Taylor September 6, 1944, telegram to FDR and C. Hull; M.C. Taylor September 10, 1944, letter to FDR; M.C. Taylor September 18, 1944, letter to FDR (all these documents are in the Taylor Papers at Cornell).

46. FDR October 9, 1944, letter to M.C. Taylor (Taylor Papers, FDR Library).

47. M.C. Taylor October 18, 1944, telegram to FDR (Taylor Papers, Cornell University). Ultimately, the Pope raised the question of possible Vatican membership in the United Nations; the State Department nixed that idea. Hull, *supra* note 1, pp. 1711-12. *See also* Blet, *supra* note 27, pp. 278-79.

48. *Id.* In 1944, Hungary constituted the largest population of Jews (approximately 800,000) that had yet to face the Nazi death machine. R. Breitman & A. Lichtman, *supra* note 1, pp. 272-73. Since the spring of 1944 the War Refugee Board had been in contact with the Apostolic Delegate to seek the Pope's help with respect to this dire situation. *Id.* p. 268; Trisco, *supra* note 34, p. 241. On May 24, Cicognani told Taylor that the Vatican was "doing everything within its power to protect and assist these people." A. Cicognani May 24, 1944, letter to M.C. Taylor (Taylor Papers, Cornell University). On June 25, the Pope sent a telegram to Admiral Horthy (the regent of Hungary), imploring him to spare the Hungarians from further pain and suffering. That intervention, as well as that of the Hungarian Papal Nuncio (Angelo Rotta), "stung Horthy" (who also received letters from the King of Sweden and FDR), and on July 7 Horthy "suspended deportations of Jews in time to save those left in Budapest." Breitman & Lichtman, *supra* note 1, p. 280. Blet, *supra* note 27, pp. 195-97.

When Taylor had raised this subject with Pius XII, the Pope was "eager to co-operate in the endeavor to save Jewish lives." M. Phayer, *Pius XI: The Holocaust and the Cold War*, p. 89 (Indiana University Press 2008). He told Taylor: "neither history nor his conscience would forgive him if he made no effort to save at this psychological juncture further threatened lives." *Id.* On October 28, Taylor gave the Pope a message from the War Refugee Board, asking that the Pope give a radio address to the Hungarian people. The Pope instead sent a message to Cardinal Seridi in Budapest, stating he had been asked by many to intervene on behalf of those who were being persecuted because of their race, religion, or political beliefs. Joining his voice with the other vocal Hungarian Bishops (e.g., Rotta, Hamvas), he implored "that, in conformity with the principles of humanity and justice, the very grave sufferings caused by this terrible conflict do not become even more horrible." Blet, *supra* note 27, pp. 196-97; Trisco, *supra* note 34, p. 242.

While hundreds of thousands of Hungarian Jews did die at the hands of the Nazis (up to and until the end of the European war), approximately

150,000-200,000 Jews were saved. Breitman & Lichtman, *supra* note 1, pp. 293-94. Even a Pius XII critic has concluded that the Pope deserves "some of the credit" for that result; that critic also concluded that "[t]here is no doubt that Pius XII did more to save the Jews in Hungary than in any other country." Phayer, *supra* note 48, p. 93. *See also* Blet, *supra* note 27, pp. 199-200; Conway, *supra* note 40, p. 149.

Curiously, Professor David Kertzer in his recent *The Pope at War* (Random House 2022) passes over Hungary with barely a mention (*see* p. 575 n.24). He does, however, reference Taylor's intercession with the Pope in July 1944 to save the thousands of Jews stranded in northern Italy, According to Kertzer, efforts by the Vatican through the German ambassador to the Vatican proved futile. Kertzer, p. 575 n.24.

Whether the Pope only deserves (some) credit for the results in Hungary (and/or elsewhere in Europe) is beyond the scope of this Taylor biography. But one key to the Hungarian result seems to have been not only the Pope's intervention but also the fact that he had forceful Church officials at the scene supporting those efforts (*e.g.*, Bishop Rotta). Conway, *supra* note 40, p. 149. That contrasts with a country like Slovakia, where the country's president, Josef Tiso, was not only an anti-Semite but was also a priest. As one high official of the Holy See bitterly complained in July of 1942: "It is a great tragedy that the President of Slovakia is a priest. Everyone knows that the Holy See cannot bring Hitler to heel. But who will understand that we can't even control a priest?" Conway, *supra* note 40, pp. 148-49.

A prominent critic of Pope Pius XII's efforts to save Jews paints Jewish leaders' "sincere praise" of those efforts in the postwar years as a form of cynical "flattery." Phayer, *supra* note 48, pp. 256-57 ("Who else, after all, could they thank?").

49. M.C. Taylor September 6, 1944, letter to FDR (Taylor Papers, FDR Library); M.C. Taylor September 22, 1944, letter to FDR (Taylor Papers, Cornell University); M.C. Taylor September 22, 1944, telegram to FDR and C. Hull (Taylor Papers, Cornell University); FDR September 28, 1944, letter to M.C. Taylor (Taylor Papers, FDR Library); M.C. Taylor October 4, 1944, letter to FDR (Taylor Papers, FDR Library); M.C. Taylor October 28, 1944, letter to FDR (Taylor Papers, Cornell University); M.C. Taylor November 16, 1944, telegram to FDR, et al. (Taylor Papers, FDR Library); M.C. Taylor December 20, 1944, telegram to E. Stettinius (Taylor Papers, FDR Library).

50. Ultimately, Cardinal Spellman vetoed Taylor (a Protestant) receiving an award from the Order of Malta (a Catholic organization). Kertzer, p. 576 n.8. Notwithstanding, Taylor subsequently received the Knight Order of Pius, First Degree (from the Pope), the Citation for Distinguished Service (from the

President of Italy), and the Citation for Distinguished Service to the Italian Red Cross and the National Committee for the Distribution of Relief in Italy (from the Prime Minister of Italy).

51. M.C. Taylor's two November 9, 1944, letters to FDR are in the Taylor Papers at Cornell.

On November 8, Harry Hooker, FDR's former law partner and one of the president's closest friends, wrote a lengthy letter to Taylor about the election night:

> I have just had dinner with the Chief. We two had dinner alone on a little table in front of the fire in the big room downstairs and he has gone to his room and I am in mine. Well it was a great victory yesterday. I arrived around 4 p.m. and joined him in a drive up to his cottage on the hill where we had tea. The others were Admirals Leahy and McIntire and Daisy Suckley [FDR's cousin]. Last night a lot of neighbors came in to hear the returns. I had dinner at a little table with Laura Delano [FDR's cousin], Daisy Suckley[,] Admiral Leahy and Serge Obilensky—Serge told us many tales of his fighting in Sicily and France with the Paratroopers. The President and a few of us here in the house did not get to bed till about 4:30 a.m. It took Dewey a long time to admit defeat and send best wishes. Today everyone went to New York except me. So we lunched together in his room and later motored about and then dined. We talked of many things and tonight at dinner of you. I told him that I knew you would perform such service as had to be done whether it came strictly under the head of your diplomatic mission or not and I recited how you had had all those men at lunch in order to aid in feeding and helping the Italian people. He spoke in the very highest terms of what you are doing and showed real appreciation and gratitude and he knew how you had helped in his election. He was in a very happy relaxed mood today—glad the election is over and happy at the size of the Electoral College vote.... Wish you had been up here during all this battle. Love to Anabel and you.

H. Hooker November 8, 1944, letter to M.C. Taylor (Taylor Papers, Cornell University). Hooker did not send the letter until the November 14 because on November 9 he suffered a heart attack. In a separate (dictated) letter on November 14, Hooker enclosed his first letter, signing off: "as I lie here in bed it is pleasant to think about you and Anabelle [sic] and what a good life you are leading." H. Hooker November 14, 1944, letter to M.C. Taylor (Taylor Papers, Cornell University).

52. M.C. Taylor's November 12, 1944, letter to FDR is in the Taylor Papers at the FDR Library.

53. In this letter (p. 5), Taylor stated that both Churchill and FDR had characterized the Pope's September 22, 1942, memorandum as "historic." *See* Chapter XII, p. 196, note 61. With respect to Taylor's 1943 "initiative" to get the Vatican to intercede with King Emmanuel to depose Mussolini (*see* Chapter XIII, p. 211, note 24), Taylor quoted (p. 6) FDR's reaction to be "the first break in the whole Axis organization." *See also* M. Richling, *Church of Spies*, p. 174 (Basic Books 2015). As to his efforts in 1944 to reinforce the unconditional surrender with the Vatican, Taylor noted (p. 8): "that task has not been an easy one[,] [although] [n]o further addresses encourage an early or "negotiated" peace have been made by His Holiness." Taylor then detailed his efforts vis-à-vis American Relief for Italy (pp. 10-11), with the hope that the various relief issues will have been solved by the time of Germany's surrender (with Taylor then able to step aside as its Chairman).

54. Blet, *supra* note 27, p. 267.

55. *Id.* pp. 267-68, 287. That said, the Pope's Christmas message nonetheless outlined his views on the conditions for a "just peace." Ongoing Vatican concerns about Soviet domination of Eastern Europe led him to stress national self-determination. Kent, *supra* note 27, p. 170. Of particular concern to the Vatican was the fate of Poland, especially after what had happened to Warsaw. Blet, *supra* note 27, pp. 270-74; Kent, *supra* note 27, pp. 170-72.

CHAPTER XV

1945: The End of the Taylor Mission (for FDR)

A s 1944 turned into 1945 Taylor continued to spend the bulk of his time on American Relief for Italy, ensuring that food and medical supplies were getting to the needy.[1] While recognition and thanks for his prodigious efforts were flowing his way from the likes of Eleanor Roosevelt and Secretary of War Henry Stimson,[2] Taylor's efforts were also publicized in the United States by Congresswoman Clare Boothe Luce in a lengthy letter published in the *New York Times*. Luce, having returned from an overseas fact-finding trip, wanted to address any public "anxiety about conditions in Italy and critici[sms] [about] the lack of aid given to the Italian people."[3] She began by identifying "the magnificent work done by Myron C. Taylor in Italy to relieve the inhabitants of that devastated peninsula; an achievement that has been somewhat overlooked because of the flood of news brought by the ending of the war in Europe." After detailing Taylor's long career, Luce moved on to his establishment of American Relief for Italy, Inc. in April of 1944. She then identified the various obstacles faced to get food and supplies to the Italian people, especially during the winter of 1944, but reported that (to date) more than a million Italians had received material aid, with an organization now in place to provide "for the relief of several times that number." Luce concluded by calling Taylor's relief work "a near-miracle."

235

Taylor was also kept busy by the constant flow of VIPs who visited Rome and wanted to meet the pope.[4] The most important of these papal audiences took place on January 30, when Taylor took Harry Hopkins—FDR's closest advisor (and a good friend of Taylor's)—for a 40-minute meeting with Pius XII.[5] The purpose of Hopkins' visit was to (hopefully) address the Vatican's concerns about the upcoming Yalta Conference and the fate of Poland.[6] While the Pope was "pleased by this attention," he was not pleased with the results of the conference and what the Vatican had feared would be the end result of the war: Russian domination of Poland and hegemony in Eastern Europe.[7]

For a good part of the early months of 1945 the Pope was sick with the flu, but he nonetheless continued to meet regularly with Taylor. In the words of the new French envoy to the Vatican: "Myron Taylor pays the Pope visits with a frequency unheard of by all other foreign diplomats. With his familiar and direct bonhomie, which has earned him unanimous sympathies, he seems to have established himself as some sort of adviser to the Holy See." The envoy attributed Taylor's success to his close relationship with the president, his substantial wealth, and his efforts to bring aid to the Italian people.[8]

In the middle of all this came an episode that is one of the most bizarre of World War II. The Office of Strategic Services (OSS) had set up an intelligence station in Rome after the city's liberation; and thereafter the OSS station paid particular attention to the diplomatic envoys to the Vatican as important sources of intelligence. From that effort came a link to a prodigious source of information, seemingly from the heart of the Vatican itself, code-named VESSEL.[9] VESSEL's reports related to a whole host of topics of interest to the OSS and the U.S. government: possible Vatican overtures to Moscow, information from the Apostolic Delegation in Japan about military and naval operations, possible Vatican mediation of the Pacific War, etc.[10]

Things took a wrong turn, however, when the VESSEL reports started to focus on Taylor. According to the Vatican spy,

Taylor with Harry Hopkins after a papal audience on January 30, 1945

Taylor met with the Pope on January 27 regarding a possible papal mediation of the Pacific War; even more incredible was the VES-SEL report that Taylor had secretly met with Ken Harada, the Japanese Ambassador to the Holy See, on February 16.[11] When the State Department read this last report, it contacted Taylor, who vehemently denied meeting Harada or having anything to do with a Japanese mediation. At that point, it was revealed that the Vatican spy was in fact Virgilio Scattolini, who (at various times) had been a journalist, film critic for the Vatican newspaper, and a pornographer.[12] Taylor gave a detailed report on the entire incident to FDR, including the fact that he had revealed "the recent Japanese episode to the personal attention of the Pope who was surprised and shocked."[13]

While a papal intervention in the Pacific War was fake, some Germans were still trying to see if the Pope might mediate with the Allies. On February 20, 1945, the German Ambassador to the Holy See met with Monsignor Tardini. Putting aside the German view that they could still choose to ally themselves with Russia if unconditional surrender continued to be mandated, Tardini told the Ambassador that he doubted very much that the Allies would change their long-articulated policy.[14] On February 25, the two men met again; Tardini concluded that the German proposal was not a diplomatic one, but rather a military one—the Germans wanted the Anglo-Allies to relax pressure in the West so that the German Army could reconstitute stronger forces against the Russians in the East. Both Tardini and the Pope could not (and would not) be party to such a protocol.[15]

Nevertheless, on February 28 the Pope met with Taylor and asked him if there was any possibility—"however remote"—of a discussion with the Germans regarding a conclusion of the war. Taylor was firm: no meetings or discussions—"nothing other than unconditional surrender."[16] The next day the Pope met with the German Ambassador. He reported that, "after testing the ground, ... no conversation or discussion with the United States or England was possible."[17]

By late March, FDR was down at Warm Springs, hoping to recharge his batteries and looking forward to spending time with Lucy Mercer Rutherford.[18] The President died on April 13, 1945, while sitting for a portrait.

The worldwide reaction to the news was instantaneous and profound.[19] The Pope immediately sent messages to the new president and to the dead president's widow. When an aide for Taylor contacted Tardini to tell him that Taylor would stay on in his post, Tardini responded: "I thank God for the news."[20]

On May 17, Harry Truman wrote to "Mr. Taylor" (in all their correspondence thereafter, it was never "Myron"). As was the new president's style, he was blunt and right to the point: "I hope you will continue in your present work—you have my confidence."[21] Just what that work would be in the future was uncertain, however. On June 12, Mr. and Mrs. Taylor left Rome for Washington so that Taylor could meet his new boss and get his marching orders.

Notes

1. H. Tittmann, *Inside the Vatican of Pius XII*, p. 212 (Doubleday 2004). *See, e.g.,* M.C. Taylor January 30, 1945, letter to FDR (Taylor Papers, Cornell University); M.C. Taylor February 12, 1945, letter to FDR (Taylor Papers, Cornell University); M.C. Taylor February 20, 1945, letter to FDR (Taylor Papers, Cornell University); M.C. Taylor March 1, 1945, letter to FDR (Taylor Papers, Cornell University); M.C. Taylor March 7, 1945, letter to FDR (Taylor Papers, Cornell University).

2. E. Roosevelt February 25, 1945, letter to M.C. Taylor (Taylor Papers, Cornell University); H. Stimson March 17, 1945, letter to M.C. Taylor (Taylor Papers, Cornell University). *See also* Chapter XIV, p. 229, note 34.

3. C. Luce, "Clare Boothe Luce Tells How Myron C. Taylor Coordinated Relief Groups," *New York Times* (May 29, 1945). For the full magnitude of Taylor's relief efforts in Italy, *see* Transcript of Meeting of Protestant Clergymen with Myron Taylor at Union Club (New York City, October 20, 1947) at pp. 36-40 (Taylor Papers, Cornell University).

4. *See* Chapter XIV, p. 230, note 40.

5. Taylor January 31, 1945, telegram to Stettinius (Taylor Papers, FDR Library) (FDR later shared this telegram with Hopkins). In his biography of Hopkins, Robert Sherwood (curiously) reported that the main topic of the meeting was Hopkins' report on his visit with General de Gaulle (about whom Hopkins and Taylor had different opinions). Sherwood also wrote that Taylor "said that when they left Hopkins was in a glow of exultation, revealing a surprisingly deep religious feeling." *Roosevelt and Hopkins*, p. 848 (Harper & Brothers 1998).

6. P. Kent, "The War Aims of the Papacy, 1938-45," *FDR, the Vatican, and the Roman Catholic Church in America, 1933-1945*, pp. 171-72 (ed. D. Woolner & R. Kurial) (Palgrave 2003). Prior to Yalta, the Apostolic Delegate had received assurances from the U.S. Secretary of State that the president would address the Vatican's concerns about Poland when he met with Stalin at Yalta. P. Blet, *Pius XII and the Second World War*, p. 274 (Paulist 1999). The Pope subsequently heard an unencouraging report about Yalta from Edward Flynn—a prominent New York Democrat (and Catholic)—who had accompanied FDR to Yalta. Kent, *supra* note 6, p. 172. Taylor was not in the loop on the Yalta Conference and U.S. plans therefor. *See, e.g.,* M.C. Taylor February 16, 1945, letter to FDR (Taylor Papers, FDR Library).

7. Kent, *supra* note 6, p. 172.

8 D. Kertzer, *The Pope at War*, pp. 445, 576, n.9 (Random House 2022). During this same period, Taylor reported to the U.S. Secretary of State that the Catholic clergy had sheltered approximately six thousand Jews during the German occupation of Rome. He further reported that "the Holy See is naturally most anxious not to give any publicity to this information lest it bring about retaliatory measures against the Catholic Clergy and communities in Nazi-controlled territories." Kertzer, p. 573, n.29.

9. A. Brown, *Wild Bill Donovan: The Last Hero*, pp. 685-705 (Times Books 1982); D. Alvarez, "American Intelligence and the Vatican, 1939-45," *FDR, the Vatican, and the Roman Catholic Church in America, 1939-1945*, pp. 253-67 (ed. D. Woolner & R. Kurial) (Palgrave Macmillan 2003).

10. *Id.* pp. 256-57.

11. *Id.* p. 257.

12. *Id.*

13. M.C. Taylor March 15, 1945, letter to FDR and E. Stettinius (Taylor Papers, FDR Library). This intelligence failure/embarrassment was later cited by President Truman for influencing his decision not to allow the OSS to continue as an intelligence agency after the war. Brown, *supra* note 9, pp. 704, 792-93.

14. Blet, *supra* note 6, pp. 268-69.

15. *Id.* p. 269.

16. *Id.* p. 270.

17. *Id. See* M.C. Taylor March 21, 1945, telegram to E. Stettinius (Taylor Papers, FDR Library). Subsequently, on April 5 Taylor sent to FDR a telegram, including a written peace proposal coming from Mussolini's son on behalf of "German authorities." M.C. Taylor April 5, 1945, telegram to FDR (Taylor Papers, Cornell University). Later that same day, Taylor sent a telegram to Stettinius ("For the President Only") asking whether he should go to Paris to meet with Eisenhower, given that he was the only one "authorized to conclude

unconditional surrender." M.C. Taylor April 5, 1945, telegram to E. Stettinius (Taylor Papers, FDR Library). The next day, the Acting Secretary of State, Dean Acheson, nixed a Taylor trip to Paris and advised that "you should refuse absolutely to accept or listen to any approaches. The danger of misinterpretation by the enemy of our position on unconditional surrender is too great, and I must therefore request you abstain from any further discussions on this subject with the Vatican." D. Acheson April 6, 1945, telegram to M.C. Taylor (Taylor Papers, Cornell University). Taylor mis-remembered this incident two years later. Transcript of Meeting with Protestant Clergymen with Myron Taylor, p. 35.

18. N. Hamilton, *War and Peace*, pp. 489-98 (Houghton Mifflin 2019).

19. When Ambassador Harriman told Stalin on April 13, the dictator held his hand for almost 30 seconds before he asked for details about FDR's death (he suspected he was poisoned). R. Dallek, *Franklin D. Roosevelt: A Political Life*, p. 620 (Penguin 2017).

Harry Hopkins wrote Taylor a long letter in which he said: "It seems incredible to realize that … the President has died. I know how devoted you were to him and his purposes and what implicit confidences he had in you." H. Hopkins April 28, 1945, letter to M.C. Taylor (Taylor Papers, Cornell University).

On June 28, 1956, Taylor sent to Eleanor Roosevelt a volume of all the messages sent and received by him about the president's death. She forwarded that volume to the FDR Library on January 23, 1957.

20. Blet, *supra* note 6, p. 279. After meeting with the Pope, General J.C.H. Lee told Taylor that he "spoke repeatedly of his hope that you might remain with him." Lee April 19, 1945, letter to Taylor (Taylor Papers, Cornell University).

21. H.S. Truman May 17, 1945, letter to M.C. Taylor (Taylor Papers, Cornell University). It appears that the first correspondence between the two men was a letter Truman wrote regarding war production issues. HST May 6, 1944, letter to M.C. Taylor (Taylor Papers, Cornell University). Prior to Truman's May 17, 1945, letter, Taylor had sent the president two letters describing the protocols by which he had communicated with FDR. M.C. Taylor April 28, 1945, letter to HST, and M.C. Taylor May 16, 1945, letter to HST (both letters are in the Taylor Papers at Cornell).

Taylor's longtime friend John W. Davis (with whom he had consulted on the United Nations draft) wrote him after the war ended in Europe that he expected that Taylor was looking forward to retirement—at last. Davis May 14, 1945, letter to Taylor (Taylor Papers, Cornell University).

CHAPTER XVI

New Taylor Mission
(for Truman)

Taylor did not get any marching orders (new or otherwise) from the President right away, because Truman was still settling in to his new job, trying to figure out how to deal with Russia, what to do about the atomic bomb, how to end the Pacific war, and countless other crises.[1] Never as willing to trust "Uncle Joe" Stalin as his predecessor, Truman, in fairly short order, made clear to his advisors that he would be tougher on Russia—and tougher he was.[2] That shift in American foreign policy would obviously have geopolitical implications for decades to follow;[3] and it would also come to cause an important change in the Taylor Mission.[4] But not right away.

Back in Rome, Taylor continued on with his relief efforts, as well as entertaining prominent VIPs who wanted an audience with Pope Pius XII.[5] At home, however, trouble seemed to be brewing. Given that Taylor's Mission had never been popular with a number of American Protestants,[6] many people believed that, with the war's conclusion, the Mission would/should end.[7]

This growing sentiment in America caused the Church (both in America and in Rome) to become quite concerned. On June 12, 1946, Archbishop Spellman made attacks on the Taylor Mission the subject of his commencement address at Fordham University. These attacks, said Spellman, constituted "bigotry," and he went on to counter the contentions of Protestant leaders that the Taylor

Taylor leaving the White House after meeting with
President Truman on July 18, 1945

Mission was meant to last only until the war ended, adding that
Taylor had much to contribute in postwar Europe.[8] The Vatican
weighed in as well, directing the Apostolic Delegate and Spellman
to assure "the continuation of the personal representative of the
President of the United States at the Vatican."[9] Key presidential
confidants were contacted (with Taylor himself talking with Truman and George Marshall, now the U.S. Secretary of State); the
report back to Rome was that nothing would be changing any
time soon (and ultimately, Truman wrote to the Pope that Taylor
would continue on in his role to facilitate "parallel endeavors for
peace and the alleviation of human suffering.").[10]

Taylor arriving at the Rome airport in 1946

While the Church was doing its best to ensure Taylor's conti-
nuity, the divide between the World War II Allies had broken out
into the open, as best exemplified by Winston Churchill's famous

"Iron Curtain" speech in Fulton, Missouri, on March 5, 1946.[11] That open fissure between the West and the Soviets appears to have prompted Taylor and Truman to think along "parallel" lines.

Perhaps reflecting back on the words the then Vatican Secretary of State had said to him when they first met in 1936 (*see* Chapter IX, page 120),[12] as well as having fresh in his mind the Vatican's ongoing concern during the war about Soviet postwar domination of Eastern Europe, Taylor wrote to the president on June 11, 1946, about the emerging cold war and the Church's role in helping the West:

> The cause of Communism versus Christianity and Democracy transcends minor differences in Christian creeds. It is the *Great Issue* of the future and thus of today.... The Pope has openly challenged Communism from the beginning. He and the Catholic Church are the great bulwark of democracy in continental Europe today.... This peninsula may well become the Mediterranean bulwark separating the Democratic West from what is fast becoming Communist Eastern Europe.[13]

That same day Taylor also sent a telegram to the Secretary of State (for the "President and Secretary Only") about various pressures in Europe concerning the fate of Trieste (a city over which both Italy and Yugoslavia were contesting sovereignty).[14] He followed up with a letter to Truman on June 25, after a meeting Taylor had had that day with the Bishop of Trieste. Taylor wrote "that if Russian influence is permitted to extend in the area in question it will only give them a foothold from which to exercise a still greater influence in both Yugoslavia, Austria and Italy and it would subordinate the population of Trieste that is eighty percent Italian to a minority of Yugoslavia."[15]

Also on June 25, Taylor sent a much longer letter to Truman about his lengthy audience with the Pope that morning, "reviewing the general situation in Europe and the expansion of Communistic

Myron Taylor is acknowledged for his work on behalf of
American Relief for Italy Inc.

political activities and control in various areas." With the situation
in Yugoslavia "terrible" ("to use the Pope's own words"), Taylor pos-
ited that "[t]he question has arisen whether it would be desirable
for me to visit our Minister in Yugoslavia" and also go to Romania.
As to the latter, Taylor referenced an open "invitation from the
Queen Mother of Romania who is an old friend and neighbor of
ours in Florence, as were her mother, the Greek Queen Sophia,
sister of the Kaiser, and her son who had until recently been King
of Greece. Princess Helene has also shown a very great desire that
we shall pay her a visit to Bucharest."[16] Truman, however, nixed
the idea, urging Taylor ("please") not to go to those countries at
the present time because of "very tense" situations in each.[17]

Later that year, on a return trip to the United States, Taylor was present for Secretary of Commerce Henry Wallace's infa-
mous speech criticizing the Truman administration's tougher
policy vis-à-vis the Russians and proposing a return to the more
friendly approach of FDR. On September 19, Taylor called on the

Taylor and Swiss Guards at Castel Gandolfo, August 1947

President and "strongly urged" him to fire Wallace. When Truman did so the following day, Taylor sent him a brief handwritten note on State Department stationary: "Dear Mr. President, Heartiest Congratulations. Sincerely, Myron C. Taylor."[18]

The growing bond between Truman and Taylor is perhaps best reflected in the president's letter to the pope on November 22, 1946. That letter, which Taylor reviewed and commented on before it went out,[19] was in sync with Taylor's June 11 letter to the President. Truman asserted to Pius XII that "this nation, as a Christian nation, prays that all moral forces of the world will unite their strength and will create ... the conditions of life and the enduring world peace to which mankind will find well-being, peace, security, and freedom in enduring world order."[20] Truman's rhetoric foreshadowed an evolving plan by the two men whereby (in the words of one historian) "the leaders of the various factions of Christendom [would hopefully unite] in a pan-religious alliance against communism. Almost 2000 years of conflict, corruption, and doctrinal disputes had rent Christianity into a dizzying array of communions, denominations, and sects. Truman and Taylor aimed for nothing less than reversing this process and bringing the Christian church back together—not around a shared confession but against a shared opponent."[21]

The Truman–Taylor plan kicked off in August of 1947, with Truman sending Taylor back to Europe—first to Rome and thereafter to various religious centers in other European countries. The plan was to promote (first to the Pope and then to all the other leaders) the idea of "meet[ing] in conference to discuss the part which religion can play in bringing peace and order back into the world."[22] Taylor's "spiritual shuttle diplomacy during August and September, 1947" led to him seeing (among others) the Pope, the Archbishop of Canterbury, the Catholic Bishop of London, the Papal Nuncio in Paris, the Archbishop of Berlin, and the Lutheran Bishop of Berlin.[23] While in Berlin Taylor also met with General Lucian Clay, commander of Allied forces, and shared copies of correspondence between the pope and Truman. Told the letters were about to be made public in the United States,[24] Clay and Taylor arranged to make them also available in Germany, reasoning "[t]he distribution will help us in raising our resistance to communism to a high level."[25] Not surprisingly, Taylor's trips (and the president's correspondence) brought on a spate of criticism by the Soviet-sponsored press.[26]

Taylor's initial report back to Truman was optimistic—there seemed to be general receptivity to the idea of a conference of religious leaders.[27] The Lutheran Bishop of Berlin (with his church in East Berlin), Otto Dibelius, was so enthusiastic in his meeting with Taylor that Taylor arranged for him to visit the White House in late October of 1947.[28]

When he arrived back in the United States,[29] Taylor took on a tougher task—one for which he had laid the groundwork before leaving for Europe—meeting with U.S. Protestant Church leaders (who had long been critical of the Taylor Mission) to gauge their interest in religious unity against communism.[30] On October 20, 1947, such a meeting took place in New York City at the Union Club on Park Avenue.[31] Meeting with Taylor were Samuel Cavert (Executive Secretary of the Federal Council of Churches), Edwin Dahlberg (President of the Northern Baptist Convention), Franklin Fry (President of the United Lutheran Church), Charles Gilbert (Bishop of the Protestant Episcopal Church), Bromley Oxman (Bishop of the Methodist Church and President of the Council of Churches), and William Pugh (Stated Clerk of the Presbyterian Church).[32]

Undoubtedly in an attempt to defuse the issue from 1939 that had never gone away—that is, Protestant unhappiness about the President (by Taylor's appointment) seeming to endorse the Pope as the head of Christianity—Taylor started by stressing that his interactions with the Pope had never dealt with "strictly religious questions" about the Catholic Church or any other church. To emphasize that point, he then detailed his efforts (at some length),

starting with the Evian Conference and Intergovernmental Committee on Refugees, to advance "the agenda of problems" given to
him by FDR.[33] In the course of recounting the sagas of unconditional surrender, the deposing of Mussolini, etc., Taylor told the
clergymen of his "secret code to the President" that bypassed the
State Department.[34] Finishing off with the end of the war and his
efforts with American Relief for Italy Inc., Taylor then moved on
to his real purpose for convening the meeting.

Handing out a color-coded map of Europe that showed the
distribution of religious groups across the continent, Taylor said
that the map demonstrated that "[i]t is unquestionably true that
the greatest single religious influence in Europe, unlike in the
United States, is the Catholic group," with that "particularly true"
in those countries behind the Iron Curtain.[35] Taylor then spoke
of his recent trip to Europe and indicated that both the Archbishop of Canterbury and the Pope were in support of "unifying
the efforts of all denominations in the looming crisis of our times
under a simple kind of formula, that all good men believe in God
and all good men believe in human liberty."[36]

No sooner did Taylor finish then the Protestant clergy, led
by Bishop Oxnam ("I am tremendously concerned about this."),
started in to object to Taylor's request, raising matters that had
been simmering/boiling for over seven years. Not only had the
president's appointment "single[d] out a single group," what Taylor was proposing would not lead to unity, but would instead lead
only to disunity. Among the most heated moments came when
Reverend Dahlburg rebutted Taylor's basic thesis: "The deadly
antagonisms in Europe are between Catholicism and communism.... I am willing to oppose communism[,] but I would hate to
see the Protestant churches pulling Catholicism out of the fire."[37]

Things did not get much better when a group of Protestant
clergy, led by Bishop Oxnam, met with the president a month later.
Oxnam repeated a suggestion he had earlier made to Taylor: that
Taylor should be appointed the President's personal representative

"to the religious leaders of the world."[38] With respect to the 1948 meeting of the World Council of Churches (WCC), Truman asked whether only Protestants would be represented. The Oxnam group responded that other Christian groups would also be represented. Unlike the flak Taylor had taken on October 20, that answer was taken by the president to be a positive development and one he wanted Taylor to explore with dispatch.[39]

Truman (according to Taylor) directed him as follows: "I wish you would call upon the World Council of Churches at Geneva, and discuss its problems, as well as the Amsterdam Conference [of the WCC] in the autumn; also meet representatives of the World Council in Europe whenever you find the opportunity to do so."[40] In the words of one historian, "Truman had dispatched Taylor on a radical mission: to reshape the internal organization, membership, and agenda of a religious community."[41] More specifically, the president wanted the Russian Orthodox Church out of the WCC, the Roman Catholic Church admitted to the WCC, and Taylor (as the president's representative) to take part in the WCC's autumn meeting.[42]

Off to London, Taylor met with the Archbishop of Canterbury to lobby for the Catholic Church's admission to the WCC.[43] From there he headed to Rome, where he got a grim report from Monsignor Tardini (now the Vatican's Secretary of State) about the Russian Orthodox Church.[44] Next stop was the WCC's headquarters in Geneva to meet with Willem Visser 't Hooft, the WCC's General Secretary. That meeting did not go well. Visser 't Hooft told Taylor point-blank: (1) that he, Taylor, would not participate in the WCC Conference; (2) that the "Church of Rome" could not attend the WCC conference (although individual Catholics—non-Church officials—might observe); and (3) the WCC did not "draw the line at the Iron Curtain," and hoped to strengthen its ties to the Russian Orthodox Church.[45] A deeply disappointed Taylor reported this back to Truman,[46] but then pivoted his efforts to try to establish a working relationship with the new head of the Greek

Orthodox Church in Istanbul, Turkey—whom he hoped would be Archbishop Athenagoras, an American he had "conferred with ... in New York on several occasions."[47] While he wanted to go to Istanbul, both the U.S. Ambassador to Turkey and the Papal Nuncio in Paris (an expert on the Orthodox Church) counseled against a trip before a final decision had been made by the Greek Orthodox Church (Athenagoras ultimately did get the job).[48]

Taylor's further religious shuttle diplomacy between high officials (religious and otherwise) in London and Paris did not make any further progress on getting a seat at the WCC table for the Vatican.[49] Truman, frustrated with the "intransigence" of so many Protestants not to rally around a common ground to fight atheistic communism, commiserated with Taylor's lack of success and "the embarrassing position in which you find yourself as a result of [that] intransigence."[50] By mid 1948, both Truman and Taylor mutually agreed that "nothing further could be done" vis-à-vis the WCC.[51]

And with that, Taylor took the rest of the summer off, touring Europe with Anabel until they sailed back to America on the *Queen Elizabeth* in September. Back in the United States, Taylor was awarded the United States Medal for Merit by President Truman shortly after his surprise reelection; Taylor was cited for "exceptionally meritorious conduct in the performance of outstanding services" to his country.[52]

The year 1949 started with Taylor and Anabel resting up in Palm Beach. Once the "season" ended, they headed back to New York City, when Taylor wound down the (completed) work of American Relief for Italy Inc.[53]

It was good that Taylor got some R&R in Florida, for May would prove to be a *very* busy month. First off was another meeting with leading Protestant leaders on May 3.[54] It was mostly the same group as before (e.g., Oxnam, Dahlberg, Cavert, Pugh), with a few new faces representing the same religious denominations from the first session. Taylor started the meeting diplomatically

("I recall very pleasantly our last meeting"), and then told the clergy group that "the President is still anxious to gather all the information he can, not only through the Pope and the Catholic cardinals, bishops and other officials of the Church, but from leaders of thought in other denominations wherever they may be."[55] He then reviewed in some detail his unsuccessful efforts in 1947-48 with respect to the WCC. This led to a back and forth as to who was to blame for that failure—Taylor: Protestant opposition; Oxnam and Cavert: the Catholic Church.[56] But it was a newcomer, Eppling Reinartz, the General Secretary of the United Lutheran Church, who challenged the basic tenet of what Truman (and Taylor) were attempting to do: "I wish our President could be disabused of the idea that there is some moral unity in Mohammedanism, in Judaism and Christianity that could be associated structurally or in an informal way to estop the on-rush of communism or of atheism."[57]

As if that were not bad enough, the day before Taylor's meeting with the Protestant clergy, Tardini had sent Archbishop Spellman a letter highly critical of the Taylor Mission.[58] The Vatican clearly did not like that Taylor was no longer exclusively focused on the Church in Rome, but was spending much of his time traveling to and in consultation with other religious leaders:

> It would seem that these other missions have been purposely assigned to him in order to engender the impression that his visit to the Pope is just one of many missions entrusted to Mr. Taylor ... and that the Holy Father is thus placed on the same level with other religious leaders who are casually interviewed. Hence, this attitude is obviously not well received here in our circles and is regarded as inconsistent with the respect which is due to the Holy See.[59]

Notwithstanding those backdrops, on May 4 Truman wrote to Taylor, expressing "special faith and confidence in you," and asking him to return to Rome at the earliest convenience.[60] The president—based on "our many conversations … in recent days" (and before)—also asked Taylor to visit "spiritual leaders and others in authority in England and Switzerland, in Paris and Berlin, and if conditions warrant, Istanbul, Turkey and Moscow, U.S.S.R."

Clearly, Truman was not giving up on his strategy to combat communism not only by military and diplomatic means but also by religious ones. The president explained that strategy to his wife after one meeting with Taylor at the White House:

> Looks as if [Taylor] and I may get the morals of the world on our side. We are talking to the Archbishop of Canterbury, the bishop at the head of the Lutheran Church, the Metropolitan of the Greek Church in Istanbul, and the Pope. I may send him to see the top Buddhist and the Grand Lama of Tibet. If I can mobilize the people who believe in a moral world against the Bolshevik materialists who believe as Henry Wallace does—"that the end justifies the means"—we can win this fight. Treaties, agreements, or the moral code mean nothing to the Communists. So we've got to organize the people who believe in honor and the Golden Rule to win the world back to peace and Christianity. Ain't it hell![61]

And on the same day Truman was formally authorizing Taylor's next Mission, Taylor was also busy on a different front—starting to fund his $1.5 million pledge to Cornell for the religious interfaith building on campus, to be named Anabel Taylor Hall (*see* Chapter III, pp. 24-27).

Back in Rome, Taylor spent a good part of the month, with the help of the Pope, trying to arrange a trip to Athens (where the Greek Orthodox Archbishop had just died) and Istanbul (where Athenagoras was now based).[62] On June 12, Taylor reported to Truman that, via the Pope's back channel, he had been able to arrange to visit with Athenagoras and the newly installed head of the Greek Orthodox Church, Archbishop Spyridion.[63] Truman responded on June 17, praising Taylor for his industry and resourcefulness, and expressing pleasure about both prospective visits (especially to "receive the confidence of men" like Athenagoras, who "is indeed in a position to exercise great influence in his exalted station in Istanbul.").[64] Truman went on to encourage Taylor to extend his travels "to pierce the Iron Curtain to negotiate with the Patriarch of Moscow along the lines we discussed before you departed for Europe."

Back in Rome on June 24, Taylor gave Truman a lengthy report on his trips to Athens and Istanbul.[65] Athenagoras was in strong support of the president's strategy and Spyridion (although reluctant at first given his church's history of relations with the Catholic Church) was ultimately agreeable to the Church having representatives at the WCC. In the words of one historian, "[t]his was no small development."[66] The threat of Russian aggression on their borders had trumped the centuries of difficult relations with the Vatican.

And while Truman was pleased with this important development, he wrote to Taylor on July 8 of the "intense and unremitting opposition to your mission … in the hearts and minds of some of our American religious leaders."[67] But it was not just pressure coming from America. Only July 1, the Pope (with Tardini present) had a candid discussion with Taylor about the nature of his mission.[68] The Vatican wanted "an official and stable" diplomatic relationship with the United States. Every other nation committed to the separation of Church and state had an official ambassador to the Holy See, but not the United States. Taylor replied that the Protestant "attacks would cease if he were at the same time the representative to the various religious groups, a thing which is evidently impossible."[69]

On July 15, Taylor reported to Truman that he would not be going to Moscow as the president had encouraged.[70] After Greece and Turkey, Taylor had gone to Germany, where he met with

Taylor arrives at reception for ambassadors to the Vatican

John McCloy (U.S. Commissioner of Germany), Robert Murphy (the U.S. Ambassador), and Cardinal von Preysing (of Berlin). All three had strongly advised Taylor not to go for a host of reasons (security, Soviet propaganda, likelihood of increased religious persecutions). By the same letter, however, Taylor reported that the Pope had issued an edict—the Church would "most warmly welcome collaboration with Protestants in the common fight of religious persons against the communist atheist." Taylor told Truman that this was "the first open offer of collaboration" by the Pope to Protestants.[71]

Perhaps emboldened by this latest development, the president on November 3 sent Taylor off to Europe with a slightly revised Mission.[72] The new job would be to convince European religious leaders of all stripes to come together at a meeting in Washington: "The sole purpose of such a gathering would be to

Taylor surrounded by papal dignitaries in Vatican City

consider ways and means to advance the just and lasting peace for which all men of good will yearn." Unfortunately, the first efforts on Truman's new idea were not encouraging. In England, the Archbishop of Canterbury and Archbishop of York were negative, believing a Washington meeting would have "a political slant."[73]

Even before he left for Europe to see if such a meeting were possible, Taylor had paid Spellman a visit to tell him he definitely intended to resign his post and would do so after representing the president at the opening of the Holy Year.[74] When Taylor told Truman of his plans is unclear. A draft resignation letter was sent to Taylor in London (with "the President's full approval") on December 1, 1949.[75] That draft became formal on December 13, when Taylor (from London) told the Pope of his intention to submit his resignation "as Personal Representative of the President to Your Holiness."[76] His letter also revealed "the President's intention, ... in accord with the desires of Your Holiness, to recommend to the Congress of the United States at an early date the appointment of a Minister to the Holy See." And Taylor lastly pitched the idea of a Washington conference of religious leaders "at an early practical date." The Pope responded on December 21, acknowledging "with a sense of real sorrow" Taylor's decision "prompted by reasons of health" (which Taylor did not reference in his letter).[77] The Pope's letter also noted "with lively satisfaction" Truman's decision to send an official ambassador to the Vatican. But as to the Washington conference idea, the letter expressed caution: "since this is a confidential matter pertaining to a domestic policy which is sponsored by the President ..., there is no reason for Our comment."

Even before he could proffer his formal resignation to the president, Taylor was back in Paris at the beginning of January 1950 pitching the Washington conference idea to Marc Bocquet, the leader of the French Protestants and a co-president of the WCC.[78] At first, Bocquet (in person) seemed open to the idea, but later that month he wrote to Taylor, predicting "grave misunderstandings which might result" from such a conference.[79]

On January 18 (Taylor's seventy-sixth birthday), Taylor formally tendered his resignation to Truman.[80] It tracked many of the same themes as his letter to the Pope (without referencing the naming of an official ambassador or a possible Washington conference). Truman responded the same day "with deep regret" and "acced[ing] to your wish most reluctantly."[81]

Nature abhors a vacuum, and when the White House did not immediately name a replacement for Taylor, on January 31, 1950, Joseph P. Kennedy wrote to Truman.[82] Purportedly concerned (as were Catholics everywhere) about the non-appointment, Kennedy started off his letter with a startling fabrication: "I write you ... as the man more responsible than anyone for the suggestion of establishing the so-called Taylor Mission at the Vatican" (see supra Chapter VIII and note 31 therein for the evidence that Kennedy was completely out of the loop on that "suggestion"). While Truman wrote back on February 3,[83] it was not until June 30 (at the outset of the Korean crisis) that Kennedy was granted an audience with the president. It must have been an odd and difficult meeting for Truman, who did not like or trust Kennedy (when his son ran for president in 1960, Truman—pre-Democratic Convention—was quoted as saying: "It's not the Pope I'm afraid of, it's the Pop"). According to a Kennedy later-written memorandum, when the conversation got to "the question of the Vatican," Kennedy got off to a strong start by saying he "thought Taylor was a horse's ass."[84] Truman responded that Taylor had done a fine job, that "he liked him ... [and] had received some fine information from Taylor ... I said if he did he got it very incidentally." As for an appointment, Truman first railed against Bishop Oxnam for "all the abuse ... [he had] been heaping on him ... for keeping Taylor there. He is going to let Congress take it from here in." But not until after the midterm elections.

No sooner had Taylor retired (yet again), and as he was basking in congratulating correspondence,[85] than the president again came calling. On July 15, 1950, Truman asked Taylor to go to Europe and "resume with such leaders as are free to talk with you."[86] Undoubtedly because the "mission [would] be personal, and quite informal," nothing of any substance (for good or ill) seems to have come out of that effort.[87] As such, on April 26, 1951, Truman tried once more, but this time bestowing a more formal sound to the task and designating Taylor "Personal Representative of the President of the United States with the rank of Ambassador."[88] And this time there seemed like there might be real progress on the Truman–Taylor plan.

First off, following up on a suggestion in Truman's April 26 letter, Taylor met with Bishop Henry Sherrill, the head of the American Episcopal Church; the two men discussed religious leaders issuing a joint statement on the world situation. Sherrill viewed that the Catholic Church's participation in such a project was "essential": "I believe that if a statement could be agreed upon, to be signed by say the Archbishop of Canterbury, Pastor Boegner, the Archbishop of Sweden, Athenagoras, and myself, with his Holiness, it would make a great impression upon the entire world."[89] When Taylor took that idea to the Pope on June 6, Taylor found him to be very receptive to the idea.[90] Not surprisingly, Truman was pleased with these two developments.[91] Within two weeks, however, the bottom fell out.

Protestant groups (in particular, the Anglican Church) had issued public broadsides against a recent papal proclamation that the Assumption of the Virgin Mary was a dogmatic article of faith.[92] The Pope and his advisors were beyond furious. On June 19, Pius XII handed Taylor a statement: "it seems difficult, not to say impossible, to arrive at a formula of a common declaration, to which ... the Holy Father could adhere."[93] A stunned Taylor wrote the Pope the next day, trying to salvage "an uneasy and fluctuating situation": while pledging to show the Pope's "memorandum" only to the president upon his return to America, Taylor wrote he could understand "perfectly well [that] the recent dogma ... might have a tendency to preclude a concert of action at this time."[94]

Not yet giving up the ship, Taylor met with Bishop Sherrill, the Archbishop of Canterbury, the Archbishop of York, and the Bishop of Chichester in London on July 3. Out of that meeting two draft statements were generated. But on September 6, the Archbishop of Canterbury wrote to Taylor (enclosing the two drafts), stating that "the prospect of getting any statement jointly signed ... is so remote that the attempt ought to be abandoned."[95]

At that point, Truman threw his hands up in frustration and publicly lashed out. At the first Washington Pilgrimage of American Churches on September 28, the president "chided" world religious leaders for their ongoing failure to unite in a common affirmation of faith at a time when "the very future of the word of God is at stake."[96] That tongue-lashing did not sit that well with many, especially with Protestant clergy, who criticized the president for seeking to mobilize Christianity, even for good political ends.[97]

Stirring up American Protestants was not a great prelude to Truman's next step. In response to ongoing pressure/lobbying by

Myron and Anabel in Rome, June 28, 1952

the American hierarchy of the Church for the appointment of an official ambassador,[98] Truman sent to the Senate on October 21, 1951, the nomination of General Mark Clark (the liberator of Rome) to be Ambassador to the Holy See. That unleashed a "furious protest" by Protestant groups, with the White House getting over 100,000 letters against the nomination.[99] But there was an even greater problem: Texas Senator Thomas Connolly, chairman of the Senate Foreign Relations Committee.[100] Secretary of State Dean Acheson was on Capitol Hill when Connolly learned of the nomination; in his memoirs, Acheson wrote that Connolly was "incoherent with rage."[101] The problem: Connolly's constituents in the 36th Infantry Division had suffered heavy casualties under Clark's leadership in Italy. With Clark's nomination literally dead on arrival in the Senate,[102] Clark's nomination was ultimately withdrawn in January of 1952.

That left one last task for Taylor to perform for Truman: to hand deliver a May 14, 1952, letter from the president explaining what had happened to the failed Clark nomination.[103] Citing not only the "deep cleavage in our population," Truman also gave the Pope an American civics lesson on Senatorial prerogatives: Clark's nomination "would not be brought before the Committee but would be indefinitely postponed" because of Connolly's "violent oppos[ition]." The president went on to conclude by praising "Mr. Taylor's extraordinary service. Throughout his long tenure as Personal Representative to Your Holiness he has constantly been beset with problems that would have thwarted a man of less steadfast purposes." Notwithstanding "an opposition from sources which few could have foreseen, ... [h]e has at all times had my complete confidence and I like to think that Your Holiness has found in him a valued friend and wise observer of world trends."

Back from his visit to the Pope and their other European travels that summer, Mr. and Mrs. Taylor presided over the dedication of Anabel Taylor Hall on October 20, 1952.[104] Then, in the final days of the Truman presidency, Taylor sent Truman a letter expressing his appreciation for all their work together and his admiration for Truman's accomplishments as president.[105] Truman responded on January 19, 1953: "I don't know when I've received a letter that I appreciated any more than I did yours of the sixteenth. My association with you has been a most pleasant one and one I shall always remember and treasure. No man could have had a more effective representative than you have been for the policies which I have been trying to implement.... Please remember me to Mrs. Taylor."[106]

264 Myron Taylor: The Man Nobody Knew

Notes

1. As Truman told reporters about becoming president: "I felt like the moon, the stars, and all the planets had fallen on me." W. LaFeber, *America, Russia and the Cold War: 1945-1975*, p. 17 (John Wiley 1976).

2. *Id.* pp. 17-18. *See also* W. LaFeber, *The American Age*, pp. 422-24 (Norton 1989).

3. *Id.* pp. 434-39.

4. P. Kent, "The War Aims of the Papacy, 1938-45," *FDR, the Vatican, and the Catholic Church in America, 1933-1945*, pp. 170-75 (ed. D. Woolner & R. Kurial) (Palgrave Macmillan 2003).

5. *See, e.g.*, R. Russell July 10, 1945, letter to M.C. Taylor (Taylor Papers, Cornell University). Taylor also kept up with his counterparts. *See, e.g.*, C. Hull August 4, 1945, letter to M.C. Taylor (reports on the U.S. Senate's approval of the U.N. Charter—it "brings again to my mind the remarkable service you rendered over a period of several years.... [The United States and the world] will always be indebted to you for the contributions you made." It was a "high privilege" to be associated with you.) (Taylor Papers, Cornell University); J. Davies March 18, 1946, letter to M.C. Taylor ("your work for Italian relief is one of the finest" in history, and a "great service" to "Peace and to Humanity"). (Taylor Papers, Cornell University); W. Churchill April 3, 1946, letter to M.C. Taylor (Taylor Papers, Cornell University).

Prior to Taylor's departure, he published *Wartime Correspondence Between President Roosevelt and Pope Pius XII* (ed. M. Taylor) (Macmillan 1947).

6. M. Carter, "American Protestant Reaction to FDR's 'Personal Representative' at the Vatican," *FDR, the Vatican, and the Catholic Church in America, 1933-1945*, pp. 179-204 (ed. D. Woolner & R. Kurial) (Palgrave Macmillan 2003).

7. G. Fogarty, *The Vatican and the American Hierarchy from 1870 to 1965*, pp. 315-16 (Anton Hiersemann 1982). In January 1946, *Newsweek* ran a story to that effect. *Id.*

8. Fogarty, *supra* note 7, p. 316.

9. *Id.* pp. 316-17.

10. *Id.* Interestingly, a lot of the Vatican's concerns were directed at changes in personnel under Taylor in Rome. Taylor's assistant after Tittmann, Franklin Gowan, was replaced by J. Graham Parsons of the Foreign Service. Parsons' oral history at the Truman Presidential Library on his short tenure (16-17 months) in that role was the first hostile (to Taylor) document the author saw in his research for the Taylor biography. Parsons does confirm, however, that his personal animus was sparked by Taylor's firing him (Parsons Transcript, Truman Library pp. 67-68, 78-79, and note 8).

11. R. Dallek, *The Lost Peace*, pp. 203-08 (Harper Collins 2008). Churchill first confronted Stalin with this concept at the Potsdam Conference, calling it an

"iron fence." C. Mee, "Churchill Called It an Iron Fence at Potsdam," *New York Times* (August 5, 1973). Stalin's response: "Fairy tales!" Dallek, p. 116.

12. As Taylor reported to the group of Protestant leaders in 1947, Pacilli's 1936 warning about a coming need to fight atheistic communism "made a very great impression on me, and I always remembered [it] as a far-sighted prophecy." Transcript of meeting of Protestant Clergymen with Myron C. Taylor at Union Club (New York City, October 21, 1947), pp. 5-6 (Taylor Papers, Cornell University).

13. M.C. Taylor June 11, 1946, letter to H.S. Truman (Taylor Papers, Truman Library). On May 21, 1946, Taylor had sent to William Hassett (FDR's Secretary, who stayed on in that same post for the duration of Truman's presidency; he would become quite close to Taylor over the next several years) a few memoranda covering his service to FDR during the war. He asked Hassett to share them with Truman (a voracious reader): "The point I am making of President Truman is that by the use we made of [Taylor's various missions] and the influence of high Catholic authority[,] we gained something otherwise not possible—a unity of plans and objectives." M.C. Taylor May 21, 1946, letter to W. Hassett (Taylor Papers, Cornell University).

14. M.C. Taylor June 11, 1946, telegram to J. Byrnes (Taylor Papers, Cornell University).

15. M.C. Taylor June 25, 1946, letter to H.S. Truman (Taylor Papers, Cornell University).

16. M.C. Taylor June 25, 1946, letter to H.S. Truman (Taylor Papers, Cornell University).

17. M.C. Taylor July 19, 1946, letter to H.S. Truman (Taylor Papers, Cornell University).

18. M.C. Taylor September 20, 1946, note to H.S. Truman (Taylor Papers, Cornell University). Interestingly, this is the only document the author has seen on which Taylor went back and made handwritten notations ("The day of his discharge of Wallace. The afternoon before this I had called on the President and strongly urged him to 'fire' Wallace. Citing our procedure in industry—any one disloyal to associates or to the Company was discharged at once—MCT"). For the Wallace incident, *see* Dallek, *supra* note 11, pp. 120-21, 127.

The growing bond between the president and Taylor is further evidenced by the exchange of correspondence between them about the disastrous (for Democrats) congressional elections in November of 1946. *See* M.C. Taylor November 7, 1946, letter to H.S. Truman; W. Hassett November 8, 1946, letter to M.C. Taylor; H.S. Truman November 9, 1946, letter to M.C. Taylor (all of these letters are in the Taylor Papers at Cornell). Truman's response is quite interesting (as a prelude to his 1948 campaign): "a definite majority in opposition is preferable to a hostile majority of my own political faith."

19. W. Hassett November 8, 1946, letter to M.C. Taylor (Taylor Papers, Cornell University).

20. H.S. Truman November 21, 1946, letter to Pope Pius XII (Official File 76-8, HST Papers, Truman Library).

21. W. Inboden, *Religion and American Foreign Policy, 1945-1960*, p. 122 (Cambridge University Press 2008). While the Inboden book is the most complete published detailing of the Truman–Taylor plan, *see also* D. Kirby, "The Cold War and American Religion" (published online May 24, 2017) *and* D. Kirby, "Harry Truman's Religious Legacy: The Holy Alliance, Containment, and the Cold War," *Religion and the Cold War*, pp. 97-102 (ed. D. Kirby) (Palgrave 2003). Unfortunately, M. Phayer's *Pius XII: The Holocaust and the Cold War* (Indiana University Press 2008) has almost no coverage of the Truman presidency's interactions with the Vatican.

This was something that Truman had been contemplating for some time. On the day after Churchill's Iron Curtain speech, the president stated that the survival of Western civilization required that all religions—Protestant, Catholic, and Jewish—come together and provide the impetus for a moral and spiritual awakening in America. Kirby, "The Cold War and American Religion," note 30.

22. W. Hassett August 7, 1947, letter to M.C. Taylor (Taylor Papers, Cornell University). That same day Truman sent Taylor a letter with similar guidance: "if people of all religious faiths would, in the present world crisis, unite upon a universal two-point declaration embodying the spirit of belief in God and belief in human liberty, to which mankind will dedicate itself, it might help temporarily and be effective permanently, in bringing people to a better basis of understanding in the interest of world peace." H.S. Truman August 7, 1947, letter to M.C. Taylor (Taylor Papers, Cornell University). The next day Hassett sent Taylor another letter, enclosing a State Department memorandum on "The Vatican Problem" (*i.e.*, the "new avalanche of protests" against the Taylor Mission), advising Taylor further about the president's press release about Taylor's trip, and relaying Truman's agreement "with you that publication of the latest correspondence simultaneously in Rome and in Washington would be highly desirable." W. Hassett August 8, 1947, letter to M.C. Taylor (Taylor Papers, Cornell University).

Just prior to his departure, Taylor had been in contact with General Lucius Clay (commander of Allied forces in Berlin) regarding his trip. L. Clay July 23, 1947, letter to M.C. Taylor (Taylor Papers, Cornell University). At the same time, Taylor was congratulating his old friend James Forrestal on becoming the nation's first Secretary of Defense. *The Forrestal Diaries*, p. 299 (ed. W. Mills) (Viking 1951) (As noted in the *Diaries*, this is the only letter of congratulations that Forrestal kept.).

23. Inboden, *supra* note 21, p. 124; W. Hassett August 23, 1947, letter to M.C. Taylor (Taylor Papers, Cornell University).

24. W. Hassett August 8, 1947, letter to M.C. Taylor (Taylor Papers, Cornell University). While Taylor was on his European trip meeting with religious leaders,

Truman told Archbishop Spellman: "I am thoroughly convinced that Mr. Taylor is doing great and constructive work." Fogarty, *supra* note 7, p. 317.

25. L. Clay September 15, 1947, letter to M.C. Taylor (Taylor Papers, Truman Library); C. Schott September 19, 1947, letter to Taylor (Taylor Papers, Cornell University).

26. Fogarty, *supra* note 7, pp. 317-18; Inboden, *supra* note 21, p. 125; C. Schott September 19, 1947, letter to M.C. Taylor (Taylor Papers, Cornell University); M.C. Taylor August 30, 1947, telegram to W. Hassett (Taylor Papers, Cornell University).

27. M.C. Taylor September 25, 1947, letter to H.S. Truman (Taylor Papers, Truman Library).

28. Inboden, *supra* note 21, pp. 125-26; W. Hassett November 7, 1947, letter to M.C. Taylor (Taylor Papers, Cornell University).

29. Back in the United States, Taylor followed up with those he had met in Europe. *See, e.g.*, M.C. Taylor October 8, 1947, letter to Fisher (Archbishop of Canterbury) (Taylor Papers, Truman Library) (the hope is "to offset the growing propaganda and accomplishments of the Soviet[s] which are contrary to our faith and imperial human liberties."); M.C. Taylor October 8, 1947, letter to Lord Halifax (Taylor Papers, Truman Library) ("arouse religious unity among all dominations in an effort to combat the propaganda and accomplishments of communism, particularly as related to Russia.").

30. W. Hassett August 7, 1947, letter to M.C. Taylor (Taylor Papers, Cornell University). *See* W. Hassett October 16, 1947, memorandum to H.S. Truman (Taylor Papers, Truman Library) (all Taylor "gets for his work is a fusillade of brickbats and dead cats").

31. Transcript of Meeting of Protestant Clergymen with Myron Taylor at Union Club (New York City, October 20, 1047) (Taylor Papers, Cornell University).

32. Boycotting the meeting was Louie Newton (President of the Southern Baptist Convention), who did not want to "imply at least tacit acknowledgement that Mr. Taylor's mission to the Vatican was thus approved." Inboden, *supra* note 21, p. 127, n.51. Given that Southern Baptists had most loudly protested FDR's 1939 appointment of Taylor (*see* Chapter IX, pp. 106-08 *and* notes 32-34), that probably was to be expected.

33. Transcript of Meeting of Protestant Clergymen, p. 2.

34. *Id.* pp. 21, 28. The revelation of this secret code seems to have had a big impact, at least on Bishop Oxnam. R. Miller, *Bishop G. Bromley Oxnam: Paladin of Liberal Protestantism*, p. 425 (Abingdon Press 1990). This secret code bypassing the State Department clearly bothered J. Graham Parsons for the brief period he served in Rome as Taylor's aide. Parsons' Oral History, Transcript, pp. 75-78 (Truman Library).

35. Transcript of Meeting of Protestant Clergymen, p. 40.

36. *Id.* pp. 40-42 (The Pope "is enthusiastic, and will do everything he can."). He went on to cite the fact that he was—to General Clay's great surprise—granted permission to visit Bishop Dibelius in the Russian zone in Berlin. According to Taylor, when his name was presented to the Russian colonel in charge of such matters, his reply was: "Myron Taylor? Certainly." *Id.* p. 41.

37. He added: "I would as much hate to be thrown into opposition to Russia by supporting what I call ecclesiastical totalitarianism as I would be against communism." In the words of one historian, Dahlberg's unvarnished broadside was stunning: "To any who doubted the intensity of Protestant hostility to Catholicism, here was stark evidence." Inboden, *supra* note 21, p. 128.

38. Inboden, *supra* note 21, p. 129.

39. W. Hassett November 20, 1947, letter to M.C. Taylor (Taylor Papers, Truman Library). Hassett also told Taylor that Truman would not act on Oxnam's suggestion: "It does not make much sense." *Id.*

40. Meeting of Protestant Clergymen with Myron C. Taylor at the Union Club (May 3, 1949), p. 4; W. Hassett March 19, 1948, letter to M.C. Taylor (Taylor Papers, Truman Library).

41. Inboden, *supra* note 21, p. 136.

42. *Id.* p. 129.

43. M.C. Taylor March 26, 1948, letter to Archbishop Fisher (Taylor Papers, Truman Library).

44. Inboden, *supra* note 21, p. 130.

45. *Id.* pp. 130-32.

46. M.C. Taylor April 29, 1948, letter to H.S. Truman (Taylor Papers, Truman Library).

47. M.C. Taylor May 22, 1948, letter to Pope Pius XII (Taylor Papers, Truman Library); M.C. Taylor May 27, 1948, letter to W. Hassett (Taylor Papers, Cornell University). *See* Inboden, *supra* note 21, pp. 132-33.

48. Inboden, *supra* note 21, p. 133.

49. Inboden, *supra* note 21, pp. 133-35.

50. H.S. Truman May 19, 1948, letter to M.C. Taylor (Taylor Papers, Truman Library).

51. W. Hassett May 24, 1948, letter to M.C. Taylor; M.C. Taylor June 1, 1948, letter to W. Hassett (both letters are in the Taylor Papers at Cornell); H.S. Truman June 18, 1948, letter to M.C. Taylor (Taylor Papers, Truman Library); W. Hassett July 2, 1948, letter to M.C. Taylor (Taylor Papers, Cornell University) (Hassett ended this letter: "I am sure you are aware of my sentiments toward you personally. It has been a privilege to work in such close association with you. The resulting friendship I count among my real blessings. It is a friendship that I know will endure until one or the other of us can enter into no further human relationships. With gratitude, appreciation and highest esteem—and every good wish to Mrs. Taylor."); H.S. Truman

September 14, 1948, letter to M.C. Taylor (Taylor Papers, Cornell University) (regarding the WCC meeting in Amsterdam "let them stew in their own joice [sic].").

52. *See* Chapter I, p. 8. On the same day of the ceremony, Hull wrote to Taylor regretting that he could not be present for the awarding of the medal by the president. C. Hull December 20, 1948, letter to M.C. Taylor (Taylor Papers, Cornell University) ("No like recognition has been more highly deserved in the light of your great ability and great public service.").

Earlier that same year the Pope had named Taylor "Knight Order of Pius, First Degree." And both the President and Prime Minister of Italy awarded him separate Citations for Distinguished Service for his relief work.

53. D. Acheson April 20, 1949, letter to M.C. Taylor (Taylor Papers, Cornell University). In January of 1949, Taylor had discussed with Acheson giving his position at the Vatican an official ambassador status. Acheson told Taylor he was in favor but said he had asked Truman to wait for a more propitious time because it "would surely start a religious controversy all over the country." D. Acheson, *Present at the Creation*, p. 735 (Norton 1969).

54. Transcript of Protestant Clergymen (May 3, 1949).

55. *Id.* pp. 2-4.

56. This back and forth is well memorialized in Inboden, *supra* note 21, pp. 138-39.

57. On top of that Pugh returned to a theme from the 1947 get-together: that the Catholic Church in Europe "is as great a problem as is communism." *Id.*

58. Fogarty, *supra* note 7, pp. 318-19.

59. Tardini also commented on Taylor's concern for Protestant attacks on him and asked Spellman to bring these matters to Truman's attention. *Id.*

60. H.S. Truman May 4, 1949, letter to M.C. Taylor (Taylor Papers, Cornell University).

61. Miller, *supra* note 34, p. 428; Inboden, *supra* note 21, pp. 139-40. *See also* L. Gardner, "The Cold War Crusade." *Passport*, p. 17 (April 2009).

62. Inboden, *supra* note 21, pp. 140-41. According to Taylor, the Pope agreed to help "as a duty to mankind and to God which he cannot shirk regardless of consequences." *Id.* p. 140. Taylor had also visited the Papal Nuncio and Cardinal Archbishop in Paris during May of 1949.

63. M.C. Taylor June 12, 1949, letter to H.S. Truman (Taylor Papers, Truman Library).

64. H.S. Truman June 17, 1949, letter to M.C. Taylor (Taylor Papers, Cornell University).

65. M.C. Taylor June 24, 1949, letter to H.S. Truman (Taylor Papers, Cornell University).

66. Inboden, *supra* note 21, p. 141.

67. H.S. Truman July 8, 1949, letter to M.C. Taylor (Taylor Papers, Cornell University).

68. Fogarty, *supra* note 7, pp. 319-20.

69. Tardini reported on the audience to Cicognani in Washington: Taylor was "so solicitous in regard to his contacts with the heads of non-Catholic churches, the questions that interest the Holy See remain generally without any positive result." *Id.*

70. M.C. Taylor July 15, 1949, letter to H.S. Truman (Taylor Papers, Truman Library); H.S. Truman July 8, 1949, letter to M.C. Taylor (Taylor Papers, Cornell University).

71. A Vatican official described the edict as a "great turning point" in the Church's relations with Protestants, akin to the 1520 papal bull denouncing Protestant reformers. Inboden, *supra* note 21, p. 143.

72. H.S. Truman November 3, 1949, letter to M.C. Taylor (Taylor Papers, Cornell University).

73. Archbishop Contuar November 30, 1949, letter to M.C. Taylor (Taylor Papers, Cornell University). Inboden, *supra* note 21, p. 146. Many have speculated that Taylor's health was a decisive factor in his decision (Fogarty, *supra* note 7, p. 720; Inboden, *supra* note 21, p. 145); but given Taylor's subsequent activities (and a lack of documentation in his papers to that effect), that seems to be merely supposition.

74. Fogarty, *supra* note 7, p. 320.

75. W. Hassett December 1, 1949, letter to M.C. Taylor (Taylor Papers, Cornell University).

76. M.C. Taylor December 13, 1949, letter to Pope Pius XII (Taylor Papers, Cornell University).

77. Pius XII December 23, 1949, letter to M.C. Taylor (Taylor Papers, Cornell University).

78. Inboden, *supra* note 21, p. 147.

79. Pastor Boegner January 30, 1950, letter to M.C. Taylor (Taylor Papers, Cornell University). Taylor shared Boegner's letter with the president and his secretary William Hassett (who was deeply involved in this matter); they all suspected Bishop Oxnam's intervention with the influential Boegner: "he has never been slow to assert his nuisance value." Inboden, *supra* note 21, p. 147.

80. M.C. Taylor January 18, 1950, letter to H.S. Truman (Taylor Papers, Cornell University).

81. H.S. Truman January 18, 1950, letter to M.C. Taylor (Taylor Papers, Cornell University).

82. D. Shaw, *The Patriarch*, p. 632 (Penguin 2012).

83. Fogarty, *supra* note 7, p. 321.

84. Shaw, *supra* note 82, p. 633; A. Smith, *Hostage to Fortune: The Letters of Joseph P. Kennedy*, p. 639 (Viking 2001).

85. *See, e.g.,* S. Welles January 24, 1950, letter to M.C. Taylor ("I have, perhaps, a better appreciation than most of the immense value [of the] contribution that your mission represented.... What you have done has been an outstanding service.") (Taylor Papers, Cornell University); W. Churchill February 21, 1950, letter to M.C. Taylor ("your influence and work for the cause of peace and freedom have been so strong") (Taylor Papers, Cornell University); C. Hull March 24, 1950, letter to M.C. Taylor ("you have done a great and lasting service to your country and the world") (Taylor Papers, Cornell University). L. Einaudi (President of Italy) June 19, 1950, letter to M.C. Taylor ("our nation owes you a debt of gratitude" for helping to relieve "the misery and suffering" caused by the war) (Taylor Papers, Cornell University).

86. H.S. Truman July 15, 1950, letter to M.C. Taylor (Taylor Papers, Cornell University).

87. Inboden, *supra* note 21, pp. 149-50. *See* M.C. Taylor February 21, 1951, letter to W. Hassett (Taylor Papers, Cornell University); M.C. Taylor February 28, 1951, letter to W. Hassett (Taylor Papers, Cornell University); M.C. Taylor April 16, 1951, letter to W. Hassett (Taylor Papers, Cornell University).

88. H.S. Truman April 26, 1951, letter to M.C. Taylor (Taylor Papers, Cornell University).

89. Inboden, *supra* note 21, p. 150.

90. M.C. Taylor June 6, 1951, letter to H.S. Truman (Taylor Papers, Truman Library).

91. H.S. Truman June 2, 1951, letter to M.C. Taylor (Taylor Papers, Truman Library) ("I agree with you that we are sowing seeds which will eventually produce a rich harvest.").

92. Inboden, *supra* note 21, p. 151.

93. June 19, 1951, Statement of Pope Pius XII (Taylor Papers, Truman Library).

94. M.C. Taylor June 20, 1951, letter to Pope Pius XII (Taylor Papers, Cornell University). One historian called Taylor's comment "a potent illustration of the curious dynamic of religion and politics wrought by the Cold War. An American Ambassador, representing the President of the United States, criticiz[ing] the pontiff of the Roman Catholic Church on a point of doctrinal conviction." Inboden, *supra* note 21, p. 152.

95. G. Cantaur September 6, 1951, letter (with attachments) to M.C. Taylor (Taylor Papers, Cornell University); Inboden, *supra* note 21, p. 152. *See also* M.C. Taylor October 25, 1951, letter to G. Cantaur (Taylor Papers, Cornell University); G. Cantaur October 30, 1951, letter to M.C. Taylor (Taylor Papers, Truman Library).

One historian has concluded that the Truman–Taylor effort did have one success. Because of the various overtures to the WCC, the Soviet Union concluded that the WCC was "controlled by Western influences" and pulled Orthodox churches in the Soviet sphere of influence from the WCC. That left a Western-dominated

Council, which "perfectly suited Truman." Kirby, "The Cold War and American Religion" (online and note 56).

96. G. Dugan, "Truman Deplores Religious Disunity," *New York Times* (September 29, 1951); R. Donovan, "Truman Reveals Effort to United World Churches in Face of Reds," *New York Herald Tribune* (September 10, 1951); Inboden, *supra* note 21, p. 153.

97. G. Dugan, "Bishop Dun Replies to Truman Chiding," *Norfolk Press* (October 1, 1951); Inboden, *supra* note 21, pp. 153-54.

98. Fogarty, *supra* note 7, pp. 321-29.

99. Inboden, *supra* note 21, p. 154.

100. M. Carter, *supra* note 6, p. 193.

101. Acheson, *supra* note 53, p. 737; Carter, *supra* note 6; Oral History of Robert F. Wagner, Jr., p. 192 (Columbia University).

102. One historian has written that had the Clark nomination gotten to the Senate floor it would have received only six votes. Carter, *supra* note 6, p. 208, n.45. But with Connolly as chairman of the committee, it would never have gotten to the floor. *See* H.S. Truman May 14, 1952, letter to Pope Pius XII (Taylor Papers, Cornell University).

103. H.S. Truman May 14, 1952, letter to Pope Pius XII (Taylor Papers, Cornell University).

104. Both Truman and Hassett sent messages to Taylor on that date, both of which are in the Taylor Papers at Cornell. Amazingly (perhaps) in light of some of their interactions, Bishop Oxnam sent a somewhat belated congratulatory note to Taylor, praising the interfaith concept of the building and its great beauty. Oxnam December 8, 1952, letter to M.C. Taylor (Taylor Papers, Cornell University).

105. M.C. Taylor January 16, 1953, letter to H.S. Truman (Truman Papers, Truman Library).

One year prior, Taylor had sent a New Year's present to the president, telling him two historical anecdotes relating to it. First: "I was told once in London that Gladstone, being asked by a young man what course he should pursue in his studies, replied: 'I would study maps.'" Second: "I recall Franklin Roosevelt once telling me, apropos of this subject, that he once asked one of the prominent members of the United States Supreme Court: 'Where is Abyssinia?' To which he replied very promptly: 'In Asia.' It is to be hoped that he keeps more nearly to the line in the decision of cases before the court." M.C. Taylor January 12, 1952, letter to H.S. Truman (Taylor Papers, Cornell University).

106. H.S. Truman January 19, 1953, letter to M.C. Taylor (Taylor Papers, Cornell University). Taylor exchanged similar letters with William Hassett. *See* M.C. Taylor February 6, 1953, letter to W. Hassett (Taylor Papers, Cornell University) ("I shall always look back upon our friendship and our work together with the greatest pleasure.").

CHAPTER XVII

Winding Down a Useful Life

This time Taylor really did retire, although in 1953 he agreed to meet with President Dwight D. Eisenhower at the White House.[1] In a systematic way, Taylor began to cut back on his various activities. A Cornell Trustee for 25 years, he went to emeritus status in 1953; that did not prevent him from subsequently endowing a third building at Cornell, naming a residence hall for law students in honor of his favorite teacher, Charles Evans Hughes (*see* Chapter XIV, pp. 218-19). And on January 12, 1956 (six days before his eighty-second birthday), Taylor stepped down as a Director and a member of the Finance Committee of U.S. Steel (a tenure of 30 years, 4 months).[2] In honor of the occasion U.S. Steel published a small volume entitled "Myron C. Taylor: An Appreciation"; not surprisingly, it principally focused on his "consummate skill" and prodigious efforts to save and revitalize the "Corporation" in the 1920s and 1930s.[3]

A long-standing Trustee of both the Metropolitan Museum of Art and the New York Public Library, Taylor also decided to step back from an active role, taking on an honorary status at each. He nonetheless continued the tradition he and Anabel began in the 1930s of donating valuable artwork to the Met.[4]

Taylor had once thought of writing his memoirs (having assembled a "good deal of material"), but by 1953 his "feet [had] grown very cold on the idea."[5]

With many colleagues "hav[ing] passed to their final rest," Taylor's correspondence dropped considerably in the mid to late

Myron C. Taylor's formal portrait

1950s, with his main concern focused on his papers being housed at the Franklin D. Roosevelt Library in Hyde Park.[6] Taylor also kept up a steady back and forth with William Hassett, his good friend and colleague from the Roosevelt and Truman administrations.[7]

Unfortunately, in 1957, Taylor broke his hip.[8] Then, in 1958, not only did the Pope die but so did Cardinal Mooney (who had been so helpful to Taylor in the early days of his Mission to the Vatican).[9] In addition, Anabel Taylor's health went into a steep decline in 1958, and she died on December 12, 1958. With his beloved wife lost to him, Taylor died five months later, on May 6, 1959.

Taylor's funeral was held at his 70-room mansion on East 70th Street in Manhattan. Presiding over the services were four clergymen, led by the Episcopal Bishop of New York, Horace Donegan. Honorary pallbearers included Sumner Welles, Deane Waldo Malott (President of Cornell), Roger Blough (Chairman of

U.S. Steel), and Benjamin Fairless and Irving Olds (former Chairmen of U.S. Steel).[10]

Notes

1. When asked upon leaving the White House whether he was going to be named the new presidential representative to the Vatican, Taylor responded: "No, no, no. That wasn't ever discussed." M.C. Taylor May 13, 1953, statement (Taylor Papers, Cornell University). *See also* M.C. Taylor September 11, 1953, letter to W. Hassett (Taylor Papers, Cornell University) ("I acquainted [Eisenhower and Dulles] with some of the pitfalls in the religious situation.").

2. That Taylor held those positions during his governmental service from 1938 to 1953 tells a lot about how the rules of public life have changed since then.

3. Only a few years later Hyman Roth would boast to Don Corleone's son: "Michael, we're bigger than U.S. Steel." *The Godfather, Part II* (Paramount 1974).

4. *E.g.*, a statue of Anukis from the Ptolemaic Period; Renoir's "Bouquet of Chrysanthemums" (purchased by Taylor in 1937; ultimately bequeathed to the Met in 2002).

5. M.C. Taylor September 11, 1953, letter to W. Hassett (Taylor Papers, Cornell University).

6. *Id. See, e.g.*, E. Roosevelt April 24, 1953, letter to M.C. Taylor (Taylor Papers, Cornell University); M.C. Taylor April 1, 1954, letter to E. Roosevelt (Taylor Papers, Cornell University); E. Roosevelt April 5, 1954, letter to M.C. Taylor (Taylor Papers, Cornell University); M.C. Taylor April 8, 1954, letter to E. Roosevelt (Taylor Papers, Cornell University); E. Roosevelt April 10, 1954, letter to M.C. Taylor (Taylor Papers, Cornell University); M.C. Taylor December 29, 1954, letter to E. Roosevelt (Taylor Papers, Cornell University); E. Roosevelt December 31, 1954, letter to M.C. Taylor (Taylor Papers, Cornell University); E. Roosevelt June 2, 1955, letter to M.C. Taylor (Taylor Papers, Cornell University); M.C. Taylor June 6, 1955, letter to E. Roosevelt (Taylor Papers, Cornell University); E. Roosevelt June 27, 1955, letter to M.C. Taylor (Taylor Papers, Cornell University); M.C. Taylor June 25, 1956, letter to E. Roosevelt (Taylor Papers, Cornell University); E. Roosevelt July 3, 1956, letter to M.C. Taylor (Taylor Papers, Cornell University).

Ultimately, various groupings of Taylor's papers ended up in five locations: the Roosevelt Library, the Truman Library, the Library of Congress, the National Archives and Records Administration, and at Cornell University.

7. *E.g.,* W. Hassett December 22, 1954, letter to M.C. Taylor (Taylor Papers, Cornell University) ("I shall always count it among my blessings that through so many years I was permitted to work with you and to feel a real inspiration in your presence and to form a friendship which I pray God may endure until one or the other of us can enter into no further human relationship.").

8. *See* H. Hooker July 19, 1957, letter to M.C. Taylor (Taylor Papers, Cornell University).

9. W. Hassett October 27, 1958, letter to M.C. Taylor (Taylor Papers, Cornell University).

10. Former President Truman paid tribute to Taylor in the *Cornell Law Quarterly* (Vol. 45, No. 2) (Winter 1960), p. 2 ("All of us should be deeply grateful for the unselfish works of this fine man and able public servant."). After his death, Taylor's New York City home was demolished and on the site *two* apartment houses were built.

A Note About Sources

Myron C. Taylor donated many of his papers, along with many wonderful photographs of his years at the Vatican, to his alma mater, Cornell University (where they are located in the University's Olin Library). Other archival sources with important Taylor documents include the Franklin D. Roosevelt Presidential Library in Hyde Park, New York; the Harry S. Truman Presidential Library in Independence, Missouri; the Library of Congress in Washington, DC; and the National Archives and Records Administration in College Park, Maryland. In addition, the Baker Library at Harvard University (papers of Thomas Lamont) and the Oral History Project at Columbia University (oral histories of Frances Perkins, George Rublee, etc.) contain many valuable materials on Taylor's life and career. The Vatican has made some, but not all, archival materials covering the World War II era available for scholars.

With respect to secondary sources utilized for this biography, all cited materials are referenced in the notes that accompany each chapter.

APPENDIX A

Myron Taylor Hall

History of Myron Taylor Hall

Myron Taylor Hall, home of the Cornell Law School, symbolizes the aspirations of the legal profession and reflects its history. The building also represents the epoch of its construction, the 1930s. It was designed to emphasize the hope that humankind would see an advance from national peace through law to world peace through law.

The building was a gift of Myron C. Taylor and his wife, Anabel Stuart Taylor. Mr. Taylor, an 1894 graduate of the Cornell Law School, served as Chairman of the Board of Trustees of United States Steel Corporation, and as personal representative, with the rank of ambassador, of the President to the Vatican during the pontificate of Pius XII from 1939 to 1950. The gift of $1.5 million was announced in December 1928; construction began in the summer of 1930. The architects were Jackson, Robertson and Adams of Providence, Rhode Island, and the contractor was the Fuller Construction Company of Washington, D.C. Through the combined efforts of the primary architect, F. Ellis Jackson '01, Charles K. Burdick, then dean of the law school, and Cornell alumnus J. duPratt White '09, every phase of the building was designed as a modern law school for a student body of moderate size.

Myron Taylor Hall is one of the last major examples of collegiate gothic style. It is constructed of native stone from the University quarries near Ithaca. Because of the extensive use of this quarry stone in buildings on the campus, it is known as "Cornell" stone. The building's exterior is ornamented by carvings done by Lee Lawrie of Easton, Maryland. Mr. Lawrie's work is also featured on a number of churches and state and public buildings throughout the country, including the Nebraska State Capitol, Rockefeller Center, and the United States Military Academy at West Point.

Myron Taylor hall was dedicated on October 15, 1932:

> If, through knowledge of and a growing respect for the law and its enforcement, it inspires increased regard for the rights of others in individual and community life; if it assists in bringing to an earlier realization an age of reason, self-control and brotherly love; if it helps to lead youth through better knowledge to wisdom, through broader perspective to higher and nobler impulses; if it leads to a better appreciation of the true relationship between that which is material and that which is spiritual; if it helps to bridge the gulf which separates the commonplace from the ideal, the temporal from the eternal, Mrs. Taylor and I shall have achieved an enduring reward.

Mr. and Mrs. Taylor presented the key to the building to University President Livingston Farrand. Dean Charles K. Burdick and Cuthbert W. Pound 1887, later Chief Judge of the New York Court of Appeals, addressed the gathering. It was the desire of the architect and faculty that the front of the building should face west, overlooking Ithaca valley and Cayuga Lake. The eastern side is commonly thought to be the front, however, because it faces College Avenue, now a main street on the campus. The original design intended the grounds on the western side to descent by terraces with a walkway which would lead pedestrians down to Stewart Avenue.

The most prominent feature of Myron Taylor Hall is the central tower, known as the Peace Tower. The tower originally divided classrooms from the portion of the building that housed the library, offices, and lounge areas. At the top of each side of the tower is a sculpture of an owl, representing wisdom. The coat of arms of the United States of America and of the State of New York respectively decorate the balconies at the top of the Peace Tower, below the owls, on the east and west sides. The Great Seal of the United States contains a shield and an eagle grasping an olive branch and arrows, symbolizing peace and the readiness of the United States to protect itself. The seal of New York State contains views of rivers and the ocean and in the center are mountain peaks with the sun rising behind them.

During the initial design stages the architect asked the dean and faulty of the Law School to select a theme for the school's new home so that it could be pictured in stone on the top of the arches at the base of the central tower. It was decided that the new building should represent the dominant aspiration of the legal profession of that day: the hope for an advance from national peace through law to world peace through law. This theme is shown most explicitly in the sculptures on the two sides of the Peace Tower. Carvings on the western side represent a future guided by international law. The eastern (or courtyard) side of the tower records the history of domestic law.

The western archway under the Peace Tower illustrates the theme of world peace through law. One carving portrays a world court comprised of judges who represent the cultures of both hemispheres. The judges sit at a bench underneath a sculpture portraying a broken sword, the torch of knowledge, and a plowshare, symbolizing the end of war and the pursuit of liberty and peace. The bench is flanked by two standing figures. On the far right the old world wears a crown and carries a shield emblazoned with the rising sun. On the far left its counterpart, wearing a crown of rays, holds a shield which shows the western hemisphere and the setting sun. Judges to the right represent Europe, wearing a wig and holding a book; Asia, wearing a turban and holding a scroll; Africa, holding one end of the scroll reading "world peace." The judges on the left side of the table include a North American Indian with a peace pipe; an Aztec; and a third figure holding the other end of the world scroll represents South America.

Through the arch, on the east side, facing the courtyard are carvings representing the history of law. At the top of the tower arch Henry II of England (1154-1189), a major figure in the development of the common law, sitting upon a throne bearing his coat of arms, is shown sending forth his judiciaries, important political and judicial officers of the Norman and later kings of England until the thirteenth century. This carving recalls the legal reforms of Henry II, who participated in the creation of trial by jury and the grand jury, and who inaugurated new court procedures and increased the jurisdiction of the common law.

Farther down and on the outside of the eastern face of the tower, eight participants in a fictional court are depicted humorously. On the left side is a judge with his wig and gavel, a clerk writing down testimony, a defending attorney, and a prisoner in leg irons. To the right are a witness taking an oath, a violently gesticulating prosecuting attorney, a jailer with his key and scroll, and a town cryer holding a lantern. On the west side of the building the sculptures are duplicated, except for the defending attorney and the prisoner.

North of the Peace Tower, facing the courtyard, is a round tower called the "New York Tower." At its tip five adjoining panels depict the stages of law and government in New York: compact, charter, decree, vox populi, and federalism. From left to right are:

> COMPACT: The unwritten compact among the Indian tribes is represented by an Indian chieftain, wearing a war bonnet, and smoking a pipe of peace. Passing before the chief in procession are two warriors, one with a spear, the other with a bow and arrows, all reflecting a spirit of conciliation.

CHARTER: In 1629, in order to encourage agriculture and industry and bring farmers and other workers to the new world, the Dutch West Indian Company issued a Charter of Freedoms and Exemptions which promised a large tract of land to any member (a patroon) who emigrated and started a colony of 50 or more families.

DECREE: By the decree of 1664 Charles II, King of England, established a province out of the territory extending from the west side of the Connecticut River to the east side of Delaware Bay, including Long Island. He appointed his brother, James, Duke of York, as Lord Proprietor.

VOX POPULI: An assembly met at Fort James in New York City on October 17, 1683, and passed 15 laws, among them a Charter of Liberties and Privileges. The Charter required that an assembly elected by freeholders and freemen be called at least once every three years; prohibited taxation without the consent of the assembly; and provided for religious liberty and trial by jury. The assembly did not meet again after the Duke of York became James II in 1685, at which time New York became a royal province.

FEDERATION: Under the leadership of Governor George Clinton (1776-95) New York forbade the Congress created by the Articles of Confederation from collecting duties at New York ports, and opposed the plan for a new federal constitution. When a majority of the Constitutional Convention in 1787 had approved the new plan, Alexander Hamilton of New York was the only delegate who did not sign it. Ultimately, through Hamilton's efforts, it was ratified by New York.

North of the New York Tower are four arched windows overlooking the courtyard. At the top of these windows the functions of the law are depicted in ornamental stone work. Above the first window is the liberty bell and the words "Liberty Within the Law." Above the second is a battle ax and the words "Protection Under the Law." Next is a ballot box and the words "Responsibility to the Law." The scales of justice are presented last, together with the words "Equality before the Law."

The oriel window of the law school's rare book room faces west, overlooking the courtyard. The window has four parts; at the bottom of each section words carved in linen-fold design correspond to symbols depicted above: scales (common law); book (statute law); scroll (constitutional law); and plowshare and broken sword (international law).

Throughout the building many small sculptures symbolize the lawyer or an aspect of the common law. Among these are the pen, quill, and gavel carved under the windows facing the courtyard to the southeast of the oriel windows.

In the passageway beneath the Peace Tower between the east/west archways, a large bronze shield recessed into the stone floor bears the seal of Cornell University. On it are inscribed the words of Ezra Cornell: "I would found an institution where any person can find instruction in any study."

Several gifts of Mr. and Mrs. Taylor are displayed in the foyer. On the south wall are portraits of Mr. and Mrs. Taylor, painted by Frank O. Salisbury. Salisbury was an English artist known for his portraits of royalty and other heads of state. Medals and awards received by Mr. Taylor are displayed in the Rare Book Room. On the north wall of the foyer, above the fireplace, is a large French tapestry, done in petitpoint needlework. It depicts a scene in the gardens of an Elizabethan palace, with courtiers and numerous figures in the foreground, and in the center Metius Curtius leaping into the chasm. The tapestry's border is woven with emblematic figures of mermaids, tritons, trophies of arms, animals and strapwork.

The north entrance of the foyer is inscribed: "Myron Taylor Hall dedicated October 15, 1932. For the promotion and study of law and its administration. To the end that justice shall prevail in human relations. This hall of the Cornell Law School is a gift of Myron C. Taylor, Cornell '94 and Anabel Stuart Taylor, his wife." Opposite this inscription a stairway leads to the reading room of the library. An imposing portrait of the founder of Cornell University, Ezra Cornell, dominates the first landing on the stairway. The painting is attributed to Frank O. Salisbury. The scene depicted is Mr. Cornell signing the charter of the University.

The top of the stairway opens into the library reading room. This room is 180 feet in length, 48 feet in width, and 50 feet high. At the eastern end is the law school's rare book room. The corridor at the northwest corner of the reading room leads to the John W. MacDonald Moot Court Room.

The Moot Court Room is at the northwest corner of the building. It was named to honor John W. MacDonald '26 (1905-1981), Professor at the Law School from 1930-1973. Though renovated in 1987, the Moot Court Room remains a replica of an appellate courtroom. In back of the bench is inscribed the first sentence of Dean Roscoe Pound's book, *Interpretations of Legal History*, "Law must be stable and yet it cannot stand still." This was also used as text by Judge Cardoza at the opening of his book, *The Growth of Law*.

The Coat of Arms of the four Inns of Court in London are carved on the doors of the Moot Court Room. The left side has those of Middle Temple and Inner Temple and the right, of Lincoln's Inn and Gray's Inn. The Inns of Court were the central institutions for training common law lawyers. Henry III (1207-1272), who favored common law and disliked the Doctors of the Civil Law, forbade the institution of a school of law in the city of London. Because the University of Cambridge and Oxford excluded those who wished to follow common law, the Inns of Court were established and students were instructed by the great judges of the time in legal learning and in the practice of the courts.

The Coats of Arms of certain Old World universities that first offered instruction in law are carved on the front of the judge's bench in the Moot Court Room. The shields, from left to right, represent the Universities of Bologna, Borges, Leyden, Paris, and Oxford.

The two buildings adjoining Myron Taylor Hall, both constructed primarily as a result of gifts of Myron C. Taylor, are Anabel Taylor Hall to the north, and Charles Evans Hughes Hall to the south. Anabel Taylor Hall is the home of the Cornell United Religious Work. It was completed in 1952 with a gift of $1.5 million from Myron Taylor in memory of his wife. Hughes Hall is a residence center for law students. Partially funded by Mr. Taylor, the hall was dedicated in 1964 and named in memory of Charles Evans Hughes, Chief Justice of the United States Supreme Court from 1930 until 1941. Hughes was a professor at the Law School from 1891 to 1893, and served as a non-resident lecturer from 1893 to 1895. Myron Taylor was one of Hughes' students during this time.

With the passage of some fifty years since the completion of Myron Taylor Hall and twenty-five years since the completion of the Charles Evans Hughes Residence Hall, it became apparent that an increase in faculty and student body and a much larger and expanding library collection required an addition to and renovation of Cornell University's fine law school complex.

In 1987 the law school began a second century of distinction announcing the capital campaign for the Cornell Law School—a $20 million campaign to finance a major building expansion and renovation project. Every effort was made to maintain the architectural integrity of Myron Taylor Hall including obtaining Llenroc for the outside of the building from the local quarry that provided the same type of stone for the original building. On April 7, 1989, more than 300 alumni, friends, students, staff, and faculty gathered in the atrium to celebrate the completion of the expansion and renovation of Myron Taylor Hall. In his remarks, President H.T. Rhodes praised the vision of three deans—Gray Thoron, Roger Cramton, and Peter Martin—in recognizing the need for expansion and change. Milton Gould '33, co-chairman of the Capital Campaign, thanked the many friends and alumni whose generous contributions made the day and called for their continuing support of legal education, "The moral fiber of the legal profession depends upon the strength of great law schools to shape the future." Dean Russell K. Osgood announced that the addition would be named in honor of Jane M.G. Foster, a member of the Class of 1918, who had been a longtime supporter of the Law School. In his presentation, Dean Osgood expressed the belief that Miss Foster's principal gift for the building would have two effects: "First, it will make our job of delivering a first-rate legal education easier to accomplish. Second, and more importantly, her gift will remind all of us that our society and our legal system are not build and should not operate to confirm the powerful in their privileges, but to empower all people to unlock their potential in the mass of us to do something and to do it well." Dean Osgood also issued a special thank you to campaign co-chairmen Milton Gould '33 and Jack G. Clarke '52. Three surprise announcements were made during the two-day celebration: Allan '63 and Frances Tessler were recognized for their $1 million gift to the Capital Campaign, the atrium was named in honor of Leo '56 and Arvilla Berger in recognition of their generous support, and the main reading room of the Law Library was named in honor of Milton '33 and Eleanor Gould for their continued and longtime dedication and support of the Law School.

Myron Taylor was dedicated to establishing world peace through law. Myron Taylor Hall still reflects this commitment which was emphasized at its opening by Dean Charles K. Burdick: "The whole symbolizes peace by law—national peace by local law, world peace by international law—to that ideal we do rededicate the Cornell Law School today."

THE CORNELLIAN COUNCIL BULLETIN

VOLUME XVIII   OCTOBER · 1932   NUMBER 1

MYRON TAYLOR HALL DEDICATED
IN IMPRESSIVE CEREMONY
Mrs. Taylor Presents Keys — Judge Pound Makes Notable Address

LAW reigned supreme on the Cornell campus on October 15. In an impressive ceremony in the beautifully appointed Moot court room Mrs. Myron C. Taylor formally handed over the keys to President Farrand, and Myron Taylor Hall, America's newest center for legal training and research, was auspiciously launched on its career.

A distinguished audience of alumni, members of the bench and bar, representatives of sister institutions and officials of the University, listened attentively to the brief exercises, ably conducted by Frank H. Hiscock '75, Chairman of the Board of Trustees and former chief judge of the Court of Appeals of the State of New York.

Seated behind the bench of the Moot Court and dressed in academic robes were those participating in the exercises. To the right of the chairman sat Myron Taylor '94, the donor of the building.

The reading of a telegram of congratulation from the Hon. Charles E. Hughes, Chief Justice of the United States Supreme Court and formerly a professor in the Cornell Law School, marked the opening of the dedication ceremonies. In his message Justice Hughes expressed his deep regret that his work at Washington made it impossible for him to be present. Following an address of welcome by Charles K. Burdick, dean of the Law School, Mr. Taylor made a brief presentation address, pausing before its conclusion to request Mrs. Taylor, who sat in the audience, to formally present the keys, because "she was a real partner in this enterprise."

President Farrand stepped down from his place beside Mr. Taylor to accept the keys and in a few remarks expressed the

Mr. and Mrs. Myron C. Taylor at Dedication Ceremony

thanks of the University and the high hopes which were entertained for the success of the school in its new home. "It is to centers such as this in our own and other countries . . . that we must look for that guidance in principle and practice, without which right living is impossible and international peace and friendship not to be attained. To contribute to those ends Cornell University dedicates Myron Taylor Hall and the efforts of those who shall work within its walls."

Judge Pound Speaks

Then followed the principal address of the day by Cuthbert W. Pound '87, chief judge of the State Court of Appeals, on the subject of "A Modern University Law School:" It was a most masterful exposition of the state of the law and of the responsibilities of our law schools.

Calling upon the legal profession to "arise to meet and solve" the problems confronting the nation, Judge Pound stated that "War is an anachronism in a world of law, which looks on private war as a breach of the peace."

As a Cornell alumnus and trustee, Judge Pound expressed the hope that the Law School, in its new home, might grow richer in the fields of jurisprudence, international law, and constitutional law, and that it may "be pushed beyond the common traffic of routine practice and may penetrate into fields where the lawyer may be prepared to serve the state outside the faithful service of private clients."

Judge Pound said that "the competence of representative government to deal with domestic and international affairs is being challenged," and that "the cost of government is being contrasted with its lack of efficiency.

"But there are now, as in the past," Judge Pound said, "lawyers to whom America looks for leadership. Lawyers were leaders in our struggle for independence."

Students of Present Needs

The bar of America must arise to meet the new problems, he continued, "not as the disciples of a rigid social philosophy, either conservative or liberal, but as students of the needs of today to be expressed in the legal formulas of the past."

Of jurisprudence he said that "law furnishes a rule; jurisprudence seeks a reason." Law schools, he said, should give "a broader view, a loftier purpose than that of the attorney who regards his check for costs as better evidence of victory than the establishment of a great principle in a well-won leading case, and who knows no philosophy except that 'water, being poured out of a cup into a glass, by filling the one doth empty the other.'"

Advocates "Peace Spirit"

Regarding international law he said that "if the peace spirit rather than the war spirit came to be regarded as the spirit of justice, custom and public opinion might soon give an efficacy to the pacts of powerful nations which could not be disturbed by war . . .

"No enduring system of international law can be built on a foundation of prejudices and hasty passions. In theory the system of law of peace among nations may seem idealistic. Practice in conformity therewith requires the patience and restraint of minds trained to a fixed belief in the efficacy of a federation of the world."

Discussing constitutional law, he said that "the most distinctive change in the government of the country in recent years has been manifest in a growing disposition to regulate the life of the people by legislation." He asked the question: "How far will the Supreme Court apply the formulas of legal decision to check the desires and professional necessities of the state?"

Tribute to Mr. Taylor

Judge Pound said Mr. Taylor, donor of the building, "takes his place with those far-sighted men, those kings and cardinals and captains of commerce, who founded the colleges of Oxford and Cambridge." Those ancient institutions, he continued, "still bear witness to the influence and importance of education in furnishing intelligent men for the service of the nation, leaving for other places the sharpening of wits for the personal profit of the lawyer in the conflicts of the courts and in the strategy of the law office."

Returning to the Cornell Law School itself, he said its success depends primarily on "the ability, character, training and skill of the teachers composing its faculty and their power to teach private as well as public law and practical as well as theoretical law. Many law graduates will not care to seek prominence in public life or public cases but will prefer the time-honored duties of faithful service to private clients. Cornell has a place for them."

Chief Justice Hughes Sends Congratulations

The good wishes of Charles Evans Hughes, chief justice of the United States Supreme Court, sped Myron Taylor Hall, new home of the Cornell Law School, upon its academic career.

The following telegram was sent by him to Dean C. K. Burdick, and was read at the dedication ceremony.

"I deeply regret that my work here makes it impossible for me to be present at the dedication of the new home of the Cornell Law School. My association with the faculty of the school in its early days was one of the most delightful experiences of my life and I have observed the development and success of the school with the keenest gratification.

"It is a far cry from the time we met on the top floor of one of the oldest buildings on the campus and when a little later we first enjoyed the advantages of Boardman Hall, to this day when Myron Taylor Hall opens its doors. The school has more than fulfilled the hopes of its founders, and its enlarged opportunities beckon it to an even higher degree of usefulness.

"The law schools have the future of the bar and bench largely in their keeping, and the administration of justice will depend not only on the technical equipment they provide but upon the professional standards they re-enforce.

"I have no doubt the new home of the school will be a power-house for the generation and distribution of the most helpful influence. I send you my hearty congratulations upon this happy occasion."

CHARLES EVANS HUGHES

Alumni Convention

Dartmouth Week End

The Twelfth Convention of the Cornell Alumni Corporation (the general alumni association) will be held in Ithaca on Friday, November 11. The program will follow the pattern of the meetings of other years, with many of the local clubs represented by accredited delegates. All Cornellians are welcome, and it is expected that the club delegates, although numerous, will be outnumbered by the unattached alumni.

Two factors calculated to help build up attendance this year are the coincidence of the Armistice Day holiday on November 11, and the Dartmouth football game scheduled for the following day.

As president of the Corporation, William W. Macon '98 of New York will open the convention in Willard Straight Hall on Friday morning. A special feature of luncheon will be the formal presentation to the University of Mennen Hall, the latest addition to the dormitory group. William G. Mennen '08, and his sister, Mrs. Elma Mennen Williams, donors of Mennen Hall, will be present, and Mr. Mennen will speak. President Farrand will respond for the University.

In the afternoon the closing hour will be given over to services in commemoration of the centenary [Continued on page 4

F. Ellis Jackson '00, Architect of Myron Taylor Hall

THE CORNELLIAN COUNCIL BULLETIN   3

Myron Taylor Hall from the lawn in front of the Old Armory

REMARKS OF
MYRON C. TAYLOR
TENDERING MYRON TAYLOR HALL TO CORNELL UNIVERSITY

*T*HOUGH *this* [*structure has visible material form and substance; though its origin can be classed as the fruits of personal activities in the arena of twentieth century civilization; though to Mrs. Taylor and me it tangibly crystallizes the conception of our minds and the result of our labours, it has to us a still higher significance, expressing inspiration, preparation, faith, cooperation, achievement, and reward.*

So, also, it should stand as a symbol of the future in those factors so vital to the great and moving current of youth preparing itself to enter upon the serious action of life. If, through greater knowledge of and a growing respect for the law and its enforcement, it inspires increased regard for the rights of others in individual and community life; if it assists in bringing to an earlier realization an age of reason, self control and brotherly love; if it helps to lead youth through better knowledge to wisdom, through broader perspective to higher and nobler impulses; if it leads to a better appreciation of the true relationship between that which is material and that which is spiritual; if it helps to bridge the gulf which separates the commonplace from the ideal, the temporal from the eternal, Mrs. Taylor and I shall have achieved an enduring reward.

Having been permitted by a friendly Providence to garner the means to build this structure embodying the actual with the symbolical, we are greatly privileged in being now able to offer it through you, Dr. Farrand, in the name of Cornell to the service of others.

Judge Hiscock, Judge Pound, Mr. Taylor, Dr. Farrand, Dean Burdick
The speakers at the Dedication.

Right: Judge Hiscock, Chairman of the Board of Trustees and J. DuPratt White '90, Vice-chairman of the Board and Chairman of The Buildings and Grounds Committee, arrive for the occasion.

United States Steel Corporation

**THE THIRTY-SEVENTH ANNUAL DINNER
OF THE**

UNITED STATES STEEL
CORPORATION

•

JANUARY 11, 1938

**MARKING THE TENTH YEAR OF MYRON C. TAYLOR'S
ACTIVE SERVICE AS CHIEF ADMINISTRATOR OF THE
CORPORATION'S AFFAIRS**

CHAIRMAN MYRON C. TAYLOR

The thirty-seventh annual dinner of the United States Steel Corporation was held at eight o'clock Tuesday evening, January 11, 1938, at the Waldorf-Astoria Hotel, New York, Chief Administrator Myron C. Taylor presiding.

◄   ◄   ◄

*M*EMBERS of the executive staff of the United States Steel Corporation, we have gathered here tonight on the occasion of the thirty-seventh annual dinner.

Several weeks ago when I was contemplating the pleasure of presiding over this dinner, I received a message from one of our dearest associates making the suggestion that inasmuch as ten years had passed and I must have exhausted annually such oratorical ability as I might possess, I might desire this year to entertain you with something of a very different character. So I am turning this dinner and the ceremonies attached to it over to one of our distinguished directors.

It is my very great pleasure to retire as Chairman of the United States Steel Corporation for the brief period of an hour or so and offer in my place—which he more than fills—Thomas W. Lamont. (*Applause*)

Mr. Thomas W. Lamont assumed the chair.

◄   ◄   ◄

MR. J. P. MORGAN

TOASTMASTER LAMONT: *Mr. Chairman, President of the United States Steel Corporation, Gentlemen: I am very greatly honored to have a chance to act as toastmaster at this dinner in commemoration of the tenth anniversary of Myron C. Taylor's pre-eminent service. I have never come to one of these dinners without being immensely heartened by them, and once more I am impressed with the character of the men that go to make up the Steel Corporation, their immense industry, their ingenuity, their energy and their tremendous loyalty. It is a privilege for us all to be here and greet you all once again.*

This is a very informal gathering—we are just a family here—so we can say about what we please. Mr. Taylor, our hearts are very full tonight, full of admiration for what you have done and for what you are. All of us come here with hearts full of admiration and respect and affection for you. I am happy too to say that this is not in the nature of a farewell dinner. As I said before, it is a commemoration dinner—the tenth anniversary of your service here.

You will recall that the Steel Corporation was organized in 1901 by the late Mr. Morgan and that a great number of steel units, at that time scattered, were brought together into one important and constructive enterprise, at a very critical moment in the history of the whole industry. I believe Mr. Morgan builded much better than he knew. His son, Mr. J. P. Morgan, came on our Board in 1909 and has seen this Corporation through many phases of success and of difficulty. He was Chairman of the Board during the interim period from 1927 to 1932, and if I do say it, as perhaps I shouldn't, he has given this Corporation the continued benefits of his steady judgment and wisdom. We should be very grateful if Mr. Morgan would say a word to us.
(Applause)

ꓥ   ꓥ   ꓥ

THANK YOU very much. As I look back over a very long period, I find that I first came to one of these dinners in 1905. I well remember that I sat next to Mr. Baker.

When I look at Mr. Taylor now and think of the ten years that have gone by, I realize it has been quite a long time. And it seems a long time to him too, I think, doesn't it? But he has been absolutely never failing.

The way it began was this: Back in 1924 and '25 the elder George F. Baker and I had a very heart-to-heart conversation on the subject of the position of the Steel Corporation. As Judge Gary was nearly eighty, it was becoming important to think of someone to succeed him. Mr. Baker felt that the Judge was getting old—in point of fact, I think Mr. Baker was a little older than the Judge! We both knew that Judge Gary did not want anybody else in sight. He didn't want to think he was old; he liked to think he would live forever. Mr. Baker and I agreed that, in spite of what the Judge felt, we ought to introduce additional strength somehow.

Mr. Baker said, "All right, now, but whom do you think we ought to have? The Board is getting to be too much composed of officers of subsidiary companies. Whom can we get?" And, as far as I can remember, Mr. Baker and I both thought of Mr. Taylor at the same time. I may say that we had quite a discussion with Judge Gary, but in the end we convinced him that something had to be done and that Mr. Taylor was a man to bring into our councils.

Our whole course was certainly justified, because within two years of that time Judge Gary passed on, and without Mr. Taylor there we should have been out of luck.

Mr. Taylor sat for two years on the Finance Committee, studying the Corporation all the time without any idea that he ever was going to take complete charge. He became Chairman of the Finance Committee on Judge Gary's death, and, when I came back from Europe some two or three months later, I found everything in perfect order. He was going along all right.

There are three things that Mr. Taylor has done which are of supreme importance to the Company. One of them, and the first one, was the extinguishment of the bonded debt, which was really entirely due to him. That was the most important thing that ever happened. That was done in 1928 and '29, and we should now be "busted" permanently if it hadn't been for that. There is no doubt about it. And we are not now close to being "busted"—not by a long shot.

The next thing: When I first came to these dinners, there were none but white heads all around the table. And now there are only a few. Those of us who are on the point of retiring are a little gray on the head, but all the rest of you are young chaps, and you are doing splendidly. New blood is what we need—provided that the old blood is properly taken care of. But you also get the younger ones in. I want each of you fellows to make sure you have behind you someone else who could, if necessary, step into your place. You want to keep watch on that, all of you, because it is important.

The third thing, which is awfully important and has given us eight to ten months of complete peace, was the peaceful discussion with Mr. Lewis last year. That was the finest performance I have ever known. No one else in the whole of industry could have done that, and I want to congratulate Mr. Taylor. I want to tell him I hope that he will go on and do some more. (*Applause*)

MR. MYRON C. TAYLOR

*M*R. LAMONT, I am very grateful to you for having presided over this dinner with such charm and interest. And I am very grateful to those friendly words that you have spoken, coming as they do from a background which we have had of more than thirty years of business and friendly association. And I want you all to know that I am very much moved by the words that Mr. Irvin, and Mr. Fairless, and Mr. Gifford, and Mr. Voorhees, and Mr. Farrell, and Mr. Filbert, and Mr. Miller, and Mr. Stettinius, and my good friend Mr. Morgan have spoken.

I feel very undeserving of such praise. My intention has been to accomplish or to assist in accomplishing in behalf of the Corporation all of those things which you gentlemen have described; but they are not accomplishments of mine—none of them. They reflect the opinions and the analyses and considered judgment of the entire organization. I have only crystallized and put in motion those policies and actions, and that may have given rise to the thought that they were mine.

This is an organization of such fine quality, of such industry and such energy, that when you come to realize what it is you discover that it is more than a business, that it is more than a place to work, and that it is more than a money-making enterprise. It is part of the economy of present-day civilization. So much so that what it does reflects in the conduct of the nation. Of that I am conscious. Therefore, it would not be safe, and of course it would not be desirable, for any individual to become so convinced of the worth of his own services and so independent of the services of the vast number of other specialists in all branches of its army of 275,000 workers, that he would consider his own services to be invaluable. The problems are such that, if one man errs, the misfortunes that follow would not always affect only those who are the owners, or only those who are the workers, or only those who are the customers, but they would reach out and affect the entire country.

And so I say in all earnestness that in the future if anyone ever gets the impression that his opinion is infallible, or his services indispensable in respect to his affairs, he must be gotten rid of at once.

Ten years might seem a long time—especially ten years filled with such a variety of experiences as we have had together. It seems like a long while if you recount all of the different episodes that have occurred. I have often said to myself that I am glad I was able to act a part in this enterprise during the troublesome times that we have had. I know that I would have felt very forlorn and very useless if I had not had a part in the trials and tribulations endured by the people of this country and without the association of such loyal partners as you have been.

So I am very glad that I have had this experience.

It is a very sad feature of the life we lead, particularly sad to the head of a corporation, to witness the constant changing of personnel which is necessary through the passing of time, the toll which the eternal laws exact of human-kind. The attachments we have formed for one another are very real and enduring. We have worked together and struggled and suffered together and our comradeship is very deep and very real. When partings come, as they have with such frequency during this ten-year period, they hurt, and they lend to it all an element of sadness which I have felt very much indeed.

The greatest compensation that I have had, and the one that I am going to cherish most of all the things that have come to me in my business experience, is the consciousness which I feel—and which I believe I am justified in feeling—of having not merely the respect—I hope I have that; not merely the admiration—and I hope I have that; but the affection of all those who are a part of the United States Steel Corporation, from the highest in position to the humblest—that is what I long to have and to retain through the years—your affection.

... The audience arose and applauded ...

◂   ◂   ◂

E, the associates and friends of
MYRON C. TAYLOR
guests at the Thirty-Seventh Annual Dinner of the
United States Steel Corporation, January 11, 1938,
marking the tenth year of his active service as
Chief Administrator of the Corporation's affairs, here-
by express our respect, admiration and affection for
him as a leader, co-worker and friend. We deeply regret his coming retirement as Chairman of the Board
and sincerely hope that the future may hold for him
many years of happy memories and the rest and
leisure which he so richly deserves.

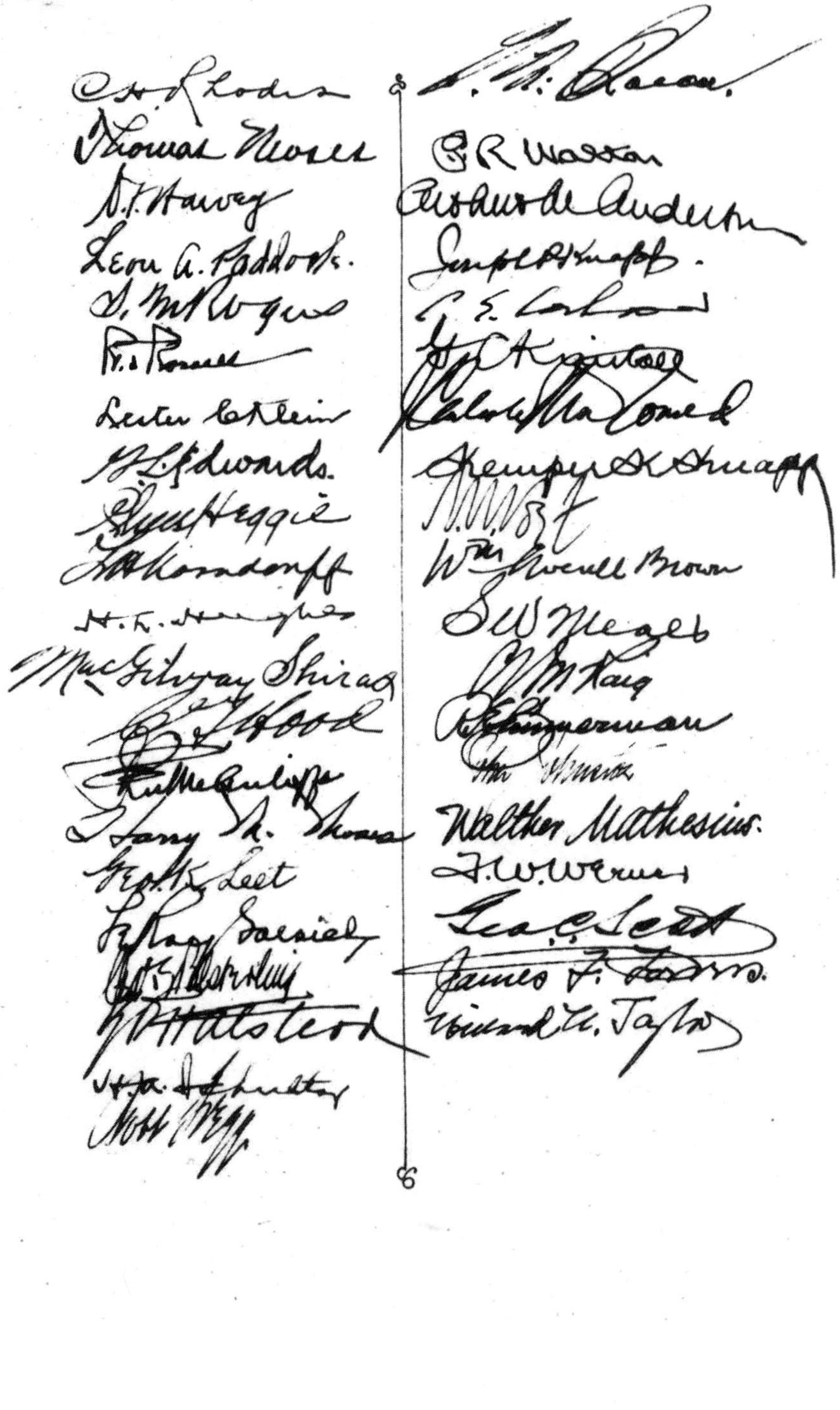
Thomas Moses
Leon A. Paddock
Lester C. Klein
Wm. Averell Brown
Walther Mathesius

Index

Page numbers in *italics* indicate photographs.

Visser 't Hooft, Willem, 242
Vita Serena, 135, 159, 253
von Preysing, Cardinal, 257
von Ribbentrop, Joachim, 141, 149n4,
    152n12, 198n83

Wallace, Henry, 247
War Refugee Board (WRB), 213n34,
    215
Welles, Sumner, 101, 104, 121, 135,
    137, 141, 149n4, 161, 167, 168,
    175, 177, 186-187, 189, 201,
    274
What the L'Bill, 13

White, Harry Dexter, 227n14
Whitman, Will (Walt), 13, 14
Willkie, Wendell, xi
Wilson, Woodrow, 217
Winant, John G., 6, 7, 186
Window envelopes, 32
Winterton, Lord, 100
World Council of Churches (WCC),
    252, 259
World War I, 39, 118
World War II, ix, 3, 4, 7

Young, Owen D., 47